The American Crisis Series
Books on the Civil War Era

*Steven E. Woodworth, Professor of History,
Texas Christian University*
Series Editor

Eric H. Walther. *The Shattering of the Union: America in the 1850s.*

Mark Thornton and Robert B. Ekelund Jr. *Tariffs, Blockades, and Inflation: The Economics of the Civil War.*

Paul Ashdown and Edward Caudill. *The Myth of Nathan Bedford Forrest.*

Michael B. Ballard. *U. S. Grant: The Making of a General, 1861–1863.*

Donald T. Collins. *The Death and Resurrection of Jefferson Davis.*

David Coffey. *Sheridan's Lieutenants: Phil Sheridan, His Generals, and the Final Year of the Civil War.*

Christopher Waldrep. *Vicksburg's Long Shadow: The Civil War Legacy of Race and Remembrance.*

J. Michael Martinez. *Carpetbaggers, Cavalry, and the Ku Klux Klan: Exposing the Invisible Empire During Reconstruction.*

Steven E. Woodworth. *Beneath a Northern Sky: A Short History of the Gettysburg Campaign, 2nd Edition.*

Sherman's March in Myth and Memory

Sherman's March in Myth and Memory

Edward Caudill and Paul Ashdown

ROWMAN & LITTLEFIELD PUBLISHERS, INC.
Lanham • Boulder • New York • Toronto • Plymouth, UK

ROWMAN & LITTLEFIELD PUBLISHERS, INC.

Published in the United States of America
by Rowman & Littlefield Publishers, Inc.
A wholly owned subsidiary of The Rowman & Littlefield Publishing Group, Inc.
4501 Forbes Boulevard, Suite 200, Lanham, Maryland 20706
www.rowmanlittlefield.com

Estover Road
Plymouth PL6 7PY
United Kingdom

British Library Cataloguing in Publication Information Available

Library of Congress Cataloging-in-Publication Data:
Caudill, Edward.
   Sherman's march in myth and memory / Edward Caudill and Paul Ashdown.
      p. cm. — (American crisis series)
   Includes bibliographical references and index.
   ISBN-13: 978-0-7425-5027-8 (cloth : alk. paper)
   ISBN-10: 0-7425-5027-3 (cloth : alk. paper)
   1. Sherman, William T. (William Tecumseh), 1820–1891—Historiography. 2.
Sherman, William T. (William Tecumseh), 1820–1891—In literature. 3. Sherman,
William T. (William Tecumseh), 1820–1891—In motion pictures. 4. Sherman's March
through the Carolinas—Historiography. 5. Sherman's March to the Sea—
Historiography. I. Ashdown, Paul, 1944– II. Title.
   E476.69.C38 2008
   973.7'378—dc22   2008004121

Printed in the United States of America

∞™ The paper used in this publication meets the minimum requirements of American
National Standard for Information Sciences—Permanence of Paper for Printed Library
Materials, ANSI/NISO Z39.48-1992.

For Robert, Daniel, and Larissa

For Audrey and Lila

Contents

Introduction
Burning the March into Memory

William Tecumseh Sherman has marched to the sea a million times in national memory, each time burning a path of barbaric havoc and ingeniously inventing a new mode of war. It depends on one's perspective. In this third volume of a trilogy, we conclude our investigation of three Civil War figures—John Mosby, Nathan Bedford Forrest, and Sherman—to explain how historical myths and legends are created by journalists, biographers, novelists, artists, filmmakers, and the subjects themselves, and how we remember the wars we fought and the people who fought them. This is an interdisciplinary study of the remembered Sherman, North and South, and the ideas that shaped the memory of him. Our subject in this volume is more Sherman's March to the Sea than Sherman himself, although the two are inextricable. The March devastated the South. But Sherman decimated more than foodstuffs, materiel, and communications. The March cut the heart out of the Old South myth, pruning its magnolia splendor to a stump. Simultaneously and conversely, it helped energize an emerging mythology in the North, one linking progress to technology, industry, and "fitness." The postwar period in which Sherman's legacy took form was a time that saw new ideas altering the American economy, society, landscape, and imagination. The Civil War was the critical experience for a generation of Americans who would see the national transition from agrarianism to industrialism, which became the context for the North's heroic Sherman. He was efficient, rational, victorious.

The newspapers and magazines of the era often loved Sherman, who hated them. During the war, and to a lesser extent afterward, covering Sherman was the journalistic equivalent of bearbaiting: the more the bear roared, the more the press provoked the bear. He was great newspaper copy, and the March was easily packaged as the big story of the war. Early in the war, the press judged him insane. His erratic behavior and nervous energy were simply additional evidence of the general's mental instability. Later, it was often the same correspondents and the same newspapers who saw those same mannerisms—such as his pacing about the camp at night, smoking cigars in his red flannels—as the eccentricities of military genius. A great drama, in a great tragedy, led by a colorful, quotable, even unpredictable general, with nothing less than the fate of the republic in the balance—it was a story that could not miss, no matter the insights or ignorance of the reporter, or the political inclinations of the publisher.

But when Southerners remembered Sherman after the war, they remembered not just destruction, but humiliation. He became a scapegoat of Southern wrath, the one to blame for what became of the Confederacy—from Reconstruction's failures, a regional malaise in an era of progress, to the simplistic stereotypes of lynch mobs and Klansmen, of sharecropper shacks built on plantation ashes. In Georgia in particular, Sherman emerged as the one to blame for wartime disaster. In myth and folklore, the general personally was accused of torching buildings, even entire cities; stealing horses (white ones were favored); plundering households. It was and is easier to create myths based upon an individual than on a faceless army.[1]

The March helped end a bloody war, and was itself a bloody wound in the corpus of the Old South and all it symbolized. Histories, legends, and myths about the March took shape at the dawn of the industrial age, which Sherman's style of war came to symbolize for many. The March meant abandoning some unstated rules of war, engaging the civilian population that supported an enemy army, and subordinating any chivalric ideals of war to the goal of winning the conflict. The industrial economy ground to dust the aristocratic culture and its ideals of war. This meant war was not army versus army, but army versus society and its values, as well as its soldiers. The Old South was a region of sharp stratification, with wealth concentrated in the landed aristocracy, the slaveholders, whose legitimacy was contrived in undocumented claims of Old World heritage. Industrialism would make such an agrarian economy an extension of the factory, identified with the rude, dirty cities of nineteenth-century America. The plantation could not be Edenesque in such a world, and its success would be measured not against a mythic garden, but a production line. In *The Destructive War*, Charles Royster insightfully sees in Sherman and his tactics an empirical mindset at work, which treated war as a "mechanical routine" in a campaign that "had the inevitability of design supported by science." With Sherman, the March was more an industrial argument against the agrarian Confederacy than a moral imperative to restore the Union, according to Royster. "His entity 'war' took on the attributes of a process of nature controlling all participants, using them, as lightning or earthquakes used matter, to establish a new equilibrium through upheaval."[2]

After the war, Southerners accused him of violating the rules of civilized conflict as he burned his way across Georgia and the Carolinas, pillaging homes and bringing war to the civilian population. He had promised to make Georgia howl, and he did. He said he would teach people that war is all hell, and he did. The South never forgave him for the lesson. But the accusations that damned him in the eyes of the romantically afflicted Dixie alerted the North to a new kind of hero, a modern one who waged battle ruthlessly, efficiently, without sentiment. His conduct of war was akin to a well-managed factory, a symbol of progress in Gilded Age America. What the South abhorred in Sherman, the North praised. No other Northern general, not even Ulysses S. Grant, was so consistently held in such infamy in the Southern mind.[3]

Sherman became a symbol of the absoluteness of the Southern defeat. Grant killed far more men, but he did so in the tradition of soldier versus soldier. Grant scarred the edges of the South, but Sherman marked its heart with footprints and flames. Even though Sherman killed comparatively few people, he made the South afraid, a self-revelation for Southerners that must have made him doubly contemptible in a culture of self-proclaimed cavalier bravado. Worse yet, he did not revel in war or sentimentalize it. He simply conducted it.[4]

Under the umbrella of progress and modernism, the North had in Sherman the modern hero. The South—looking backward at an idealized, agrarian culture—had the model of a modern villain. Grant only defeated an army. Sherman killed a culture.

History and Public Memory

Memory is a veil that blurs historical reality and filters the past through a flimsy cloth colored for the wearer's preferences or the dictates of fashion. This is a history of those veils, North and South, and how they are manifest in popular culture, then and now. The conventions of biographical and institutional media histories are expanded to include not only newspapers and magazines, but also film, theater, literature, monuments, and museums. They are engaged as more than a panel in the ever-changing diorama of America, and used instead as the fabric upon which the panels are painted. That fabric is a weave of events, myths, legends, history, family stories, and countless other threads of public memory that comprise cultural identities. A number of histories have taken such a tack in recent years, linking past and present in unique ways. They include, to name only a few, Gary Gallagher's *Lee and His Generals in War and Memory*, Carol Reardon's *Pickett's Charge in History and Memory*, Tony Horwitz's *Confederates in the Attic*, William L. Davis's *The Cause Lost: Myths and Realities of the Confederacy*, David W. Blight's *Race and Reunion: The Civil War in American Memory*, and Michael Kammen's *Mystic Chords of Memory: The Transformation of Tradition in American Culture*.

The press and war has become a popular subject in recent decades, not just in the wake of the Vietnam tragedy, which a consensus seems to agree was the first "TV war," but also with the proliferation of new media outlets to meet the market for popular history and war subject matter. The History Channel is exemplary in this category. And Ken Burns's *The Civil War* must have catalyzed both audience and media interest in the Civil War. However, some recent scholarship regarding the press, the Civil War, and the prewar decade has turned to complex issues such as the impact of the press on public opinion, the impact of public sentiment on coverage, and the relationship between the press and broad social movements. Such studies include Lorman A. Ratner and Dwight L. Teeter, Jr.'s *Fanatics and Fire-Eaters*; and David B. Sachsman et al.'s *The Civil War and the Press* and *Memory and Myth*.

History involving public perceptions is both treacherous and promising. It is the latter because the "public" is not revealed by conventional historical sources, usually documentary. The promise resides in the opportunities for historians to explore new perspectives and gain new insights. The sources for such history are inevitably a step removed from the subject. Other historians have noted the problem in even defining public opinion. D. G. Boyce criticized others for treating public opinion as a mystical entity and proposed simply abandoning private letters and turning to the press for a greater understanding of public opinion. In the press, he said, one could find opinions in articles and letters that were written by and for the public. The trove should be expanded even further to include public performances and displays, including museums, parks, and monuments, as some of the above authors have done. And now we have the all-pervasive Internet.[5]

Public opinion is not everyone's ideas about all issues. Boyce asserted, instead, that since the historian "invariably studies public opinion with reference to specific issues (such as the Boer War, the New Deal) he can use the press and the other organs of communication to discover how issues were first identified, defined and treated." Boyce believed a newspaper could not be too

far ahead of readers' opinions. This idea of confining public opinion to man-
ageable dimensions is not new. As early as 1937, D. W. Harding outlined
what he deemed "the range of permissible opinion" within which a newspaper could operate. He said opinions in the press would be within the publicly
permissible range because newspapers could not isolate themselves from audiences, and needed to remain fairly central in the wide range of public opinion pertaining to major issues. Though he spoke of newspapers, the same
logic would hold for other media and public displays, which would also have
to exist within a certain range of opinion relative to their audiences.[6]

The sources for this book include numerous popular media, not just newspapers, in the search for popular memory and its creation. The focus here is
on the March to Savannah, which remains the foundation of the Sherman
myth and overshadows the important, and probably underappreciated, march
through the Carolinas.

Scorching Southern Soil and Myth

Sherman was especially reviled as a conqueror because he was the antithesis
of romantic war and heroism. He made defeat for the South akin to being
beaten by a corporate magnate good at reading balance sheets but indifferent
to glory and legacy. The South had in Sherman its antihero, an individualis-
tic Yankee soldier who outsmarted and outfought some of the South's best,
bared the culture's scars, and turned war into an industrial exercise. Sherman's tactics exacerbated Southern bitterness, as he denuded numerous
myths at the center of the Old South fantasy, including the superiority of the
Southern warrior, the romantic ideal of war, and the contented slave. Worse
yet, the destroyer was the very personification of the Yankee and common
man. Rumpled in appearance, coarse in language, Sherman was as un-cava-
lier as a soldier could be. His habit of living rough and his casual attitude toward dress endeared him to his own troops, but to Southerners these traits
were just further proof that he was an uncouth barbarian. Its military had
crumbled before him, however, and its mythology evaporated behind him.

The myth of the March and the man gained momentum for the rest of his
life. Old soldiers told tales and reminisced, while Sherman lectured and
wrote his memoirs. By the time of his death in 1891, *the March* was a term
that meant one march, embodied in one man in American history. Ironically,
the "Old South" and "the March" had become intimately linked as thesis and
antithesis—agrarian and industrial, tradition and modernism, spiritual and
material. The March was reinvigorated in the 1920s, when a distinctive
event and an amorphous group energized a revival of the Old South myth.

The 1925 trial of John Thomas Scopes in Dayton, Tennessee, for teaching evolution in public schools provoked a storm of ridicule from the North, personified in Baltimore journalist H. L. Mencken. Turning to the trial's central theme of biblical fundamentalism versus modernism and science, he skewered the South as an intellectual vacuum, devoid of culture and populated by hillbillies and bumpkins. The embarrassment provoked a countercharge by a group loosely associated with Vanderbilt University. In 1930 the Nashville Agrarians, which included many Southern literary luminaries of the day, published *I'll Take My Stand*, a manifesto setting a luminous Old South against the corruption and filth of modernism and industry. Even if the Old South myth failed the test of factuality in some of its details, they argued, it was essentially true in its nobility and spirituality. Sherman never became a central figure in the Agrarian ideology in the same fashion as his Tennessee nemesis, General Nathan Bedford Forrest. But Sherman was for them what he was to Georgians who were not even in the path of his march—a presence lurking just beyond the horizons of their imaginations. One writer at the core of the Agrarians, Donald Davidson, wrote in his regional history of the river valley, *The Tennessee*, that Sherman and Grant's idea of "total war" evolved from campaigns in Tennessee, where "casual destruction" emerged as Federal policy. "During the later years of the war, therefore, the Federal invasion . . . could hardly be distinguished from the inroads of a Genghis Khan or an Attila." For Davidson and other Agrarians, the campaign was only the beginning of a war that accelerated with the Tennessee Valley Authority's dam building in the 1930s. [7]

The memory endured in the South and became a national one, encapsulated in a few seconds from a film now three-quarters of a century old, *Gone with the Wind*: "And the wind swept through Georgia: Sherman!" in giant letters as the screen goes up in flames. The March has even been recalled in more recent popular music to evoke some Southern distinctiveness. In "They Laid Waste to Our Land," Waylon Jennings laments the defeat, bemoans the scars, and wonders if it was worth all the pain just to live under one flag.[8]

The postwar era, the empirical-industrial age, was the foundation for the national memory of Sherman. He showed that the certainty of Southern cultural superiority was ephemeral, grounded in beliefs appropriate to an earlier age and without foundation in the modern world. In the North, his legend blossomed, changing Northern spirits with the capture of Atlanta and then Savannah, with his March redefining the war, in Victor Davis Hansen's words, "as a death struggle between yeomen farmers and the privilege of aristocratic plantationists, and the verdict of that ideological contest was plain for all to see in the burning estates of central Georgia."[9]

In *Gone with the Wind*, Scarlett O'Hara condemns Sherman's soldiers for destroying her way of life. The real Sherman roils up the romantic narrative because the dazzle disappears, along with the cavaliers. It's raw power and advantage, which complements the reigning philosophy of the Gilded Age. Sherman still appeals to unregenerate sectionalists in contemporary America, North and South. For the former, his triumph is proof of Northern superiority. For the latter, the triumph of such a mode of war is proof of Southern superiority. A third, and more ambiguous, narrative subsumes Sherman within the national mythology in which the March reveals something inherently American, a restless, relentless, outward movement toward an ocean.

Notes

1. Lee B. Kennett, *Marching through Georgia: The Story of Soldiers and Civilians during Sherman's Campaign* (New York: Harper Perennial, 2001), 321–22.

2. Charles Royster, *The Destructive War: William Tecumseh Sherman, Stonewall Jackson, and the Americans* (New York: Knopf, 1991), 329, 227, 341, 354–55.

3. Robert K. Murray, "General Sherman, the Negro, and Slavery: The Story of an Unrecognized Rebel," *The Negro History Bulletin* 22 (March 1959), 125.

4. Marion B. Lucas, "William Tecumseh Sherman *v.* the Historians," *Proteus* 17:2 (2000), 15.

5. D. G. Boyce, "Public Opinion and Historians," *History* 63 (1978), 214–26.

6. D. W. Harding, "General Conceptions in the Study of the Press and Public Opinion," *Sociological Review* 29 (1937), 370–90.

7. Paul Ashdown and Edward Caudill, *The Myth of Nathan Bedford Forrest* (Lanham, MD: Rowman & Littlefield, 2005), 103–20; Donald Davidson, *The Tennessee, Vol. 2: The New River, Civil War to TVA* (New York: Rinehart, 1948), 108, 112; Paul V. Murphy, *The Rebuke of History: The Southern Agrarians and American Conservative Thought* (Chapel Hill: University of North Carolina Press, 2001), 111.

8. Waylon Jennings, "They Laid Waste to Our Land," cited in James Reston, Jr., *Sherman's March and Vietnam* (New York: Macmillan, 1984), 114.

9. Victor Davis Hansen, *The Soul of Battle: From Ancient Times to the Present Day, How Three Great Liberators Vanquished Tyranny* (New York: Anchor Books, 1999), 245–46.

Sherman faces down the camera in this iconic photograph of a determined general, with a menacing countenance, confirming in image his reputation for ruthlessness. But the photo is representative of more than the man, as it reflects the problem of interpreting Sherman. He may be for some the scowling killer of culture, while for others he is the very picture of martial discipline and determination. Historians would have to struggle to create their own image. Library of Congress

CHAPTER ONE

Sherman

War is cruelty and you cannot refine it; and those who brought war into our country deserve all the curses and maledictions a people can pour out.

William Tecumseh Sherman to James Calhoun,
mayor of Atlanta, September 12, 1864[1]

William Tecumseh Sherman's early years seemed to anticipate a life that was a mixture of well-to-do circumstances and difficulties. His family came to Ohio from Connecticut in the early nineteenth century and settled in Lancaster, where his father, Charles, was a successful attorney. Tecumseh Sherman was born February 8, 1820. His father died when Tecumseh was only nine, leaving his mother with nine children still at home, whom she could not support. She kept the three youngest children and sent the remaining six to live with family and friends. Young "Cump" Sherman was taken in by Thomas Ewing, a family friend who lived near the Shermans in Lancaster. Ewing was a well-respected, successful businessman. He and his wife already had four children of their own, including Ellen, who was four years younger than Sherman and one day would become his wife.[2]

The name Tecumseh was a minor issue for the Catholic Ewing family. Naming one's son for the Shawnee chief was an unusual action in early nineteenth-century America, which was still in the midst of its Indian wars. In 1830, with consent of Mary Sherman, the youngster was baptized into the Catholic church. The baptizing priest insisted on adding a Christian name, and so anointed him "William Tecumseh," who never became a practicing Catholic and never used the name "William." He was "Cump" to the Ewings, and simply "Sherman" when he went to school at West Point a few years later, and during his military career generally.[3]

Sherman was commissioned a second lieutenant upon graduation from West Point in 1840, and assigned to Fort Pierce, Florida, where he would be part of a war of raids and skirmishes with the Seminoles. Before Sherman's arrival in the fall of 1840, there was an ongoing guerrilla war of raids against white settlements and military units, which meant Sherman saw no real combat. His arrival coincided with a new strategy, which was to keep the army afield year-round, and not recoil from the summer heat. Though difficult for the soldiers, maneuvering in the summer meant destroying the Indians' crops. By 1842, enough Seminoles had been removed to the West to allow the military to declare victory. Though Sherman believed the war was a waste of time, he learned that conventional military tactics had their limits, and that military success was also a matter of food supply and the will of a whole society, not just warriors.[4]

In the spring of 1846, Sherman eagerly waited to be part of the growing conflict with Mexico. In July, he finally departed with Company F, Third Artillery for California, its destination either San Francisco or Monterey, and its mission unstated. Because the voyage around Cape Horn took six and one-half months, the company never saw action against Mexico. Arriving in Monterey on January 26, 1847, the troops found a quiet city. Sherman was appointed assistant adjutant general for the Tenth Military District, a poor, sparsely settled region. He still was not involved in the war, which ended in August 1848, and California became U.S. territory. Sherman believed the peace treaty inadequate because it failed to "impress the Mexican with respect for us." He thought more severe measures, such as burning down the Mexican capital, were in order.[5]

Married, Still Moving

Sherman and Ellen had not seen each other in four years, and his career was still an issue: the Army versus managing her father's saltworks in nearby Chauncey. Though they also had not settled the question of his religion, they were married in May 1850. For the next several years, Sherman and his wife would keep moving—apart and together. Sherman received his commission as captain on September 27, 1850, in the Commissary Corps offices in St. Louis. Their first child was born in January 1851. In March, he returned to Ohio to bring his family back to St. Louis with him. But in the spring of

1852, Ellen, pregnant again, decided to return to Lancaster. In August, Sherman was ordered south to become commissary officer in New Orleans, where corruption apparently permeated the operation.[6]

Sherman quickly reformed operations in New Orleans, improving the prices and quality, and getting a backlog of correspondence and paperwork in order. His family arrived in late December 1853, but the expense of living in New Orleans and his wife's inclination for living comfortably made his Army salary more inadequate than ever. An Army friend from his days in California, Henry S. Turner, offered Sherman a partnership in a California bank branch, which Sherman decided to accept provisionally, taking a six-month leave from the Army to do so. In February 1853, Sherman sent his family back to Lancaster, and in March he left for San Francisco to manage Lucas, Turner, & Co. Sherman liked San Francisco, and resigned his commission effective September 6. He returned to Lancaster for his family, and brought them to San Francisco in October.[7]

The Banker versus the Press

At the beginning of 1855, Sherman's bank was in good order. But in February news came of the collapse of the Page & Bacon bank of St. Louis, which was also the largest bank in San Francisco. This set up a run on banks in San Francisco. Sherman was able to meet the bank's obligations, having seen the business through a very real and close crisis, during which seven of nineteen banks had failed.[8]

In the spring of 1856, Sherman found himself in a new dilemma. Governor J. Neely Johnson had appointed him commander of the Second Division of the California Militia, whose district included San Francisco. The city was pretty much what one would expect in a gold rush boomtown: corruption included, but was not limited to, bribery of officials, jury tampering, and the stuffing of ballot boxes. The frustrated citizenry had replaced the corrupt government with vigilantes. At the center of the situation in which the new militia commander would be embroiled were a man accused of killing a policeman and an editor who shot a fellow journalist. A grand jury had refused to indict a man named Charles Cora, who was accused of shooting the policeman. In the other case, the editor of the *Sunday Times*, James Casey, shot the editor of the *Daily Evening Bulletin*, an individual with the unusual name James King of William, who had documented the fact that Casey once served time in a New York prison. Casey shot King on May 14, and turned himself in to the sheriff, a political associate.

After the newspaperman was shot, the "Vigilance Committee" took control of the city. A mob of about 2,500 took Cora and Casey from the jail on

May 20, and publicly hanged them several days later. Sherman's neutrality in the affair may have been made suspect by the fact that he had threatened during an earlier financial panic to throw Casey out of his building's third-story window for publishing anti-bank commentaries in his newspaper. Sherman resigned command on June 9, and the Vigilance Committee remained the effective government of the city until fall elections. Sherman had performed poorly. He was overly sensitive to the press, which was lambasting other public officials as well, and he resigned command at the height of conflict. The episode further soured Sherman on political life and the press. He later told a friend that his mistrust of the press was conceived in California.[9]

In August, Sherman accepted the position of superintendent at the Louisiana Seminary of Learning and Military Academy. Rising sectional animosities made it poor timing for any Midwesterner to be taking a job in Louisiana, even if Sherman's personal views on slavery would have been no problem for Southerners. He felt that ending slavery would cause "utter ruin to immense numbers." His brother John's abolition sentiments in the U.S. Senate put Sherman in an awkward position. As tensions mounted in late 1859, Sherman condemned abolitionism but decided not to tolerate criticism of his brother. He told the academy's board of supervisors he would accept slavery, but not disunion.[10]

Unionist Professor in the South

The seminary opened January 2, 1860, and by May, more than sixty students were enrolled. Sherman was clear in his support of the Union, and equally clear in his disdain for the abolitionists. But his brother's and stepfather's positions would face strong enmity in the South. Abraham Lincoln's victory in November heightened concerns about secession. The downward spiral increased with South Carolina's withdrawal from the Union. In his *Memoirs*, Sherman said, "I think my general opinions were well known and understood, viz., that 'secession was treason, was war.'" He stated publicly in mid-December that as long as Louisiana was in the Union, he would serve the state faithfully, but he would quit if the state seceded. When Louisiana troops seized Federal forts on the Mississippi in mid-December, Sherman asked to be relieved of his job. The board had no replacement for Sherman and persuaded him to stay. Some friends even encouraged him to join the Confederate army. In January, though, troops captured the arsenal at Baton Rouge and sent captured weapons to the seminary's arsenal, which was under Sherman's supervision. Dejected, and still with good feelings toward the people around him, Sherman resigned on January 18, 1861. Louisiana seceded on January 26, and Sherman left for Lancaster at the end of February.[11]

War Begins

On April 14, 1861, Confederate cannons opened fire on Fort Sumter in Charleston. Sherman was summoned to Washington to command a new regiment of the Regular Army, the Thirteenth U.S. Infantry. He assumed command of the Third Brigade, First Division, on June 30. His 3,400 troops were largely inexperienced volunteers, who had signed on for only ninety days, which for many was nearly up by the time they signed the official muster book in Washington. The first Battle of Bull Run on July 21 was Sherman's initiation into major combat. The Union advance had started at dawn, and Sherman's unit was one of the two that were to attack the Confederate left flank. His brigade helped push the Confederates from Mathews Hill to Henry House Hill, where General Thomas J. "Stonewall" Jackson's brigade stopped the Federal troops. The subsequent retreat turned into a panic, proving to Sherman that his contempt for volunteers was justified. Sherman regained some control of what had become a milling mob as he ordered men to get with their units, posted guards on bridges leading to Washington, and ordered the ferry to stop transporting men who were not with their units.[12]

General George McClellan took command in late July, and Sherman was unexpectedly promoted to brigadier general of volunteers. Shortly thereafter, General Robert Anderson, a friend from Sherman's Fort Moultrie days and of Fort Sumter fame, asked Sherman to be his deputy in the Department of the Cumberland. Sherman went to Kentucky with the intent, and the promise from Lincoln, of being second in command. But Anderson resigned on October 8, probably as a result of fatigue, and Sherman was in charge. As he fretted about having too few troops, he also concluded that a Confederate attack was imminent. Worrying constantly, sleeping little, smoking incessantly, drinking excessively, Sherman did not slip comfortably into the cloak of command. Reporting his forces at less than 20,000, Sherman told Secretary of War Simon Cameron and Adjutant General Lorenzo Thomas that pushing Confederates out of Kentucky would require 60,000 men, and a successful offensive would eventually require 200,000 men. As he generated a stream of pessimistic reports and letters, Sherman wanted to get out of Kentucky and return to his old command in Washington. Thomas W. Scott, the assistant secretary of war, put into words what others had only been thinking: "Sherman's gone in the head, he's luny [sic]." In mid-November, General Don Carlos

Buell succeeded Sherman, who reported to General Henry Halleck, commander of the Department of the Missouri, in St. Louis.[13]

He arrived in St. Louis in late November on an assignment to inspect troops. One of his first actions was to order troops concentrated in anticipation of Confederate attack, which some saw as symptomatic of too much stress. Halleck countermanded the order and sent Sherman home to Lancaster for a twenty-day furlough. Then, the nation's press managed to justify the general's past animosity and to earn his eternal contempt. A December 11 headline in the Cincinnati *Commercial* screamed "General William T. Sherman Insane." It went on to report that Sherman was "stark mad" in Kentucky, demonstrated by his exaggerated reports of enemy strength, frequent telegraphing of the War Department, and allegedly ridiculous orders that subordinates would not obey. In short order, the story spread to St. Louis, then to New York newspapers, the *Herald* on December 19, and *Frank Leslie's Illustrated Newspaper* on December 15. Years later, in his *Memoirs*, Sherman remained convinced that mere malice had motivated the press. He devoted several pages to the episode in his *Memoirs*, in which he claimed newspapermen distorted his memorandum to Cameron concerning the "insane request for two hundred thousand men." It was, Sherman wrote, turned into a charge of Sherman himself being crazy.[14]

Redemption at Shiloh

In March, Sherman assumed command of the Fifth Division, Army of the Tennessee, at Pittsburg Landing, Tennessee. The Union forces were targeting Corinth, Mississippi, an important rail juncture. Grant had amassed nearly 40,000 troops at Pittsburg Landing, and another 20,000 were on the way under Buell. They were to meet around Corinth. Confederate General Albert Sidney Johnston had about 44,000 troops in Corinth. On April 3, the Confederates marched out of Corinth toward the Union encampment. A two-day march put them within only a few miles of the Union forces. Sherman was encamped about three miles from the landing near a small Methodist church, which he chose for his headquarters. It was named Shiloh.[15]

Despite numerous reports that the Rebels were advancing in force, Sherman failed to act, chiding nervous officers who raised the alarm. His reluctance to act may have been a result, in part, of his overreaction earlier in the war to perceived Confederate threats. Steven E. Woodworth notes that despite Sherman's high intelligence he had "played the fool" in the days before the battle of Shiloh. He had "formed a theory about the strategic situation and then simply made the data fit that theory."[16]

Early Sunday morning, April 6, the battle began. The ferocity and scale of killing and bloodletting was a shock for the inexperienced Union troops. Sherman had three or four horses shot out from under him and was wounded by buckshot in his hand. His hat was even pierced by a projectile. Wounded, bloody, dirty, he was calm and in command as he ordered artillery into position just in time to stop a Confederate charge against the line. Sherman engaged the bulk of the Rebel army in his stand along Shiloh Ridge, in the counterattacks that followed, and in the ferocious fighting back to Jones Field. In mid-afternoon, Johnston bled to death after being shot in the leg. General P. G. T. Beauregard took over command, and stopped the attack a few hours later. That night, as it rained, Sherman bumped into a disheveled, soaked Grant, leaning against a tree. Grant agreed with Sherman's comment that it had been "the devil's own day" for them. Incredibly, though—and perhaps apocryphally in terms of the way the two came to wage war—Grant famously added that they would "lick 'em tomorrow." Early the next morning, Grant attacked, and the pattern of the first day was reversed. Beauregard began retreating to Corinth, and Grant sent Sherman and cavalry in pursuit. Sherman ran into a Confederate commander who would become his nemesis, a man he deemed "that devil," Forrest. The Confederate was legendary for his ferocity in battle and brilliance in tactics. He charged Sherman's exposed cavalry and infantry, forcing the ranks to break and run. Sherman rallied his troops and soon repulsed the attack, wounding Forrest in the process. Sherman's troops were exhausted after three days of bloody fighting. Confederate casualties were 9,740 killed or wounded, compared to 10,162 Union soldiers killed or wounded. The Union had twice the number missing or captured, a total that Woodworth deems less comparable because several Union regiments had surrendered. Union missing or captured were 2,103; Confederate, 957.[17]

Halleck credited Sherman's skill and judgment with a great contribution to the Union victory and wired Lincoln, recommending promotion to major general. In his report, Grant cited Sherman's "great judgment and skill." He had redeemed himself from the Kentucky episode. Shiloh linked Sherman and Grant for the rest of their lives, and Sherman not only restored his reputation but also saw Grant's determined leadership and its results.[18]

War with Civilians

The months following Shiloh were important ones in the development of Sherman's thinking about conducting war not just between two armies but with hostile civilians. Sherman arrived in Memphis on July 21 as its new military governor. Two major issues were fugitive slaves and guerrilla warfare. Sherman put fugitives to work on fortifications, as teamsters, or as cooks, and he fed and clothed them. Sherman disagreed strongly with abolitionists, but the issue was settled for him when Lincoln issued the Emancipation Proclamation on September 22, 1862. The second major problem was guerrilla warfare, which usually meant armed civilians who fired on riverboats, disrupted trade, and sniped at Federal troops. In late September, guerrillas fired on a riverboat carrying civilians and private goods. Sherman had warned them earlier. Without further investigation, he sent a regiment to destroy the town of Randolph, Tennessee, which was near the site of the incident. A few days later, he issued special order no. 254, in which he said he would expel ten families of Confederate soldiers or sympathizers from Memphis for every boat attacked. Memphians were shocked. How could he condone such uncivilized action? His retort was simple: How could the Confederates defend firing on civilians in an undefended boat? He was true to his word. A few weeks later, four Union boats were fired on. Sherman expelled thirty-two individuals and two families, and ordered the destruction of all houses, farms, and cornfields on the Arkansas bank of the Mississippi River for fifteen miles downriver from Memphis. It was, he reasoned, a page from the lesson book in the Seminole wars. It would have been senseless to chase the culprits around the countryside, and subjugation of the Confederate military would only come with the destruction of its underlying support system.[19]

Scores to Settle

In late November, he left Memphis to take part in the attack against Vicksburg, which also culminated in his boldest and most audacious assault ever on the press. Sherman would be part of a three-pronged attack on the so called Gibraltar of Dixie, which overlooked the Mississippi from high bluffs, making it difficult to attack and also giving the Confederacy control of river traffic, as well as access to its trans-Mississippi territories. It also was the Confederate juncture of two important east–west rail lines, operated safely under the guns of Vicksburg. Sherman was to gather troops and supplies in Memphis and attack from the north, while Grant advanced from the south along the Mississippi Central Railroad. Sherman's troops left Memphis on December 19. He had unconfirmed reports that on December 20 Confederates had raided a supply depot at Holly Springs, Mississippi, causing Grant to turn back. On December 26, Sherman reached the Yazoo River, just north of Vicksburg, and three days later he attacked Confederate defenses on bluffs above Chickasaw Bayou. It was a failure. Heavy rain made the swampy terrain even worse, as a rising river threatened to put even their encampments under water. In the uphill fight, Sherman's troops faced deadly Confederate fire. Sherman ended the failed assault, suffering nearly 1,800 casualties out of the 36,000-man force.[20]

The beginning of 1863 saw Sherman again under fire from the newspapers, which blamed him for the failure and in a few cases even resurrected the charges of insanity. John A. McClernand, a political general for whom Sherman had little regard, arrived on January 4 under special order of President Lincoln to take over the river expedition, relegating Sherman to command of the Fifteenth Army Corps. Sherman's repulse at Chickasaw Bayou showed that McClernand's strategy would not work, leaving the political general without a plan of action or the quick glory he had hoped to achieve. Sherman suggested going downriver to Milliken's Bend, Louisiana, against Fort Hindman, also known as Arkansas Post. The fort, about fifty miles up the Arkansas River, had been a nuisance to Union supply lines. After two days of fighting, it was taken on January 12.[21]

Though somewhat acquitted for the Vicksburg debacle, Sherman still had scores to settle. The press was, for the general, an obvious culprit. And among the members of the press, one correspondent made himself an easy target, becoming the chief culprit and lightning rod of the general's wrath. Thomas Knox, a reporter for the New York *Herald*, which had doled out substantial criticism of Sherman in the past, had written an especially harsh report of the Vicksburg failure. His caustic commentary included the remark that he wished Sherman and his troops had acted with as much energy against the Confederates as they used against the press. Sherman had him arrested, to be court-martialed for spying.[22]

Knox had disobeyed Sherman's order that excluded reporters from accompanying the Chickasaw Bayou expedition against Vicksburg. When Knox heard of Sherman's plans, he wrote a conciliatory letter to the general, and explained that he was ignorant of the order forbidding reporters on the Chickasaw Bayou action. He believed his original stories were accurate, though based on limited information, and he acknowledged that subsequent information allowed him to see that he had committed several errors, which he offered to correct. Sherman was unmoved. Knox was charged with giving intelligence to the enemy, being a spy, and disobeying orders. His court martial began on February 5, and Sherman was the only witness and the whole case against Knox. Ultimately, Knox was found not guilty of the first two charges, and guilty of disobeying orders. He was banished outside army lines, under threat of being arrested if he returned. It was a limited victory.

Intimidation may have been the more substantial triumph for Sherman, as not even the *Herald* commented. The episode was not quite over, however. Two reporters, one each from the New York *Times* and the New York *Tribune*, asked Lincoln to reverse the sentence. The president was in the difficult position of choosing between the press and his generals, but he demonstrated his masterful political skills with a letter that pointed out that Knox's offense was "technical rather than wilfull [sic]." The reporter could proceed to Grant's camp, but Grant would get to decide whether to allow Knox to stay. When Knox showed up in early April with the letter, Grant refused to let him stay unless Sherman agreed. He did not. So Knox returned to cover the war in the East. Such was the mood and context for one of Sherman's more memorable remarks about the press. Learning that three correspondents had been blown out of the Mississippi near Vicksburg, he was to say, "Good! Now we'll have news from hell before breakfast."[23]

Travails and Triumphs

After a series of maneuvers and skirmishes, Grant and Sherman made new assaults on Vicksburg on May 19 and 23, both times with bad results. Grant began the siege. Sherman's careful troop placement kept General Joseph Johnston from reinforcing the city, which suffered incessant bombardment and growing disease. General John Pemberton surrendered to Grant on July 4. With General Robert E. Lee retreating from Gettysburg, it meant major victories in both theaters of the war.[24]

In late September, Sherman was ordered to move his headquarters from Memphis to Chattanooga, where he was to provide support for General William Rosecrans's Army of the Cumberland. On October 16, Halleck appointed Grant commander of the departments of the Ohio, Cumberland, and Tennessee. Grant, in turn, named Sherman commander of the Army of the Tennessee. He reached Chattanooga in mid-November and met with Grant. He crossed the Tennessee River the night of November 23–24 with four divisions, to threaten the right flank of General Braxton Bragg's Army of Tennessee, which was entrenched along Missionary Ridge, overlooking Chattanooga. Grant's chief engineer, General William F. "Baldy" Smith, had drawn up a battle plan that made the northernmost point of Missionary Ridge Sherman's primary objective. With about 20,000 men, Sherman was to take the point and sweep south along the ridge, while Generals George Henry Thomas and Joseph Hooker would tie down Confederates in Chattanooga and Lookout Mountain, south of the city. Difficult terrain and muddy roads delayed Sherman. His troops were finally in position to begin their advance on Missionary Ridge on the afternoon of November 24. Sherman attacked the next morning and gained a position at the ridge's northern extremity. The Confederates had been reinforced and repeatedly turned back Sherman's assaults, which had been launched against a hump of the main ridge called Tunnel Hill. Grant saw the dilemma, and ordered Thomas forward from his position west of Missionary Ridge. Though Grant's exact orders are unknown because he gave them verbally, it is believed he wanted Thomas's troops to drive the Confederates from rifle pits at the base of the ridge, then stop. But after taking the pits, the men continued of their own initiative and took the ridge. Thomas's successful assault and Hooker's triumph at Lookout Mountain meant Bragg's only recourse was to save his army. Grant embraced the triumph, even though it radically differed from the original plan, and then commended Sherman in writing for taking so much ground and contributing to Thomas's success by tying up so many enemy troops. Both Grant and Sherman helped this version of the battle gain credence when, in later years, they gave similar accounts of the battle plan in their memoirs. Both changed Sherman's role from conducting the main assault to putting him in the secondary position of supporting Thomas.[25]

Civilians and Seawater

Before taking a brief furlough with his family in late December, Sherman met with Grant and the high command in Nashville, where he won approval for a raid on Meridian, Mississippi, with the goal of clearing the valley of guerrillas and, if possible, his old nemesis Forrest. In his plan to destroy the Confederate infrastructure, Sherman made no secret of his intent to punish those who supported the rebellion. He told General A. J. Smith to take livestock from hostile inhabitants in west Tennessee and to banish from the area anyone deemed to be in opposition to restoring civil order. It was better, he believed, to destroy property than lives. On February 3, he began the march from Vicksburg to Meridian. He had ordered that his 25,000 men travel light, not even carrying tents. To any who objected to his tactics, he cited historical precedent, and he reminded Southerners that they were responsible for their own suffering. In order to end the suffering, they only needed to end the rebellion. By the time Union forces reached Meridian on February 14, Confederates had abandoned the city. Two days later, Sherman put Union troops to work at destroying the city's usefulness as a supply depot, destroying rail lines, bridges, warehouses, hotels, hospitals, and arsenals. In mid-March, Sherman went to Nashville to meet with Grant, who had been named general-in-chief of the Union army and would move to the Eastern theater of the war. This meant Sherman would be in charge of operations in the West. Grant was to move against Lee's Army of Northern Virginia, while Sherman would attack Johnston's Army of Tennessee in Georgia.[26]

Atlanta

Atlanta was important for both military and political reasons. It was an industrial center, with warehouses of provisions and materiel, as well as an important rail center. In April 1864, Grant ordered Sherman to pursue Johnston, who was entrenched with 50,000 troops near Dalton, Georgia. Sherman wrote in his *Memoirs* that he had begun to convert his army into a "mobile machine," dispensing with such things as wall tents and keeping the "mess establishment . . . less in bulk than that of any of the brigade commanders." He wanted to set an example, have his troops prepared to move out at a moment's notice and subsist on a minimum of rations. Meanwhile, he contemplated U.S. census tables for Georgia and statistics from the state controller, studying population and statistics for every county. Sherman left for Chattanooga on May 7 to begin the Atlanta campaign with 100,000 troops. He had under his command the Army of the Tennessee, led by General James Birdseye McPherson; the Army of the Cumberland, under Thomas; and the Army of the Ohio, under General John Schofield.[27]

The Atlanta campaign became a series of flanking maneuvers, which kept Johnston in retreat. Johnston dug in, Sherman flanked, and Johnston retreated at Dalton, Resaca, and Cassville. Sherman began another flanking movement designed to force Johnston out of Allatoona Pass, which protected Atlanta. Sherman planned to move against Dallas, between Allatoona and the Etowah River, over steep, woody terrain, blocked with thickets of dense underbrush. Creeks and quicksand became bogs when heavy rains started on May 25. Johnston figured out Sherman's plans and moved to block him, and three days of heavy fighting ensued at New Hope Church, just outside Dallas. Sherman lost about 1,600 men at Pickett's Mill, as he tried again to flank the Confederates, and he inflicted only about 500 casualties on the Confederates. With the incessant pressure, Johnston kept moving, and Sherman reached the railroad south of Allatoona Pass.[28]

Johnston had fallen back by mid-June toward Kennesaw Mountain, near Marietta. Sherman was familiar with the area from his travels in 1840, and he knew the 700-foot mountain would be a formidable defensive position. Sherman's attack on June 27 failed dismally, with Sherman losing about 2,500 men to the Confederate losses of 800. Schofield had managed to get several brigades in Johnston's rear, however. Sherman went back to his flanking tactics. On July 1 and 2, he sent McPherson behind Thomas and Schofield to threaten Johnston's rear. The Confederate saw little choice but to withdraw again, and on July 9 retreated to Atlanta.[29]

After Johnston's retreat across the Chattahoochee River and into Atlanta, Union forces destroyed mills north and west of the river. The mills included those in Roswell Factory (now Roswell), which employed hundreds of women. Sherman concluded that, since the factories had been working for the Confederate government for a number of years by supplying military goods, the women employees were "as much governed by the rules of war as if in the ranks." They were, in the general's estimation, as traitorous as the men who governed and fought for the Confederacy. He ordered about four hundred women arrested and deported by rail to Indiana, where he figured they could be dispersed to find employment again, but not for the benefit of the Confederacy. The order became symbolic of either the barbarism to come, or of the "modern" conception of war, one waged against all of society and not just its military. Just what it symbolized depended on one's sympathies.[30]

Newspapers in Tennessee, New York, Indiana, and Kentucky reported harsh treatment of the women, some deeming them "destitute," their condition "deplorable." One of the more severe assessments came from the New York *Commercial Advertiser*, which stated that it was "hardly conceivable that an officer bearing a United States commission of Major General should have so far forgotten the commonest dictates of decency and humanity, (Christianity apart) as to drive four hundred penniless girls hundreds of miles away from their homes and friends to seek their livelihood amid strange and hostile people." Historically, there is no evidence of mistreatment of the women, although their plight was real enough.[31]

Johnston's consistent retreating, however justified militarily, provided the excuse that President Jefferson Davis needed to replace him. Their relationship had been an uneasy one for some time. On July 17, Davis named General John Bell Hood the new corps commander. When Sherman read of the action in an Atlanta newspaper, he asked Schofield, who had attended West Point with Hood, what to expect of Hood. He was, Schofield said, extremely courageous, but to a degree that took him to "rashness." He told Sherman to expect an attack. A few days later, Hood ordered assaults on the Army of the Cumberland and the Army of the Tennessee. Though both attacks were repulsed, Sherman suffered a serious loss when McPherson was killed on July 22. Sherman named General Oliver O. Howard to replace McPherson, and directed Howard to cut the rail line from Macon to Atlanta. But supply lines were not cut, so Confederates barricaded themselves in the city. With an open line of fire to the city, Sherman settled in for the quasisiege. Military

targets were scattered about Atlanta, so the bombardment of the city inevitably and unintentionally found civilian targets. Meanwhile, Sherman extended his trench lines as he tried to completely surround the city and cut
Confederate supply lines.[32]

Nearly encircled, Hood had little choice but to pull out of the city, which
he did on September 2. Sherman's troops entered the city September 2, but
he personally took his time, getting there five days later, almost as if to say
"so what?" to the accomplishment, and that he didn't need a conqueror's
march at the head of the troops. When he did arrive, he ordered the expulsion of the whole population within five days. The Southern press was
aghast, the Northern press attentive, but any criticism was muted by the accomplishment of taking the city. The move had precedent. General Philip
Henry Sheridan had laid waste to the Shenandoah Valley; Sherman's foster
brother, General Thomas Ewing, had banished about 20,000 people from
several Missouri counties; and Sherman had in the previous year expelled the
people of Iuka, Mississippi, for sniping on Union boats. But Atlanta was big-
ger, more important, and in the heart of the South.[33]

Atlanta officials protested to Sherman, citing the consequences for the
women, children, and elderly. Though Sherman was sympathetic, he dismissed the protest because, he said, "The use of Atlanta for warlike purposes
is inconsistent with its character as a home for families. . . . War is cruelty
and you cannot refine it." Here was Sherman the realist, scolding Southerners for their genteel concept of war. Hood, too, objected, writing Sherman
that the order "transcends, in studious and ingenious cruelty, all acts ever before brought to my attention in the dark history of war." Sherman countered
that Confederates had started the war, and were responsible for the consequences. The correspondence with Hood and the mayor of Atlanta on the
morality of expelling civilians was widely reprinted in the North, where
Sherman was praised for his action.[34]

Sherman and Grant had been discussing a march on either Savannah or
Macon. With the Vicksburg triumph, the South was divided at the Mississippi River. An eastward march would cut the Confederacy again, and slic-
ing it along the Atlanta–Milledgeville–Savannah rail line would seriously
impair supplies to Lee's Army of Northern Virginia. Sherman was well aware
of the psychological benefits if such a plan succeeded.[35]

Stories have grown up about Sherman's destruction of Atlanta as he left
the city. Although it is not possible to know with certainty what damage
Sherman inflicted, it is clear that the Confederates share some of the blame.
Hood had destroyed a number of buildings, including ammunition depots, as
he left the city in September. Sherman did order the destruction of factories,

depots, and any other facilities that would be of use to the Confederates. In at least one case, a hidden ammunition depot ignited in a machine shop that was being destroyed, sending sparks through the night of November 15, and resulting in a number of houses burning. But the general did not burn the entire city. Some of the looting was at the hand of Atlanta's own.[36]

The March to the Sea

On November 16, Sherman left Atlanta with 62,000 of his best troops, selected for a tough, physical campaign, having culled those he deemed "sick, wounded and worthless." Thomas was sent north to block Hood, who had departed Georgia to attack Kentucky. The Union troops destroyed the rail line behind them, which also must have caused some concern because they were, in effect, wrecking their own supply line. They were not even burdened by tents. Each man carried only a blanket; a shirt and spare socks; a few cooking utensils; a ration of coffee, sugar, salt, and hard tack; and his gun with forty rounds of ammunition. The general split his command into two wings, Howard's Army of the Tennessee on the right, and General Henry Warner Slocum's newly designated Army of Georgia on the left. General Judson Kilpatrick's cavalry would go where needed, protecting flanks, skirmishing with guerrillas, and scouting. Sherman's historic field order no. 120 informed his command that it would "forage liberally on the country" in order to feed itself. Foragers were ordered to refrain from "abusive or threatening language," and to leave a written receipt with those from whom they took food. Troops were not to enter houses and were to leave some food with the family for its own sustenance. Destruction of any structure, including houses, was only to be done under order of corps commanders.[37]

The character of the March to the Sea was evident fairly quickly. Sherman's troops not only "foraged liberally," a term they interpreted liberally, but also began the destruction of the infrastructure, including railroads and factories. Sherman's "bummers," the troops assigned to scavenging the countryside for sustenance, became legendary in their ability to find hidden food and loot, whether it was buried or stashed in nearby swamps or woods. They were the very personification of Yankee villainy in the eyes of Georgians. The fighting was in the form of skirmishes and ambushes, mostly by Confederate cavalry and state militia, which by now consisted of young boys and old men. In addition, a large and growing contingent of former slaves fell in step behind Sherman's columns. Some were taken on as laborers, cooks, and teamsters. But for the most part Sherman saw them as a nuisance, a small army of refugees that needed food and care, and which could only slow his advance.[38]

Looting occurred, but fell out of fashion as troops discovered that anything they stole much larger than a silver spoon would soon become a burden; so candelabras, clocks, and paintings often were quickly discarded along the road. They took not only foodstuffs but livestock, oftentimes killing what they didn't consume or need in order to undermine any support for the enemy and further crush morale. They replaced worn out horses and mules with fresh ones plucked along the way. Though Sherman had ordered soldiers to "forage liberally," he did not approve of out-and-out plunder. But he also did not punish plunderers severely, if at all, even when he saw soldiers marching along, burdened with far more foodstuffs than would be consumed in the near future. They were fighting not just Southern soldiers, but also the civilians, in order to demoralize them and to make more evident the fact that their government could not protect them. Undoubtedly, some homes were ransacked and destroyed, some civilians assaulted, some atrocities committed. But such things were comparatively rare, given the size of the force sweeping through the countryside and the conditions under which it was operating.[39]

The two wings moved rapidly, at ten to fifteen miles per day, from twenty to sixty miles apart, a distance that would provide plenty of countryside from which to supply the troops. The general traveled with the left wing of his army, which feinted toward Augusta, while the right wing threatened Macon. The paucity of the Confederate resistance was exemplified by three brigades defending Griswoldsville, a village just outside the state capital of Milledgeville. On November 22, about 2,000 militiamen charged about 1,500 men of Sherman's Fifteenth Corps. After an afternoon of fighting, the militiamen left the field to the Union forces. Nearly a third of the Confederates remained on the battlefield, and the Yankees—veterans who had seen the blood and carnage of battle—were appalled by what they saw once the firing ceased and they ventured out. An Illinois officer recorded in his diary, "I was never so affected at the sight of wounded and dead before. Old grey-haired and weakly looking men and little boys, not over fifteen years old, lay dead or writhing in pain." Such comments would later add fuel to the myth—whether Sherman's unstoppable power or his unfathomable cruelty.[40]

A day later, the two wings converged on Milledgeville, which was undefended. Union troops destroyed various materiel, including gunpowder and ammunition, as well as about a thousand cotton bales, and they divided up about 1,500 pounds of tobacco. Legislators and the governor had fled, after the latter issued a proclamation calling into service all Georgia males age sixteen to fifty-five. Sherman's troops took it upon themselves to hold a legislative session, one lubricated by liquor, in which they mocked the bravado of the lawmakers with fiery rhetoric, and showed theatrical terror upon notification of the Yankees' approach.[41]

Griswoldsville would be the only real battle, though a limited one, of the campaign. More characteristic of the fighting that would ensue was that involving each side's cavalry, led by Kilpatrick and by Confederate General Joseph Wheeler. The Confederate cavalry was too small to risk a major engagement, and so was limited to a campaign of harassment all the way to Savannah. The drawn-out skirmish between Kilpatrick and Wheeler also revealed a dark side to war. When the Confederates caught a foraging party in action, the Union soldiers often were killed, their bodies left unburied as a sort of warning. Such action provoked Kilpatrick's men in turn. The generals corresponded, each charging the other with atrocities. In one instance, Kilpatrick informed Sherman of finding bodies of Union soldiers with their throats slit and rope burns on their necks. Sherman responded that when such acts occurred, Kilpatrick "may hang and mutilate man for man without regard to rank."[42]

Sherman marched. His foragers roamed. Their stated job was to find food for the troops and forage for livestock. But given the size and rapidity of the March, it would have been difficult in any circumstances for a given contingent to know how much to take and which territory to cover. As it was, several forage parties might descend on a farm over the course of several days, and those parties might range in size from only two or three to as many as twenty. And they were wasteful of the forage, often killing livestock in order to deprive the Confederates of it, or taking only choice cuts if they were already loaded with food. They took far more horses and mules than they needed to replenish those used in the March. Those not used were shot. Confederate cavalry at times found up to 150 mules and horses shot by the roadside. The zealous foragers were no doubt wasteful and inefficient, but it was an issue that seemed of little concern to their commander, who in his *Memoirs* refers to the "skill and success" of his foragers.[43]

Though the foraging was excessive, the general has been unjustly credited with another excess, and that is the use of fire, of literally burning his way across Georgia. In special field order no. 127, Sherman stated that if the enemy were to burn corn and forage on the route of the March, then "houses, barns, and cotton gins must also be burned to keep them company." It was a standing order that if troops were fired on from a building, then it would be torched. If a bridge were burned to impede the March, then the house of the person who did the burning would be burned. The folklore has Sherman burning thousands of houses, leaving "Sherman's sentinels," the brick chimneys, standing across the countryside. But most houses were left standing, according to a number of recent historical studies. Marion B. Lucas acknowledges that the Southern view of Sherman as a barbarian has been the most enduring one, but questions whether "total war" was ever an appropriate label for the Civil War, let alone for Sherman's March. Lucas points out that the presumed excesses of the March may have been due in part to Sherman's excesses with language, rather than actual deeds: "(H)e carried a big stick and spoke loudly. . . . Words spewed from Sherman's mouth like barbed wire." Likewise, according to Lee B. Kennett, there is no evidence of any more personal crimes—rapes and murders—than in earlier campaigns. In fact, the Southerners' own, Wheeler's cavalry, came to be seen by some Georgians as more destructive than Sherman's foragers.[44]

Any reservations the troops may have had about foraging liberally or any inclination to tread lightly across Georgia also were alleviated by what they saw of Union prisoners of war. At Millen, Georgia, they found a stockade, without shelter or water, that held three hundred Union prisoners. They also found seven hundred unmarked graves. Escapees from Andersonville confirmed the terror of the Confederate prison camps. The Union soldiers would have found the starvation even more damnable in the middle of such a wealthy countryside.

Because of the speed of the March and the general lack of communications lines, including access to both rail and telegraph lines, news about the expedition dried up. Sherman's antipathy to reporters probably contributed also, since he was not inclined to be very accommodating to correspondents. In the North, people were left to speculate, and even Lincoln was at a loss for information when Senator John Sherman inquired as to the whereabouts of his brother. Lincoln replied, "Oh, no, we have heard nothing from him. We know what hole he went in, but we don't know what hole he will come out of." Even the formerly antagonistic Cincinnati *Commercial*, which a few years earlier had accused Sherman of being insane, expressed great confidence in the general. The lack of information may have served only to enhance the drama and excitement of the March. The news coming out of the Confederate press probably did little to allay Southern fears or to feed Northern reservations. Southern newspapers would regularly make note of Sherman's pending doom, or his "retreat to the sea." Sherman and news of his March finally did arrive when he appeared at the outskirts of Savannah on December 10.[45]

A Christmas Present for Lincoln

The capture of Savannah was a fairly brief and bloodless affair. On December 13, Union forces took Fort McAllister in a brief engagement with few casualties. Its fall opened up a supply line to the ocean, where Union vessels were waiting. General William Hardee still defended the city with about

9,000 men, no match for Sherman's forces. The Confederate general on December 17 refused Sherman's surrender demand, and then four days later slipped out and into South Carolina on the only remaining escape route. Sherman moved into the city and sent the memorable telegram to Lincoln, offering the city as a Christmas present.

It was at this point that one of Sherman's more hard-line views finally demanded a response from Washington. Sherman's argument was with secession, not slavery, which he made clear before and during the war. During the March, slaves along the route would greet him and his troops as saviors. They had aided Sherman, acting as spies and giving directions. Sherman saw them as a burden, a growing mob to feed and care for who slowed down the March. The low point for Sherman's command in this respect occurred on December 9 at a crossing of Ebenezer Creek, just outside Savannah. There, the Fourteenth Corps commander, with the unlikely name of Jeff Davis, was crossing the river, Wheeler's cavalry not far behind in pursuit. After crossing, Davis ordered the pontoon bridge pulled up, which his men did, stranding trailing slaves on the other side. As the Confederate cavalry moved in, terrified men, women, and children began jumping into the river. An undetermined number drowned, though soldiers did help some ashore. The incident did nothing to soften Sherman's attitude, but the secretary of war was sent to visit Savannah as a result.

Stanton arrived on January 11, 1865. But Sherman defended Davis. Stanton arranged a meeting with about twenty blacks, mostly ministers, which Sherman thought an odd thing to do. Stanton wanted something done for the newly freed slaves, so he and Sherman, after much discussion, drafted special field order no. 15. In it, Sherman set aside land on South Carolina's Sea Islands for the former slaves and forbade whites from going there. Given Sherman's attitude toward blacks, it was quite a surprise. However, it appears to have been more the work of Stanton than Sherman. Once it was issued, Sherman did nothing to enact its terms.[46]

Sherman was already planning his next move, and at the beginning of 1865 he received Grant's approval for a march through the Carolinas. On January 19, Sherman issued orders for the northward march, and he began the advance on February 1. With entry into the cradle of secession, the mood of the troops changed, and the destruction of homes and property was more severe than it had been in Georgia. In spite of South Carolinians' dire threats, there was little resistance. Sherman's forces entered Columbia on February 17, and that night much of the city was destroyed by fire and looted by soldiers. Sherman ordered the destruction of arsenals, munitions, and other government facilities. Southerners blamed Sherman for the burning of

Columbia, and Sherman blamed Southerners, cavalry and artillery commander Wade Hampton in particular. Sherman said putting cotton bales in the streets was careless and caused fires to spread. Whoever was to blame—Sherman, Hampton, drunken soldiers, or former slaves—Columbia did burn, and Sherman did not apologize. Lucas concludes that both Union and Confederate forces were to blame, and that Sherman was not personally responsible.[47]

He left Columbia on February 20, going north on a path about thirty miles wide. Sherman reached the Confederate arsenal in Fayetteville, North Carolina, on March 11, and ordered its destruction. Johnston and Sherman collided again near Bentonville, on March 19, when Johnston attacked Sherman's left wing. The Confederates were repulsed, and Johnston withdrew two days later. Confederate collapse became inevitable. On April 6, Sherman learned of the fall of Richmond and Lee's westward retreat. Sherman began to march west in pursuit of Johnston. The Army of Northern Virginia surrendered on April 9, and on April 14 in Raleigh Sherman received Johnston's proposal for a cease-fire. As Sherman was en route to meet Johnston, he learned of Lincoln's assassination. When he showed the telegram to Johnston, the Confederate general pronounced it a disaster, and denied the Southern government had any role in it.

Meeting outside Durham on April 18, Johnston and Sherman agreed to surrender terms that went beyond military issues and into political terms for peace, which included recognition of existing state governments, guaranteed political rights, and a general amnesty. Unlike the terms of Lee's surrender at Appomattox, this surrender did not require that Confederates surrender their weaponry. Sherman apparently calculated that if civil unrest occurred, Southern officials would need armed forces to keep order. President Andrew Johnson and his cabinet almost immediately rejected the surrender terms. New terms were given Johnston, the same as those given the Army of Northern Virginia. Sherman received Johnston's surrender on April 26.[48]

As the nation began lurching toward reconciliation, and sometimes away from it, war stories became a staple of popular culture. Sherman and his boys were beginning another march, this time into the culture's imagination.

After Bentonville

Sherman and his family returned to Lancaster, where he received orders in summer 1865 assigning him to command of the Military Division of the Mississippi, which stretched from the Mississippi River to the Rocky Mountains, and from the Canadian to the Mexican borders, excluding Texas. The assignment also placed Sherman at the center of another critical issue for the westward-moving nation. Kennett has pointed out that Sherman was facing a complex issue that involved the Department of the Interior and its bureaucracy, the unfamiliar cultures of the American Indians, the Western settlers who wanted them simply gone, and a Congress that had no coherent policy. Anyone would have needed great diplomatic finesse and political acumen to find a route through such a political wilderness. Sherman did not have such skills. The fighting between the end of the war and 1890 almost always involved a relatively small number of soldiers and Indians. Despite the fact that he was named for an Indian chief, Sherman shared the commonly held opinion that the Indians were an inferior race and were impediments to progress. His feelings about Indians echoed his earlier words about blacks—they were inherently inferior to whites, and could not attain a higher, civilized culture without the assistance of whites. He saw two alternatives for Indians: extinction or confinement.[49]

When Sherman became commanding general in 1869, a number of Civil War generals were part of the Indian wars, but Sherman and Sheridan were the most vocal advocates of a harsh Indian policy. Grant had appointed Sherman in the summer of 1867 to a seven-man Indian Commission. Though the Indians had their defenders, those who would deal compassionately and fairly with them lost ground when, in June 1876, Chief Crazy Horse and somewhere between 2,000 and 4,000 Indian braves annihilated Lieutenant Colonel George Armstrong Custer and about 250 of his men at the Little Big Horn River in Montana. Militarily, it was a minor engagement. But it mobilized public opinion against the Indians and in favor of the hard war that Sherman advocated. As in the Civil War, he believed that compassion only prolonged the war and suffering.[50]

A Very Public General

Sherman had worried about the version of the war that would prevail—in particular the Lost Cause mythology that was emerging in the South. He believed it was historically inaccurate, and diminished his own accomplishments in the war. Sherman had started his memoirs in 1873, and within a month of their release in May 1875, more than 10,000 copies were sold. Reviews of the two-volume *Memoirs* were favorable, in spite of obvious flaws. His narrative started in 1846, meaning he ignored his own early years in Ohio. Not surprisingly, he was sharply critical of the war's "political generals," many of whom were still alive, and who did not always silently accept Sherman's condemnation. Sherman provoked special attention from Orville

Babcock, Grant's personal secretary. Babcock hired Washington journalist Henry Van Ness Boynton—a correspondent for the Cincinnati *Gazette*, an old news nemesis from the "insanity" episode—to attack the *Memoirs* and Sherman's war record. A series of newspaper articles, then a book, *Sherman's Historical Raid: The Memoirs in Light of the Record*, described the volumes as "intensely egotistical, unreliable, and cruelly unjust to nearly all his distinguished associates." Boynton pointed to, among other things, Sherman's surprise at Shiloh, the plunge into swamps at Chickasaw Bayou, and an overly critical assessment of Thomas at Kennesaw Mountain. He declared that Grant, not Sherman, conceived the March to the Sea. Sherman worked with his brother-in-law, Charles Moulton, to publish *The Review of General Sherman's Memoirs Examined, Chiefly in the Light of Its Own Evidence.*[51]

In the ensuing years, Sherman's characteristic restlessness manifested itself in public speaking, travel, meetings with fraternal organizations, and official functions, what Lloyd Lewis calls "one long chicken dinner." He was in great demand as a speaker, and apparently was a good one. He was especially popular with veterans, and regularly attended the annual meetings of the Society of the Army of the Tennessee (of which he was president for twenty-two years), the Society of the Army of the Cumberland, the Society of the Army of the Potomac, and the Grand Army of the Republic. Though Sherman was never one to sell himself short in his own accounts, he did not present the March as an extraordinary innovation in war or a departure from convention. Instead, he wrote in an article for *Century* magazine, it was simply a "shift of base" with the ultimate purpose of crippling Lee's army.

He could not resist the occasional blunt insult. In his analysis of the war, he noted, "Of course Charleston, ever arrogant, felt secure; but it was regarded by us as a 'dead cock in the pit,' and fell of itself when its inland communications were cut." If putting Charleston in its place was not enough, Sherman, in another article, lambasted the Confederacy's chief icon, Lee. It was in response to an article in *McMillan's Magazine*, which deemed Lee "the great American of the nineteenth century, whose statue is well worthy to stand on an equal pedestal with that of Washington," that Sherman retorted that Lee's "sphere of action was . . . local," and that he was not an "aggressive soldier." Sherman offered Grant and Thomas as both military and moral superiors to Lee, who failed to remain "true to his oath" by resigning his U.S. Army commission. In a *North American Review* article, Sherman wrote that Lee battled flames on his front porch while "the kitchen and house were burning, sure in the end to consume the whole." It was not only a rebuke of Lee, but of the whole Lost Cause movement's idea of the moral and martial superiority of the Confederacy.[52]

Sherman gave his most famous speech in August 1880, in Columbus, Ohio, where he accompanied President Rutherford B. Hayes to an encampment of the Grand Army of the Republic. After the president spoke, the crowd of veterans started calling for Sherman to speak. He had prepared no remarks. It was the occasion for his most famous words, "War is hell," though he never said exactly those words. In his brief remarks, he joked about rain that had begun to fall and how they had often camped in just such weather during the war; commented on his affection for all of them; and then said of war: "You all know this is not soldiering here. There is many a boy here today who looks on war as all glory, but, boys it is all hell." Kennett notes that the words "war is hell" do not appear in any surviving texts of Sherman's remarks. And John F. Marszalek points out that Sherman used similar words many times both before and after the Columbus speech and had commonly characterized the Civil War as "hell." The words and the idea were popular with the public, and the New York *Times* praised his condemnation of war.[53]

Still Fighting

Since the end of the war, Sherman had promoted development of the South as he traveled and socialized in the region. Generally, he retained his prewar fondness for the region and the people. His hard feelings about Confederates—those who would destroy the Union—were as severe as ever. When he had toured the South in 1879, he had been well received, and he had returned the good feelings. But there had been a glaring exception to his willingness to reconcile. Sherman's forgiveness came with a price, and that was loyalty to the Union, and not a qualified loyalty, whether it be subscribing to the Lost Cause mythology or just being an apologist for the rebellion. When, in that 1879 trip, he was asked to exchange greetings with Jefferson Davis, who was in another car on a train in which Sherman was riding, Sherman refused, no doubt due largely to the fact that Davis had continued to defend the South's justification in secession.

Two years later, Davis published *The Rise and Fall of the Confederate Government*, in which he defended secession, deemed the expulsion of Atlanta civilians an act of savagery, and called the March cruel, barbaric, and an absurd military maneuver. Implicitly acknowledging the South's ineffectiveness in the face of Sherman's March, Davis lauded Wheeler for "daringly and persistently" harassing Sherman, for delaying the March, for "attacking and defeating exposed detachments, deterring his foragers from venturing far from the main body," and for defending towns and protecting rail lines and depots. Davis accused Sherman of "infamous disregard" of the rule of war and the dictates of humanity. He called Sherman a hypocrite for blaming the burning of Columbia on Hampton. The March itself, Davis wrote, only succeeded because the Confederacy was weak. The volume is a masterpiece of myopic self-interest and self-promotion. At every turn, others are to blame; the Confederacy is a bastion of righteousness and bravery; and the Union soldiers are little more than armed hoodlums who loot and pillage.[54]

Sherman said he was more convinced than ever that Davis "is the type of a class that must be wiped off the face of the earth." His temper cooled within a few months, by which time he figured no one was reading Davis's volumes anyway. When he visited Atlanta in November, his anger had turned to bemusement, as he termed himself "the Vandal Sherman." But the hard feelings endured, and, two years later, Sherman renewed the imbroglio by calling the war a conspiracy, not a rebellion or secession. He said Davis's actions against the United States began when Davis was a part of its government, apparently referring to Davis's tenure as a U.S. senator and secretary of war. Sherman cited a letter from Davis to a Confederate governor that purportedly said Davis would use Lee's army against that state if it tried to secede from the Confederacy. The story spread in papers across the nation. Davis raged. He challenged Sherman to produce the letter, which Sherman could not find. He said it must have been in Chicago, where Sherman sent many of Davis's papers after he captured them. Sherman thought they were destroyed in the fire of 1871. His dislike of Davis, among others, was genuine and deep. That it was a personal issue for Sherman—and not one with the South—is demonstrated by the fact that in 1881, while the fight with Davis ground on, Sherman also visited the Atlanta International Cotton Exposition, to which he had subscribed $2,000. He continued the earlier habit of traveling and promoting the South.[55]

A Social Soldier

On his sixty-fourth birthday, February 8, 1884, Sherman retired from the U.S. Army. Within a few months, he was set upon again to run for office, the presidency no less. Again, he refused. And in so doing, he also managed to do so in a fashion both quotable and memorable: "I will not accept if nominated and will not serve if elected." He visited his old friend Grant, who was writing his memoirs and suffering from cancer, in New York. Grant died in July 1885, which meant Sherman was the Union's leading, living icon of the Civil War era. The demands on him continued as dinner speaker and club member—everything from theater clubs to scientific societies to veterans' groups to charities. He continued to read voraciously, especially Civil War material. Ever sensitive to the "wrong" version of the war that might be offered up to the public—namely, the Confederate's Lost Cause mythology—Sherman began work on revising his memoirs in 1885, in which he added chapters about his prewar and postwar years. In the new edition, Sherman remained unsentimental about his first twenty-six years of life, covering them in a chapter of modest length, most of which was devoted to the time from his West Point appointment to the Mexican War. The new concluding chapter, "After the War," was about twice the length of the new introductory chapter. Like the first chapter, the conclusion also managed to cover its years rather quickly. In short, the *Memoirs* was dedicated to the singular great event of his life, the Civil War, and his role in it.[56]

In addition to his *Memoirs*, Sherman turned to the popular press to see that the "correct" version of the war was presented to the public and to posterity. Both *Century* and *North American Review* published numerous articles by Sherman, including, in *Century* magazine, "The Grand Strategy of the War of Rebellion," notable in particular for Sherman's use of the more deprecating term, *war of rebellion*, rather than the more conventional *civil war*. He continued to hold in contempt, and to insult, the traitors, especially Davis. "No one has ever questioned the personal integrity of Mr. Davis, but we his antagonists have ever held him as impersonating a bad cause, from ambitious motives, often exhibiting malice, arrogance, and pride."[57] Though he continued to shun politics, he could not shed the habit of speaking out on an issue. In the October 1888 issue of *North American Review*, he argued that black Americans should be assured of the right to vote. He warned of another civil war if blacks continued to be denied suffrage. States that denied the right to black Americans—which largely meant Southern states—should have reduced representation in Congress. Sherman's racism seemed to have mellowed, but he was as perplexing as ever in terms of the South. He was on good terms with the South and Southerners, but would harshly rebuke them. And he did so in the context of a subject—the rights of blacks—to which he had appeared rather indifferent most of his life. In earlier years, he had said he had fought to save the Union, not to end slavery.[58]

"Last of the Mohicans"

He and Ellen moved in 1886 to New York City, where life suited him well. There were ample opportunities for the celebrity-general to socialize, address innumerable clubs, and attend events. By 1887, Ellen's health was declining, but Sherman—uncharacteristically in denial of reality—insisted that she would get better, noting that she had been a chronic complainer about health problems all her life. She apparently suffered from heart problems, and died in their New York home on November 28, 1888. Sherman slowed considerably after his wife's death, but still attended the theater and social events, speaking at the occasional veterans' reunion. The ranks of the Civil War generals were fading, and Sherman felt it. Grant had died in 1885, and Sheridan in 1888. He took to calling himself "the last of the Mohicans," as bouts of depression again plagued him.

On February 4, 1891, he went with a group in bad weather to the theater. He awoke the next morning with cold symptoms, which worsened over the next few days. A physician was called in on February 8, the general's seventy-first birthday, as his condition worsened. Despite Sherman's lifetime of indifference to religion, the family had a priest administer last rites as the general lay unconscious several days later. He died on Sunday, February 14. His Jesuit son Thomas officiated at a private service, and a public funeral procession in New York City included President Benjamin Harrison. Crowds gathered along the train route to St. Louis, where Sherman was buried alongside Ellen and his sons Willie and Charles. Among the pallbearers at the funeral had been eighty-four-year-old Joseph Johnston, who stubbornly refused to cover his head against the cold. He died the next month of pneumonia. The war was long over, most of its old soldiers dead. But the battle lines were drawn starkly in the contest for American memory.

Notes

1. William Tecumseh Sherman, *Memoirs of W. T. Sherman* (New York: Library of America, 1984; orig. pub. 1875), 600–601.

2. Lloyd Lewis, *Sherman: Fighting Prophet* (New York: Harcourt, Brace, 1932), 31–33, 46; Sherman, *Memoirs*, 13–14.

3. Lewis, *Sherman*, 34, 52–59; Sherman, *Memoirs*, 11–14.

4. Lee B. Kennett, *Sherman: A Soldier's Life* (New York: HarperCollins, 2001), 26–27; Lewis, *Sherman*, 67–69; John F. Marszalek, *Sherman: A Soldier's Passion for Order* (New York: Free Press, 1993), 39; Sherman, *Memoirs*, 17–21.

5. Marszalek, *Sherman*, 48–51; Sherman, *Memoirs*, 35–44, 64–65, 80; Lewis, *Sherman*, 77–79.

6. Marszalek, *Sherman*, 76–89; Sherman, *Memoirs*, 106–7, 113; Kennett, *Sherman*, 54–55; Lewis, *Sherman*, 85–87.

7. Kennett, *Sherman*, 58–61; Lewis, *Sherman*, 85–88; Marszalek, *Sherman*, 91–92; Sherman, *Memoirs*, 121.

8. Kennett, *Sherman*, 66–68; Sherman, *Memoirs*, 128–37.

9. Kennett, *Sherman*, 68–71; Lewis, *Sherman*, 91–93; Sherman, *Memoirs*, 137–43.

10. Kennett, *Sherman*, 86–87; Lewis, *Sherman*, 112–18; Sherman, *Memoirs*, 160–68.

11. Marszalek, *Sherman*, 125–35; Sherman, *Memoirs*, 164–73, 184.

12. Lewis, *Sherman*, 162–77; Marszalek, *Sherman*, 147–50; Sherman, *Memoirs*, 192–205.

13. Lewis, *Sherman*, 181–94; Sherman, *Memoirs*, 209–20, 223–32; Marszalek, *Sherman*, 160–63.

14. Marszalek, *Sherman*, 165–66; Sherman, *Memoirs*, 221–22, 234–35.

15. Lewis, *Sherman*, 212–14; Sherman, *Memoirs*, 245–49.

16. Steven E. Woodworth, *Nothing but Victory: The Army of the Tennessee, 1861–1865* (New York: Knopf, 2005), 157–58.

17. Woodworth, 202; Lewis, *Sherman*, 219–29; Marszalek, *Sherman*, 175–80; Sherman, *Memoirs*, 250–68.

18. Woodworth, *Nothing but Victory*, 197–99; Lewis, *Sherman*, 219–36; Kennett, *Sherman*, 161–62, 170.

19. Lewis, *Sherman*, 242–50; Kennett, *Sherman*, 172–75; Sherman, *Memoirs*, 278–79, 285, 301; Marszalek, *Sherman*, 194–96.

20. Kennett, *Sherman*, 187–95; Sherman, *Memoirs*, 308.

21. Marszalek, *Sherman*, 207–11; Sherman, *Memoirs*, 318–20, 339; Woodworth, *Nothing but Victory*, 250–53, 260–64.

22. Lewis, *Sherman*, 263–64; Marszalek, *Sherman*, 211–13.

23. Lewis, *Sherman*, 263–67; John F. Marszalek, *Sherman's Other War: The General and the Civil War Press* (Kent, OH: Kent State University Press, 1982), 137–61.

24. Sherman, *Memoirs*, 351–57; Woodworth, *Nothing but Victory*, 390–424.

25. Kennett, *Sherman*, 210–16: Lewis, *Sherman*, 314–23; Sherman, *Memoirs*, 379–83, 386–92; Woodworth, *Nothing but Victory*, 468–77.

26. Marszalek, *Sherman*, 249–54; Sherman, *Memoirs*, 417–21, 429–30, 463, 468, 489.

27. Lewis, *Sherman*, 366; Sherman, *Memoirs*, 467–68, 472–73, 495–96.

28. Marszalek, *Sherman*, 264–70; Sherman, *Memoirs*, 496–518, 521–23.

29. Marszalek, *Sherman*, 271–74; Sherman, *Memoirs*, 520, 525–42.

30. Hartwell T. Bynum, "Sherman's Expulsion of the Roswell Women in 1864," *Georgia Historical Quarterly* 54 (1970), 169–81.

31. Ibid.

32. Sherman, *Memoirs*, 548–59.

33. Kennett, *Sherman*, 252; Sherman, *Memoirs*, 582–84.

34. Kennett, *Sherman*, 210–11; Marszalek, *Sherman*, 285; Sherman, *Memoirs*, 585–604.

35. Lee B. Kennett, *Marching through Georgia: The Story of Soldiers and Civilians during Sherman's Campaign* (New York: Harper Perennial, 2001), 226–27; Sherman, *Memoirs*, 614–15, 619, 621, 627–28, 640–41.

36. Sherman, *Memoirs*, 649–55.

37. Kennett, *Sherman*, 262–64; Kennett, *Marching through Georgia*, 242–43; Sherman, *Memoirs*, 660–61.

38. Kennett, *Marching through Georgia*, 247; Sherman, *Memoirs*, 657–58.

39. Lewis, *Sherman*, 452–54; Sherman, *Memoirs*, 658–60.

40. Kennett, *Marching through Georgia*, 254–55; Sherman, *Memoirs*, 663–64; Charles Wright Wills, *Army Life of an Illinois Soldier, Including a Day by Day Record of Sherman's March to the Sea* (Washington, DC: Globe Printing, 1906), 324.

41. Kennett, *Marching through Georgia*, 257–62; Sherman, *Memoirs*, 666–67.

42. Kennett, *Marching through Georgia*, 264; Lewis, *Sherman*, 448.

43. Kennett, *Marching through Georgia*, 269–73; Sherman, *Memoirs*, 658.

44. Kennett, *Marching through Georgia*, 275–78; Marion B. Lucas, "William Tecumseh Sherman v. the Historians," *Proteus* 17:2 (2000), 15–21.

45. Lewis, *Sherman*, 457–58; Marszalek, *Sherman*, 306.

46. Marszalek, *Sherman*, 312–15.

47. Lewis, *Sherman*, 504–7; Marion B. Lucas, *Sherman and the Burning of Columbia* (College Station: Texas A&M University Press, 1976), 163–67.

48. Lewis, *Sherman*, 555; Marszalek, *Sherman*, 346–50.

49. Kennett, *Sherman*, 292–97.

50. Lewis, *Sherman*, 596–99; B. H. Liddell Hart, *Sherman: Soldier, Realist, American* (New York: Dodd, Mead, 1929), 408–9; Marszalek, *Sherman*, 380–82, 389–90, 398.

51. Kennett, *Sherman*, 317–20; Lewis, *Sherman*, 615–17; Marszalek, *Sherman*, 465.

52. Kennett, *Sherman*, 327–28; Lewis, *Sherman*, 631–33; Marszalek, *Sherman*, 468–71; William T. Sherman, "The Grand Strategy of the War of the Rebellion," *Century* 13 (February 1888), 582–98; William T. Sherman, "Grant, Thomas, Lee," *North American Review* 144 (May 1887), 437–50.

53. Kennett, *Sherman*, 328; Lewis, *Sherman*, 635–36; Marszalek, *Sherman*, 477.

54. Jefferson Davis, *The Rise and Fall of the Confederate Government, Vol. 2* (New York: Appleton, 1881), 564, 571–72, 627, 701–2.

55. Marszalek, *Sherman*, 473.

56. Lewis, *Sherman*, 631.

57. Sherman, "The Grand Strategy of the War of the Rebellion," 582–98.

58. William T. Sherman, "Old Shady, with a Moral," *North American Review* 147 (October 1888), 361–68.

$\backsim$

Industrial-Strength Sherman
The Press, the Idea, the Myth

A sea rolls between them and us—a sea of blood.

Civil War diarist, November 1864, in Columbia,
South Carolina, on Sherman's approach[1]

Time and legend have given the March to the Sea far more significance than the march north from Savannah through the Carolinas. Sherman, in his *Memoirs*, deemed the second march ten times as important as the march from Atlanta to Savannah. The Carolinas campaign was critical to ending the war, but the Sherman legend was born in the March to the Sea, and his legacy to this day almost reflexively makes Sherman and the March to the Sea, not the campaign northward, synonymous. There are good reasons for the attention going to the Atlanta–Savannah March: Sherman faced more powerful Confederate forces in Tennessee and Georgia; the idea of abandoning supply and communications lines was radical and untested; and the political atmosphere was far more tenuous before the Georgia campaign than it was after the capture of Savannah.

Mark Twain and Charles Dudley Warner branded the period the "Gilded Age" with their 1873 satire of the same title, which lambasted greed, politicking, and profiteering. The Gilded Age came to symbolize the dark side of capitalism and the need for reform. Concerns were justified. By 1900, a few large corporations dominated critical industries, such as oil and steel, and by 1904 a mere 4 percent of businesses were responsible for 57 percent of American production. From the Civil War, the new managers learned hierarchical management and organization, and the importance of communication and transportation. Command extended from individual section leaders at the base of a pyramid to a company president and board of directors at the top. That corporate America took lessons from war is not surprising, considering that many Northern and Southern generals worked for the railroads after the Civil War.[2]

The collapse of the Southern plantation system and the rise of the robber barons in the North were harbingers of radical change in American society. The last three decades of the nineteenth century were ones of conquest, not only of the geographic frontier, but also of social, political, and economic frontiers. War symbols were imbued with new meaning. The Confederate flag could be both a reminder of slavery and the banner of the ennobling Lost Cause. An individual such as Sherman could be both heroic and villainous. On the one hand, he was a man ahead of his time, who was said to have invented a new mode of industrial war, baring a stark reality stripped of pretentiousness, and bringing a speedy end to a great tragedy. On the other hand, he could be seen simply as a new version of a barbaric Vandal, one with a singular goal of conquest, unburdened by sacred tradition and honor.

And so the story of Sherman became two competing narratives. The Northern, or Yankee, mind enshrined an individual who exemplified opportunism and efficiency, a man who was bold and creative in making the system meets its goals. That same person, for the still-defensive South, symbolized the soulless machine of industrialism, in which cultural values and traditions were sacrificed for mere results. Well before the March to the Sea ever began, the essential elements of what would become the Sherman myth were in place—a homely, eccentric, intellectual character, sometimes ruthless and at other times charitable, so driven and purposeful a leader that on occasion he seemed close to a breakdown. He was an innovative general, but one who made errors. He took command and assumed personal responsibility, and when things went wrong he might assail others, especially the press. The aura of menace, which took on new vitality and served military goals during the March, had its beginnings well before Atlanta, and probably as early as Memphis.

Newspapers of the war era and the decades following offered to the public a variety of Shermans, ranging from a fiery, eccentric, effective commander to an unpredictable, menacing, even irrational mob leader. What in some accounts was an innovative wartime commander was in others the head of an invading force. In the South, Sherman's perceived role changed from that of mere invader to that of violator as the fate of the Old South became more dire. The conduct of war itself changed in similar fashion, and what began as a grand, romantic adventure for many in the South eventually became a gross violation of a civil society. In the North, Sherman evolved from madman to military genius. The foundations of what would become the competing Sherman mythologies were a result of stories that were "negotiated" with the audiences of a mass press, which had to create a narrative that its audiences would appreciate as both stories and morality tales. So a peculiar, volatile character disappears into the Georgia countryside, destination unknown, and puts the finishing touches on renegade Confederates.

Sherman versus the Press: Before the March

Newspapers and magazines may have been at the zenith of their influence in nineteenth-century America, and they were the principal conduit of a public discourse that defined the standards for evaluating leaders. The press ranged from the phenomenal circulations and vulgarity of the "Yellow Press" to the idealism of reform-minded muckrakers. The press also varied widely, even extremely, during the war itself in terms of circulations, propaganda function, and resources for gathering information. In the North, Grant and Lincoln both were generally hospitable to the press, with a more or less tolerant attitude toward reporters and newspapers. In the South, the Davis administration rarely indulged the press. Southern newspapermen were exempted from conscription, however, along with some state officials and teachers, all under the rubric of providing vital services to the Confederacy. Toward the end of the war, Davis asked the Confederate Congress to end the professional exemptions, a move that provoked virulent opposition from the Southern press. Davis called for the change in law in November 1864, as the South was weakening and as Sherman was setting out from a burning Atlanta. The Confederate president's timing was poor, making the call appear to be not only a desperate action, which it was, but an attempt to manipulate the press, which it apparently was not.[3]

Though most Southern newspapers supported the Confederacy and the war, numerous papers were critical of both. The Richmond *Examiner* consistently criticized Davis and his cabinet, as did the Mobile *Daily Tribune* and *Daily Advertiser and Register*. In Knoxville, Tennessee, the *Whig's* editor, William "Parson" Brownlow, was accused of treason for opposing secession and was banished to the North in March 1863. In Raleigh, North Carolina, a Georgia brigade passing through the city to fight at Chickamauga wrecked the offices of the *Standard*. Its editor had been accused by no less than Robert E. Lee of "disgraceful 'peace' sentiments." The editor, W. W. Holden, another Davis critic, initially had urged peace negotiations, and later said North Carolina should negotiate its own treaty. Dissent, though, may have been more a matter of absolute numbers than proportions in the South. By February 1864, the number of Southern newspapers had shrunk from eighty to only thirty-five. Most pro-Union newspapers in the South quickly became supporters of the Confederacy. The Northern contrast was both in degree and in number. The South had numerous sympathizers in the Northern press, and even staunchly pro-Union papers were often critical of Lincoln and the war effort.[4]

Civil War era newspapers were truly mass media—widely available, cheap, fueled by competition in both midsize and large cities. As publishers looked to entice readers, they often degenerated into the sensational. Along with these changes, the idea of "news" changed from a more passive mode of printing what came to the office, to seeking out the news. The greater power of the press—both economically and in shaping public opinion—did not necessarily mean a more responsible press. In fact, newspapers often were quite irresponsible in reporting. The limits of irresponsibility appeared simply to be a matter of how much readers would tolerate.[5]

Sherman was never on good terms with the press. By war's beginning, the First Amendment protection of free speech or free press did not loom large in Sherman's conception of Constitutional guarantees. The insanity episode in late 1861, provoked by the Cincinnati *Commercial* blaring "General William T. Sherman Insane," was picked up in other papers, including the New York *Herald*, the Cincinnati *Gazette*, and *Frank Leslie's Illustrated Newspaper*. Though the topic was short lived in the press, it was not out of Sherman's memory.[6]

Memphis fell to the Union in June 1862, and Sherman became the city's military governor the next month. Three influential Confederate newspapers in that city—the *Appeal*, the *Avalanche*, and the *Argus*—only exacerbated the general's feelings about the press. He quickly drew up rules for the city's newspapers, informing them that their job was to help maintain order, to be devoted to the United States, and not to be "personal, abusive, [deal in] innuendoes." People engaged in such activities, he stated, were "greater enemies" to the Union than the Confederate soldiers. The Northern papers usually were safely out of the general's reach. But in the course of his military governorship, he gladly arrested a reporter for the Chicago *Times* (on order from Grant) for a story "false in fact and mischievous in character"; had the editor of the Army's own newspaper, the *Union Appeal*, arrested for an article critical of a general in Arkansas; and had the *Argus* take out a $10,000 bond to ensure future good behavior after the editors printed material that Sherman felt showed "a spirit of insubordination and resistance to authority." Marszalek argues persuasively that the Memphis period showed the depth of

Sherman's antipress bias, and his willingness to disregard the First Amendment and to suppress publications.[7]

Sherman's most significant collision with the press took place during the Vicksburg campaign in December 1862, when he court-martialed New York *Herald* correspondent Thomas Knox as a spy. The court found Knox guilty of disobeying orders, but found no criminality involved and ordered him outside Union lines. At its core, the action was not about aiding the enemy, but the general's enduring animosity toward the press. He was in the extreme in believing that any news about the war or specific battles was useful to the enemy.[8]

The Fall of Atlanta

The press coverage of the Atlanta campaign was a microcosm of the whole Sherman-press relationship to date. Newspapers praised his character, criticized his shortcomings as a tactician, admired his shrewd maneuvers, condemned his brutality, and commended his realist's view of war. The image of his barbarism blossomed with the capture of Roswell Factory in July 1864. It was as though he were confirming Southern fears of a ruthless invader. He burned the textile mills and expelled four hundred or so women who worked in the factories. The New York *Commercial Advertiser* cringed at the violation of the "dictates of decency and humanity . . . the frightful disgrace." The New Albany (Indiana) *Daily Ledger* reported that the exiles were in "very destitute condition," and the article was picked up by papers in Louisville and in Madison, Indiana. Both of the latter cities had been way stations and stopping points for some of the women. The New York *Tribune* may have had the recent court-martial of Thomas Knox in mind when it reported the burnings in obfuscated fashion: "Major Tompkins, who was ordered to clear the place and destroy the mill, performed his duty in the most soldierly manner, giving the people all the time it was possible to save their household furniture in the tenement houses." Though minor as an event in the war, the expulsion was recalled and studied for decades: fifty years later a legal scholar declared Sherman's action a deviation from the accepted rules of conduct; and seventy years later the Atlanta *Journal* interviewed a man who claimed he and his mother were among those expelled. It would be a catalyst for the myth of a brutal Sherman. In destroying Roswell Factory, Sherman justified his actions on the grounds that it was an operational base for Confederate guerrillas.[9]

Sherman's move toward Atlanta did not generate special excitement in the coverage of the general or his maneuvers, probably because the Eastern theater was getting more attention. The New York *Herald* seemed blase about

Sherman in June 1864, about three months before Atlanta fell. The paper showed respect for the general but was not awed by his actions or intentions:

> Sherman's victories in Georgia are somewhat dwarfed in popular estimation by the nearness of the struggle in Virginia; but alone they would have been sufficient to decide the fate of the rebellion. He also initiated his campaign by flanking Johnston out of a tremendously strong position at Buzzard's Roost and Dalton, continued it by flanking him out of Ressacca [sic], and has finally driven him, by maneauvres and by battle, to the city of Atlanta—one hundred miles.[10]

But the *Herald*, in a style common to the time, ran dramatic narratives and first-person accounts from correspondents when possible, replete with opinion and speculation. On the same day the paper pointed out that the Georgia campaign was dwarfed by battles in the East, nearly an entire inside page was devoted to a detailed account of a battle at New Hope Church—complete with maps and multiple-deck headlines, one trumpeting the "Brilliant Operations of Our Armies in Georgia," and concluding in true dramatic fashion with a hint of mystery, implying inside knowledge on the part of the reporter about Sherman's intentions:

> The operations of General Sherman's army, though very inadequately understood by the people, cannot yet safely be explained. His campaign is one of enormous dimensions, and is second only to Richmond. In fact, it is as important as Richmond; for the success of either one depends upon the success of the other. But it is better to say nothing on this subject now.[11]

It may have been some license taken by the reporter. More likely, and given Sherman's record of press relations, the reporter was attempting to endear himself to the general or to minimize the animosity. Any praise was temporary, however, and Sherman would have to earn his praise. A month later the *Herald* speculated that Johnston would keep retreating before Sherman and avoid a "final fight," which would "perhaps complicate matters elsewhere." In such a course of action, the *Herald* found a "peculiar military genius by Johnston" in his ability even to sustain operations in the face of so much adversity. Furthermore, "General Sherman has not the intuitive perception of military genius. He has less vigor than he was credited with at the commencement of this campaign. Johnston is his superior in both these particulars."[12]

In early August, the *Herald* announced Sherman's progress and its own daring in even relaying news of the military situation. A page-one report noted that transmission of the news to follow was not permitted, but that it would be of no military use by the time the paper ran the story. The correspondent believed Sherman was avoiding a direct engagement with the Confederates by advancing and delaying toward Atlanta. The Confederates' choice, in short, was "a siege or a skedaddle." The newspaper, which only a few weeks earlier had found Sherman inferior to Johnston, praised Sherman for his tactics: "All this is highly favorable to Sherman's plans, and he will as certainly outgeneral Hood as he has outgeneraled Johnston." This could have been a turning point in the public image of Sherman. The very attributes that had been part of the evidence of insanity a few years earlier were now eccentricities, even inspiring those around him. In a sketch of Sherman in the article, the *Herald* stated: "The salient point—the most striking feature—of Gen. Sherman's character is a peculiar nervous energy that shows no cessation, and which is resisting and inspiring. It gives energy to others." The paper described the general as untiring, attentive to detail, and decisive, as he paced ceaselessly, "smoking segar after segar" and, of course, as absent-minded. It also recognized something that later became critical to the memory of the war—differing perspectives between North and South. One, the correspondent said, saw it as a "great struggle between two races," and the other saw it as a "personal quarrel." In raising the issue of whether Union troops should guard the property and lives of "secessionists," the article noted that many people believed "the rebellion can be put down by persecuting the women and children whose natural protectors have run away and left them to our mercy." The *Herald* was assailing Southern men, who had "run away." Sherman, too, came to embody the assault on Southern masculinity, as they fled before him or failed to confront him.[13]

With the fall of Atlanta in early September, Sherman's reputation went up, at least in the North, as the rebels' military reputation shrank. The *Herald* said Sherman's "masterly strategic movements" were a prelude to capturing the whole state of Georgia, which Hood was defending by conscripting "numerous boys and old men." The Richmond papers were reported to be telling readers that it was actually Sherman in retreat, which in the face of reality appeared to make the Confederate words desperately silly. Northern newspapers transformed Sherman into a brilliant strategist, an "enterprising commander." Atlanta became a juncture in the war, recognized in the press both North and South. It also saw shifting perceptions, from the genius generals and their warriors in gray to commanders of incessant retreat, the ranks a "contemptible crowd of trembling, nerveless old men and barefooted boys."[14]

War's hard heel had begun crushing Southern confidence, and Sherman was wearing the boot. The Washington *Chronicle*, with its Confederate sympathies, cast about for solace in other Southern papers. Several weeks after Sherman took Atlanta, and while his intentions were a topic of speculation North and South, the Richmond *Examiner* reported that Confederate armies "maintained" their positions while Sherman arranged for "another campaign." Some officers even expected no further advance in Georgia for the year. In a separate dispatch, the *Examiner* went beyond the military story, striking at the cultural issues of Southern dignity and Northern disgrace. The paper reported a train of Atlanta exiles to have been robbed by Union troops carrying out that "inhumane and unprecedented military order" to evacuate Atlanta. Even worse, though, was a "grand ball and blowout" the Yankees held shortly after entering Atlanta. About a dozen women attended, it was reported, "not a decent lady among them." As evidence of the lowliness, it continued, "Several respectable negro women, who were invited and sent after in carriages, with Yankee officers for escorts, refused to go. . . . They looked on it as an indignity to be asked by the enemies of their country to associate with the white women who attended the ball." The reported event was a crude parody of a Southern ball, as though Northerners longed to emulate Southern traditions, but failed to comprehend the rituals, like a pretender to Christianity gluttonously guzzling the communion wine. In other words, a white woman who was friendly to the Yankees was even lower than blacks had been. The *Examiner*'s exhortation was a warning of the new, lowly status created by war, a status now even beneath the blacks. It was a status that would eventually serve to pit poor whites against blacks and against the North.[15]

The *Chronicle* and many other papers, North and South, also reprinted Sherman's letter to General Hood, in which Sherman logically dissected an appeal concerning the Atlanta expulsion:

> In the name of common sense I ask you not to "appeal to a just God" in such a sacrilegious manner—you who, in the midst of peace and prosperity, have plunged a nation into war, dark and cruel war; who dared and badgered us to battle; insulted our flag; seized our arsenals and forts that were left in the honorable custody of a peaceful ordnance sergeant; seized and made prisoners of even the very first garrisons sent to protect your people against negroes and Indians, long before any other act was committed by the, to you, "hateful Lincoln Government." . . . turned loose your privateers to plunder unarmed ships; expelled Union families by the thousands, burned their houses, and declared by act of your Congress the confiscation of all debts due Northern men for goods had and received. Talk . . . not to me, who has seen these things, and who will this day make as much sacrifice for the peace and honor of the South as the best born Southerner among you. If *we must be enemies, let us be men,*

and fight it out as we propose to-day, and not deal in such hypocritical appeals to God and humanity. [emphasis added]

God will judge us in due time, and He will pronounce whether it be more humane to fight with a town full of women and the families of "a brave people" at our back, or to remove them in time to places of safety among their own friends and people."[16]

The letter is notable because it was such a harsh rebuke—the logic of war in the face of a losing soldier's appeal to God. The letter reminded Hood of Southern actions, of who initiated the action, and of the consequences of those actions. The coup de grace was to call into question Southern masculinity. In a turn of events, it was now the Northerner—Sherman—belittling the Southerner's martial spirit and thus his masculinity: "let us be men." Though Sherman did not create the crisis of Southern identity that followed the war, his comment to Hood illustrated the issue clearly, as the March would foreshadow the crumbling Old South myth. The letter shows, at the least, indifference to Southern myth.

In the North, the same event—the evacuation of Atlanta—prompted praise for Sherman. The *Herald* found the letter to Hood to be a "noble piece of scorn well thrown at one who had fought as long as he could and then snivelled at his defeat." The article also cited a letter from the mayor of Atlanta asking that families not be removed, an idea the *Herald* dismissed as a ruse to keep spies in the city. The letter "does not read like the defiant documents that were wont to emanate from Southern functionaries when the war was at a safe distance."[17]

The exchange of letters anticipates the cultural conflict to come—which set of values, what standard of judgment, the emergence of two Shermans. His reputation was growing as a soldier of action and plain words. The *Herald* found in him "a Titan in both spheres—whose great acts challenge the admiration of the world, and whose utterances the people learn to seize with the most eager avidity."[18] It was the sort of praise that made a historically ideal prelude to the March. Sherman was being cast as hero, a man of action and wisdom, a bit mysterious in some respects, leaving the public to guess as to his next move.

The Press and the March

Given the magnitude and importance of the March, press coverage was relatively sparse, both North and South. This was simply a matter of access—reporters' lack of access to the action, and poor access to telegraph, rail, and shipping lines by which to send copy back to newspapers. The nature of the March to the Sea was problematic for the press, insofar as it was a fight that was strung out from Atlanta to Savannah and took place over the course of months rather than a few days. Once the fighting left Atlanta, there was no single battle to define it, no momentous action or decision around which to build a news story. In fact, it was, on a daily basis, a rather dull story: "Sherman's troops walk another 20 miles, steal more chickens and cows, steal more mules and horses, march through another Georgia village without resistance, few casualties," to parody what the daily story might have looked like. There were "big events" such as the taking of Savannah and, after the March to the Sea, Columbia. But they were almost anticlimactic, mere affirmations of the inevitable, demonstrating what the March made evident: that the North was stronger and the South increasingly defenseless. Newspapers often simply had to print a "no news" bulletin. Though doing nothing in the way of informing the public, such notices may have heightened the mystery and drama of the March. Viewed from afar, either in terms of time or distance or both, one can see how such non-news helped build to a dramatic crescendo in which Sherman suddenly appeared, after weeks of speculation as to his whereabouts and the terror-inspiring rumors, at Savannah's doorstep.

Access, non-events, and telegraph lines were press issues in both North and South. In the latter, the issues were exacerbated. The South had fewer telegraph lines and fewer newspapers, and, like the Southern generals, the Southern reporters could only guess about Sherman's next move. Like the "no news" bulletins of the North, the speculation and rumor in Southern newspapers could have increased apprehension, and enhanced myths, about the March. Sherman would not have minded.

His restrictions on the press had worked well during the Atlanta campaign, with many reports consisting of generalities about his army's location and successes. The same would be true after Sherman left Atlanta—destination unknown—but the flow of information would be more than a matter of Sherman's policies. Communication suffered not just from the nature of the March, but from the fact that even the goal was uncertain: Richmond? Columbia? Savannah and the Atlantic Ocean? Sherman issued no new order concerning the press when he left Atlanta on November 15, 1864. Only eight to ten correspondents accompanied his army, and they would have been acutely aware of Sherman's disinclinations about press freedom. "No news from Sherman" was a common report in Northern newspapers. The initial stories summed up the dilemma for the press fairly well: "Where is Sherman?" the Chicago *Tribune* asked on November 19. The following day, the New York *Herald* wondered, too, "Where Has Sherman Gone?" Not even

Lincoln appeared to know. The drying up of news during the March in itself made the general's Christmas present to Lincoln—the city of Savannah—all the more exciting. The Chicago *Tribune*, a bit hyperbolic but probably sincere, compared Sherman to Anabasis, Marlborough, Wellington, and Napoleon. It was quite a comparison coming from a paper that had been a consistent critic of Sherman.[19]

Confederate newspapers, due obviously to very different circumstances, provided even less information about the March. Sometimes it was misinformation. By this time, newspapers had suffered from a lack of paper, ink, and personnel. One unusual newspaper, the *Countryman*, published on a plantation in Putnam County, Georgia, has the historical distinction of being the only periodical published on a Southern plantation. A literary publication, it circulated widely and was quoted extensively in the Southern press, and it provided a window on the Southern planter's fears and mindset concerning Sherman. Its publisher, Joseph Addison Turner, ran the family plantation, including more than three hundred slaves, while his brother and brother-in-law were in the military. Turner did not become a soldier because a childhood ailment had left him lame. Reports in the *Countryman* illustrated too well the communications breakdown, and the fact that rumor and speculation would fill the information void.

At the end of July 1864, as Sherman was making his way to Atlanta, Yankee foragers visited one of Turner's neighbors, who reported that the Union soldiers behaved well, taking only food and horses and treating the women with respect. A few days later, on August 2, a "squad" of Yankees passed through the neighborhood, "variously estimated at from 75 to 75,000." As though those numbers were not sufficiently indicative of the confusion and unreliability of information, the newspaper reported on the same day, in another story, that three Yankees had visited Turner's plantation, which he and the others had fled, and had taken only corn. "We suspected, immediately, that this was a squad of our cavalry, who had taken one of our negroes, as a pilot; but we could not know it. Afterwards, it turned out to be so." Not only was he unable to give any reasonable estimate on the number of troops in the area, but he could not even be sure of whether Rebels or Yankees were at the plantation. The *Countryman* acknowledged that it often was dealing in innuendo, as it chronicled several visits to the plantation after the March to the Sea had commenced. Turner's accounts typically reported the solders to be well behaved, but willing to take what they pleased.

On one occasion, the Yankee humor did not resonate, understandably, with the Southerners, who reported that a group of four Yankees had visited the plantation. Their names included "T. W. Sherman" and "John Smith," at least according to the Yankees. When questioned by the Southerners, the Yankees said they were unrelated, respectively, to the general or to Pocahontas. Turner's losses in various raids included a gold watch, silverware, saddles, a wagon, horses and mules, and three slaves. The soldier who took the watch was the one who called himself "T. W. Sherman." A report on November 26 concerning Sherman—the general, this time—reflected the continuing dearth of information, as well as a degree of Southern self-delusion: "The Yankees did not go to Macon at all [as reported earlier], but are fleeing towards the coast—Wheeler on their right flank, Hampton on their left, and our forces gathering in front."[20]

Though Sherman's March had been deemed many things, few called it a flight. In the same issue, the *Countryman* reported on another Yankee visit to the plantation, and it reflected both the fears for and the fighting spirit of Southern women, in which the much heralded fighting spirit resided:

A mob of savage yankees, and some Europeans, surrounding us with a pistol, and the torch—our children frightened—a mother and sister calling upon us for counsel, and assistance—our wife put away in her room, by our own hand, where we begged her to stay—our fears excited all the while, lest she should betray her indignation, and give vent to her feelings, in words which might cause the hyenas to insult her—this is what we have had to endure, and this is what thousands upon thousands of other people, at the south have had to endure.[21]

The wife was not only the one most willing to fight, but also to fight in spite of being well aware of the personal risk. A few weeks after Sherman's troops had reached Savannah, Turner found himself embarrassed for Georgia and the entire Confederacy:

Well, Sherman has marched through Georgia from one end to the other; and though we have no idea his march was half so "agreeable" as he represents it, yet he has gone through, comparatively uninjured—hardly receiving a scratch. This should mantle with the blush of shame the cheek of every Georgian, and every Confederate. We, for one, feel deeply mortified—humbled, chagrined— even degraded. It is a bitter draught we have had to quaff: and yet God pressed the chalice to our lips. We must accept the lesson which he has taught us.[22]

The North also noticed that Southern bravado had diminished. In a long report taking up all of page 1 on January 2, 1865, the Cincinnati *Daily Gazette* cast the war as a moral conflict in which the "heathen" fled before "our army . . . an instrument of Divine wrath." Comparing Sherman to kings and ancient Greek heroes, the newspaper recalled the nation "in suspense . . . our war kings . . . crashing through the very center of the Confederacy, sweeping towns and cities, and cultivated lands with the terrible scourge of a destroying army." According to the report, not only had the South lost any claim to morality it may have had, but Sherman's forces were anointed the historical descendants of royalty. It was far more than a military victory, as the Union forces were credited with destroying slave pens and "implements of this modern Inquisition." Even Southern editors were rebuked: "[The editors'] knowledge of confederate affairs has suddenly become as limited as their circulation, and that reaches no farther than South Carolina. . . . [T]hey stand dumb as the tomb, or, in very mockery of the questioners, exclaim, '. . . Peace and independence are at hand.'"[23]

Newspapers in neighboring states apparently did little to assuage Georgians' pride. Governor Joseph Shaw, when the Georgia legislature reconvened in early 1865, alluded to press taunts for the failure of Georgians to confront and defeat the enemy, and added:

> General Sherman ought to have been totally defeated and ruined, but the sad fact will be handed down to posterity that while Sherman's minions were devastating the country with fire and committing outrages upon defenseless women, the men of Georgia staid [sic] at home or at least a large portion of them, trying to save what they had.[24]

The New York *Times* noted Georgians' apathy, too, the nominal resistance and minimal sacrifice, and contrasted Georgians' martial reticence to the fighting spirit and sacrifice of Russians and Tyrolese who had harassed Napoleon.[25] As one myth incubated, another decayed.

When news flowed again with Sherman's appearance in Savannah, the contrast in coverage had taken distinctive, predictable turns: celebration in the North, dismay and defeat in the South, for those newspapers that still published. News of the March had gone from a simple, honest "no news" to fabrications of Sherman's "flight to the sea" to describing the appearance in Savannah in prophetic terms, replete with resurrection and avenging-angel references. Sherman's triumph became, in many Northern papers, a call to account for the moral transgressions of Southern culture.

When Union troops marched into Savannah on December 21, it was almost without incident. There was some minor looting, and the groups blamed for it—Union troops, Wheeler's fleeing cavalrymen, blacks, or Irish Americans who were city residents—depended on who told the story. Savannah did not go unscathed, of course. The New York *Times* reported on, and endorsed, the need for food in the city, and noted the charitable attitude held by Northerners and the general. This charity, the *Times* pointed out, flowed in spite of earlier exhortations by Georgians to their fellows to "Let every woman have a torch, every child, a firebrand—let the loved homes of youth be made ashes, and the fields of heritage be made desolate . . . preferring even for those loved ones the charnel house as a home than loathsome vassalage to a nation already sunk below the contempt of the civilized world." The article made note of the wound to Southern pride—something that would become an enduring wound—that followed from such a "bloodless victory." It may have reflected the necessity, for the sake of pride, of calling up images of fire and desolation. The Southern temperament could be shown in word if not in fact, and honor might be preserved.[26]

Extensive coverage in *Frank Leslie's Illustrated Newspaper* was similar, in that it made much of the North supplying food to the people of Savannah and included an extravagant layout of illustrations that blared the military triumph of the North, replete with fire and explosions. The Southerners were no longer feared, but pitied—nearly helpless before the Northern military machine, stubbornly and foolishly refusing to surrender, and finding themselves objects of civic charity rather than military respect.[27]

The Carolinas Campaign: "A Sea of Blood"

Before Sherman left Savannah, his reputation—his myth—preceded him and proved a valuable weapon. His opposition often evaporated before him, as Confederate soldiers abandoned positions before an assault was ever made. South Carolinians were certain Columbia would be burned. Such fears began as early as November 1864. With Sherman only a few days out of Atlanta, a diarist in Columbia lamented, "Fire and sword are for us here; that is the word."[28] A few days after Sherman took Savannah, similar sentiments came from another diarist:

> They are preparing to hurl destruction upon the State they hate most of all, and Sherman the brute avows his intention of converting South Carolina into a wilderness. Not one house, he says, shall be left standing, and his licentious troops—whites and negroes—shall be turned loose to ravage and violate. . . . A sea rolls between them and us—a sea of blood. Smoking houses; outraged women, murdered fathers, brothers and husbands forbid such a union.[29]

Such fears were common, and not unwarranted. South Carolina had reason to presume itself a special target. Recent scholarship has revealed that the destruction of property and violence against citizens did not, in reality, measure up to the reported or presumed level of such atrocities. The making of Sherman's myth accelerated with his entry into South Carolina, where revenge by the torch occurred at a much higher rate than it did during the March to Savannah. Tales began to take hold—the prowess of Sherman's troops, their roughness in dress and manner, their toughness as soldiers, and even their "noses like hounds" that could sniff out livestock hidden in swamps. The general's name could be invoked like a pardon, as happened when some troops entered a South Carolina woman's property and began their pillaging. She invoked Sherman's name by showing their sergeant a book from the general, and the inscription to her from 1845. The sergeant placed a guard over the property. With such power and benevolence must go the chivalric impulse. One story has it that when Sherman came to Cheraw, South Carolina, blacks told him that just the mention of his name sent whites running. It was here that, in a private home, he apparently came upon a collection of Sir Walter Scott novels, the general's favorite reading during the march. He took a few volumes, and left the others in place. So Sherman indulged himself in chivalric literature as he leveled the pretenders to its tradition. [30]

As the war neared an end, Sherman was in the unusual position of having been lionized, at least in the North, by an institution he despised and with which he consistently clashed. From bank failure in San Francisco, to "insanity" in Kentucky, to a reporter's court-martial in Tennessee, he appeared to be anything but a savior of American democracy. But he was quotable, moody, colorful, and—most of all—successful. He had become a story.

After Bennett Place: Only the Guns Go Silent

The surrenders at Appomattox and Bennett Place were, naturally, major news stories, worthy of lavish attention. Bennett Place received wide and extensive coverage, even more than Lee's surrender in some cases, for several reasons. First, Johnston's surrender meant it was over—no credible second force lingering elsewhere in the country could mount a sustained campaign. There could, and would, be some noisy posturing and showy maneuvering along the Mexican border, and scattered guerrilla raids, unauthorized and uncoordinated. But the war was over. Second, the Bennett Place surrender dragged on over the course of ten days, and three meetings between Sherman and Johnston, and was spiced with political imbroglios from Washington. Third, unlike the Grant-Lee surrender, the Sherman-Johnston negotiations were conducted in the shadow of Lincoln's assassination, which helped fuel the acrimony of Johnson and Stanton toward Sherman's generous peace terms. This gave Bennett Place more depth and complexity in the theme of the story as a national tragedy. And, finally, the American press had in place its structure for war, with hundreds of correspondents, audience expectations, and pages to fill. With no battles to cover, the reporters turned to the nature of the peace that would follow. Bennett Place turned into a high drama, preceded by assassination, enriched with political infighting and intrigue, heightened by the uncertainty of the Southern response, and with a colorful, quixotic general at center stage. Sherman came in for a new round of rebuke in the press after Stanton leaked the surrender terms to reporters. The New York *Times* said Sherman had been "outwitted" by Johnston. The New York *Herald* accused Sherman of negotiating under a "temporary absence of mind," perhaps alluding to the old insanity episode from earlier in the war. The Chicago *Tribune* said Sherman was guilty of treason. On April 26, Johnston signed a surrender based on the terms offered at Appomattox.[31]

A Nation Divided

More than 600,000 men were dead, the Union affirmed. Northern industrialism prevailed, then thrived, while the defeated South's agrarian economy withered, its secondary industrial capacity destroyed. The slaves were freed, but only legally, not socially or economically. Union troops occupied the South, where bitterness and resentfulness over the war grew ever deeper. In the shadow of Reconstruction, corruption, and Southern resentment, the Old South was crudely resurrected in the form of the Ku Klux Klan, poll taxes, and tenant farming, which left blacks and poor whites barely removed from literal slavery. Economic and social progress foundered in the retrenchment.

It was more than a fight for power, which was an immediate goal. It was a battle over the future—for the memory of the war. Michael Kammen calls it the "imperative of remembering versus the comforting convenience of amnesia; reconciliation versus intransigence; the virtues of a New South versus the romance of a Lost Cause." War veterans and journalists were at the forefront of those who would construct the nation's war memories. People wanted to remember, and built the machinery of memory. An example of the memory contest is how the idea of a memorial day for the war dead caught on in various communities. The Grand Army of the Republic (GAR), in upstate New York, began sponsoring Memorial Day in 1868. It was a mandated holiday in thirty-one states within a year—a sort of "instant tradition." The South's Memorial Day originated in Columbus, Mississippi, in 1866, and came to be linked in many places with sentiments for reconciliation. The

GAR would continue to organize public celebrations and commemorations in almost any available public venue—churches, public halls, academies of music. In the 1870s, the South took seriously the responsibility of memory and tradition. The Southern Historical Society was founded in New Orleans in 1869, with the idea of having affiliates in all the former Confederate states and Washington, D.C.[32]

Its first president was former general Jubal Early, whose 1872 speech on the anniversary of Lee's birthday was the genesis for several Lost Cause themes: the superiority of Lee; the special gallantry of the Army of Northern Virginia; its defeat at the hands of a Northern machine; and the special pride that Southerners could take in their leaders. The celebration of Southern valor resonated across the South and swayed Southern historiography for the rest of the century, with former Confederate soldiers even sending their manuscripts to Early for his approval before publication. The cult of the Lost Cause shifted the focus to Lee and his army, and away from Davis and Confederate political history. In such a framework, it would also become easier to vilify Sherman, not for destroying a rogue state, but as a cog in the gears that ground a noble civilization and its noble traditions into submission. A Lost Cause adherent, accepting the idea that it was a war of an agrarian culture's right to self-determination in the face of invasive urban industrialism, could easily cast Sherman as vulgar modernism, corrupting the Garden of Southern history.[33]

A story from the Atlanta *Constitution* in July 1868 summed up, symbolically, the Southern righteousness and futility in challenging Sherman's heroic status. A short piece recounted the theft of a valuable thoroughbred horse by officers of the Twentieth Connecticut during Sherman's March. The horse eventually showed up at an auction. The Northern doctor who purchased it "denied the validity" of the claim made by the Southerner. The item only noted that the case would likely end up in court. So it has gone in reassessing the March—one side calling it horse thievery on a grand scale, the other dismissing the loser's lament in the face of a perfectly legal action.[34]

The *Constitution*, in general, did not assume the backward-looking stance of resentment and recrimination so common to the Reconstruction-era South. In response to the New York *Tribune*'s declaration that the war "ended too soon"—leaving too many unreconstructed rebels in power—the *Constitution* remarked that, by *Tribune* logic, "the neck of the Southern States is not yet sufficiently fashioned to the Federal yoke." The article referred in passing to a remark that Sherman should have stayed in Atlanta for another year before commencing his March, in order to lessen the postwar compromise with Democrats. Sometimes the newspaper seemed even admiring of Sherman, as in a story reporting on the general's remark that the March was not the result of a study of classics of warfare but simply of observation and experience. He referred to his days in California, and to having watched "caravans of immigrants . . . who reached their destinations in health and strength." It was a neutral item, neither praising nor condemning, but simply giving space to a national figure. When the *Constitution* defended the South, it was tempered in its defense. The Confederate defense was a heroic exercise, the paper said, admitting that old men and boys comprised much of the military manpower toward the end of the war. But this fact, the paper insisted, was a testament to the high quality of Southern men. In the same edition, the paper recommended to readers a new book on the siege of Savannah, written by a Confederate officer who was there. The book and the *Constitution's* review recalled Sherman's harsh words about depopulating and destroying Atlanta, and his intent to "make Georgia howl." The coverage and commentary, in this case, reflected the dilemma for advocates of the "New South," an idea that *Constitution* editor Henry Grady had popularized a few years earlier in New York. It meant a residual respect for the Old South, but a deference to modernism, which Sherman symbolized. And Grady touted the power of experience over tradition. This was, in part, what Sherman was describing in the remark about learning by observation rather than by studying the classics.[35]

Even when it seemed the occasion would understandably provoke some excoriation of Sherman, the *Constitution* remained reserved in its criticism. Reviewing Sherman's *Memoirs* in 1875, the newspaper praised the general's tactical skill, citing the fall of Atlanta and "that brilliant march through Georgia to the sea which has given immortality to Sherman's name." It noted that Sherman, at the time, was an example to his men, with his own meager accommodations during the March and his ability "to start at a moment's notice and to subsist on the scantiest food." The review was not a "pro-Sherman" story, though, as it recounted the general's having made Confederate prisoners into an advance guard to remove torpedoes in the Federal troops' path.[36]

War Remembered

In the post-Reconstruction years of the late 1870s and throughout the 1880s, the general turned his nervous energy to making and addressing memories of war. His legend flourished, North and South, as he tirelessly spoke to veterans and the public in thousands of speeches, dedicated monuments, toured the country—including the South—and worked on his *Memoirs*. His warm reception in New Orleans in 1869 and 1870 seems surprising, given the ill feelings that must have existed toward someone who had conducted such merciless war through the middle of the Confederacy. But newspapers, too, were businesses first, and as boosters would be expected to laud anyone who might benefit the balance sheet. At the time of the 1879 tour, the political climate for Sherman was mixed. Hayes was president and was living up to his politically inspired promise to end Reconstruction. But even as an envoy from a sympathetic administration, and as a genuine friend of the South, Sherman still was a conqueror. Though the casualties caused by his hand were relatively few in comparison to Grant's, Sherman was the one who had conducted a psychological war against the Confederacy, succeeding in that he humbled the would-be aristocrats as the rhetorical warriors fled before him. It was this humiliation that struck the soul of the Southern myth, not the historical Sherman—destroyer of property, not people. A barbaric killer was a better cover for the shame of defeat than a general who simply marched through the countryside, taking what he wanted.[37]

An editor was the catalyst for what may have been the general's most notable comments of the tour. After having been through Chattanooga and Atlanta in late January, Sherman was in St. Augustine, Florida, when Atlanta *Constitution* editor Even P. Howell asked the general to reiterate his favorable remarks—in writing—on Atlanta's growth and future. Howell wanted a public-relations document to use with Northern investors, and Sherman responded with praise not only for Atlanta's economic potential, but for the whole South. Newspapers across the nation picked up and reprinted the general's praise for Southern potential. The remarks were treated as an endorsement for the South, where major newspapers that reprinted them included the Charleston *News and Courier* and the Savannah *Morning News*. The general stated, "I know that no section is more favored in climate, health, soil, minerals, water, and everything which man needs for his material wants, and to contribute to his physical and intellectual development." He noted everything from railroads to fruit orchards, and said the region needed a few million immigrants, which could be diverted from the West. The only admonition, and a slight one at that, was as much to the editor as to the region: "Excuse me if I ask you, as an editor, to let up somewhat on the favorite hobby of 'carpetbaggers.'" Even in the amiable exchange, a bit of the old edginess about the press endured. He warned Howell that many of his readers would construe the term too broadly and negatively: "I have resided in San Francisco, Leavenworth, and St. Louis, and of the men who have built up these great cities, I assert that not one in fifty was a native of the place. All, or substantially all, were carpet-baggers, i.e., emigrants from all parts of the world, many of them from the South."[38]

The *Constitution* took the mild rebuke about emigration to heart, and said that not just Georgia but the whole South should remember that "American emigration is prompted by enterprise, and that the distinctive American idea is that one man is just as good as another. 'Look ahead and not behind' is the general's counsel on his closing lines; when the south can do this the day of her prosperity will dawn."[39]

Sherman's sins had not been forgotten, however. The *Constitution* recalled the bombardment and evacuation of the city by reprinting the mayor's September 1864 letter to the general pleading for him to rescind the evacuation order. Sherman's blunt refusal was reprinted under the headline: "Major General Sherman won't listen." Atlanta, the general stated, was used "for warlike purposes. . . . You might as well appeal against the thunder-storm as against these terrible hardships of war." The *Constitution* was an especially important newspaper and institution after the war because, as the voice of Henry Grady, it was at the forefront of the New South movement, advocating a progressive economic perspective to move the Old South into the modern era. But the Old South defensiveness had not disappeared from its pages. Responding to the Buffalo *Express's* concern that the *Constitution* could not be amiable to Sherman without forgetting his March, the Atlanta newspaper asked why the South should forget it if the March could be remembered "without rancor" while keeping its sights set firmly on the future. Feeling "slandered," the *Constitution* sounded a bit peevish in commenting, "[T]hey beg us to be patient while they malign us."[40]

Like the South in general, Southern newspapers were slow to recover from war. Though often on the economic margins, the Southern press had not lost its political edge, as it regularly clashed loudly and angrily with Republican rule in Reconstruction. Even by 1880, newspapers in several states—especially Louisiana, Virginia, and South Carolina—had not recovered to prewar circulation levels. The "New South" idea, which emphasized industrialization and diversified agriculture, found its chief advocate in two newspaper editors. Grady, who had purchased one-quarter interest in the Atlanta *Constitution* in 1880, became a leader of the movement with a New York speech in 1886. Henry Watterson, editor of the Louisville *Courier-Journal*, campaigned for reconciliation, promoting investments from the North and modernized farming in the South. Both were promoters of their own interests and regional interests. Their allegiance to the South and to progress put them in the position of articulating an idea that resonated with Northern investors while maintaining Southern dignity and identity.[41]

The *Constitution* was noteworthy for its conciliatory tone, and coverage of anything to do with Sherman would have been a test of that attitude. Sherman was a problem for Southerners in that he was easy to damn for his infamous March, but in postwar years was a genuine friend of the South, which many newspapers noted. The Chattanooga *Daily News*, at the time of the Atlanta visit, pointed out that Sherman was "cursed from one end of the State road to the other" for his "cruel" warfare, and noted that the general's "grand effort" to restore the South to its prewar position was "utterly forgotten." The newspaper said it was curious that people should be so willing to welcome Grant, whose eight years as president injured the South more than four years of war. When Sherman did show up in Chattanooga, the *Daily News* noted that he was received by both ex-Confederate and ex-Federal officers, and was certain that both nation and region were on the threshold of "unexampled prosperity."[42]

"War Is Hell"

Sherman's most famous words arose from a brief, impromptu speech before a gathering of veterans in Columbus, Ohio, not far from his hometown of Lancaster. The general and Hayes were visiting an encampment of as many as 10,000 members of the GAR in August 1880. As Hayes addressed the crowd, rain began to fall, and the crowd called for the general to speak. He took the podium, joked about how they had braved the rain before, and observed, "You know this is not soldiering here. There is many a boy here to-day who looks on war as all glory, but, boys, it is all hell." He concluded by commending the men for their role in bringing peace to the nation, and took his seat.[43]

Newspapers North and South picked up on the remark, some with simple reprints of the short speech, others with long commentary. The Ohio *Journal* reprinted the speech in its entirety among other reports on the GAR event. The New York *Times* saw the Sherman character in the "two-minute" speech, describing his "terse, picturesque, and original mode of expression." The *Times* also pointed out that it was not the first time Sherman had expressed such sentiments, citing his letter to Hood on the evacuation of Atlanta. The *Times* stressed the condemnation of romantic war, as it recounted the Hood-Sherman correspondence in 1864:

> At Atlanta, the two generals were in correspondence over the method of conducting the war. Sherman's view of war as a terrible scourge, not a knightly tournament, was urged strongly by him. In fact, Sherman only represented in this respect the sentiment of the majority of the Nation, while Gen. Hood, a very gallant and dashing fighter, was by no means disposed to take so somber a

view of the business he and other Southern insurrectionary leaders were engaged in.[44]

The *Times* justified the war because "the very existence of our Government
was involved. . . . The punishment of treason, and the raising of a whole race
from chattel bondage to human freedom." Compare such war to those con-
flicts, the *Times* said, "that spring from the jealousy of a Court beauty, the am-
bition of a General, the pride of a Premier, the drunken fury of a Prince." The
newspaper had turned Sherman's short speech into a commentary of justifi-
able war and cruelty, concluding with the lesson: "But the frenzy for resort to
war may be gradually lessened by putting its horrors in their true light; and
from none can this duty come with better grace or more impressiveness than
from famous soldiers themselves."[45]

The Atlanta *Constitution* did not reprint the speech or comment on it, but
in reporting of the Hayes-Sherman tour described the general succinctly and
colorfully, aboard a train from Columbus:

> The General looks remarkably well, and stood, with his sunburnt face, on the
> platform puffing his cigar smoke in the face of a forty mile current of air. . . .
>   The General wore a black felt hat and a long linen duster while he puffed
> away and received congratulations of his fellow passengers, all of whom felt at
> liberty to take him by the hand and wish him God speed.[46]

It was the celebrity Sherman, unpretentious, with trademark cigar, and
facing into the wind. The significance of the comment "war is hell" is probably due to a number of factors, many having to do with the nature of news
and newspapers. First, Sherman was famous in his own right, and he was traveling with the president of the nation. The event was planned and staged,
and reporters were ready to cover it, which may not have been the case with
any number of other impromptu appearances and speeches. The remark itself
is quotable, succinct, and fits very nicely into a one-column headline. And,
as the *Times* noted, the plain, direct language reflected Sherman himself—
original and blunt, efficient in both words and war.

"War is hell" became a defining remark, both by and about Sherman.
Though most found merit in the austere observation that stripped war of
heroic adornment and romance, some did not. A University of Georgia historian, E. Merton Coulter, writing in 1931, cited the remark in stating: "Because Sherman believed in this variety of warfare and more particularly because he used it with great efficiency, the South came to detest him most and
understand him least of all the Union generals who practiced their art in the
former Confederacy."[47]

Though Coulter carefully pointed out that Sherman was a friend of the South in peacetime and had offered generous surrender terms to Johnston, he cited this idea and method of war as being at the core of Southern contempt for the man. "This nineteenth century efficiency expert" was misunderstood in that he was not vindictive, and was not so cruel as his words would indicate. Coulter deemed the general a "hyper-Yankee" in his ambitiousness, and "typically American" in his work ethic and loquaciousness. But, for Southerners, he served the wrong God—the "American God efficiency," according to Coulter. The historian had synopsized an essential truth of the era in which he wrote and the place he wrote about—that so many saw modernism and industry, and anyone who advocated them, as the enemy.

The suspicion of modernism and other things "Northern," such as manufacturing, was by no means a universal sentiment in the late nineteenth-century South. The Southern embrace of industrialism came most visibly from Grady. In an 1886 speech in New York City, Grady eloquently outlined his New South vision. The South of slavery and secession, he said, was dead. In its place, a South of "union and freedom . . . is living, breathing, growing every hour." He said the issues of the war were settled, and appealed to audience sentiments with a conciliatory vision of the Southern accomplishments in industry, agriculture, education, and even progress on race problems. He not only spoke the words of reconciliation, but demonstrated them at the event. The dinner of the New England Society, on December 22, 1886, was a celebration of the 266th anniversary of the landing of the Pilgrims at Plymouth Rock. The business and political leaders who packed the ceremony included Sherman, who was saluted and spoke briefly. When he finished, the orchestra broke into "Marching through Georgia." Grady spoke next, and deftly deflected any tensions over the orchestra's selection by acknowledging Sherman:

> I want to say to General Sherman, who is considered an able man in our part, though some people think he is a kind of careless man about fire, that from the ashes he left us in 1864 we have raised a brave and beautiful city, that somehow or other we have caught the sunshine in the bricks and mortar of our homes, and have builded [sic] therein not one ignoble prejudice or memory.[48]

Grady had successfully defended Southern honor and offered a progressive vision. The speech was notable not only for its statement on a New South, but because Grady accommodated Sherman, that very living and vivid symbol of the utter destruction of the Old South.

The war wounds left by Sherman would never completely heal. And even the generally accommodating *Constitution* adopted a harder tone at times in the 1880s. For example, in an interview with the newspaper, a William Markham referred to the March as an "afterthought," and said the general did not intend to go to Savannah "until General Hood got in his rear" and disrupted Sherman's supplies. Markham identified himself as a member of an 1864 Atlanta citizens' committee organized to meet with Sherman, to ask that his evacuation order be rescinded. The elderly man still carried the grudge in 1888. He called Hood's action a "perfect surprise to Sherman," who had planned to make Atlanta his permanent headquarters. It was a contest between cruelty and gentility. So Sherman had stumbled into heroism, thanks to the heroic and cunning maneuvers of a Confederate general. In 1889, the newspaper portrayed him as a man still burning with "hatred and malice," citing the "ferocious and inhuman instincts that guided his march through Georgia," a man who incited "negroes . . . to incendiarism, rapine, pillage and murder." The crimes of the past were equated with a continued meanness in spirit, and so he was deemed a "malignant crank."[49]

Death and Remembrance

Newspapers North and South, and even in Europe, bled ink in praise of Sherman after his death in 1891. The inevitably heroic paeans, though, faced a quixotic protagonist—one whose legend was arising not out of a warrior's gallantry but from his brute efficiency in the conduct of war. Such a hero left his chroniclers to build a myth on his ability to practice "all hell." But he was, of course, lauded as a soldier, and the lingering war prejudices would emerge, as in the Chicago Herald's remark that Sherman was evidence of the "superior intellectual acumen and moral strength of the northern leadership." Even so, the Herald said, he was a modest and stubborn man, of "simple, honest, genial nature." The New York Times, citing his magnanimity and lack of pomposity, put Sherman alongside Lincoln and George Washington as a great hero of the nation. Newspapers consistently found the "common man" in Sherman to be a laudatory trait, echoing a familiar theme from his war days of rough dress and living and mixing with soldiers. The New York World said he was "in some respects the most popular soldier of his day. In every fibre of his character he was an American." According to the World, he reflected the character of his countrymen in his "simplicity and straightforwardness," which appealed to "the democratic heart and mind." As a strategist, he was masterful and prevailed in "the game of grand strategy with the skill and coolness of the scientific soldier that he was." It was a persistent theme in Sherman's life and legend—that he was a "common man," personifying the character of American democracy, and, being implicitly dismissive of the old-world ideals of romantic war, was a man of the modern world, rational, purposeful, and guided by the facts of reality.

The New York *Herald* also saw the "American character" in him, noting that he was "a man of simple manners, a product of our peculiar institutions, as pure minded and honest as Coriolanus. He was blunt, brusque. . . . His sword was forged in fire and tempered in blood." The Atlanta *Constitution*, the day before the general's death, had joined in with the comparison to classic greatness, this time to nothing less than Alexander the Great: "His way of settling a difficulty was to cut the Gordian knot with his sword." After Sherman's death, the *Constitution* remembered that it was Atlanta "which gave him his fame in war," noted the harshness of his actions in war, and recalled his appearance, which was in sharp contrast to the "glitter and glaring colors" of the staff around him.[50] But the *Constitution* may have been unusual among Southern papers in its praise of Sherman. A few weeks later, in a story from Fremont, Ohio, concerning a memorial service for the general, the *Constitution* reported on the speaker's comparison of Lee and Sherman, and found the latter superior:

> Lee had the same opportunity, only it was ten times better than that Sherman had in Atlanta. . . . Washington at that time lay completely in the power of an enterprising and daring commander, and with Washington captured, intervention from abroad would have come. . . . [B]ut at Washington was the chance of liberty, and Lee failed to take it. . . . Lee did not dare lose communication with his base of supplies. . . . Had Sherman been at the head of that army, and that distance between him and the pursuing forces, he would have gone to Philadelphia, Pittsburg, Buffalo, Cleveland, Cincinnati, and then cut his road back into Virginia. . . . Lee with his great army, with nothing before him but wealth and supplies and cities able to pay tribute for not being burned, is not to be compared with Sherman.[51]

Castigating Lee and aggrandizing Sherman was a daring action to take in the heart of the South, even a generation removed from the war. Why such a bold statement provoked little, if any, reaction is difficult to know. It may have been that readers were attributing the accolades to the customary effusions of obituaries, or that the lionization of Lee was still a work in progress, especially outside Virginia. Also effusive in praise of Sherman, the Knoxville *Sentinel* said he was "the hero of no idle tale" and a "great leader," and had few equals as a "military chieftain." But Knoxville was in a region with strong Union sentiments during the war.[52]

Other Southern newspapers were not so generous. The Richmond *Times* remembered the "useless vandalism and inhumanity" of the March, the "warfare thus made upon women and children and helpless non-combatants." Though admitting that Sherman at least maintained a "neutral position" toward the South after the war and so did not add to sectional hatred, the *Times* still could not admit that Sherman was a conqueror. The paper deferred to him as the "best general officer which that section produced during the late war between the States—that is, after any Northern general was able to make any reputation at all." However, and curiously, the paper insisted, "The transcendent genius of Southern military leaders, backed up by the vigor and young manhood of the South, was more than a match for any army."[53] With similar sentiments, the Louisville *Times* stated:

> The death of General Sherman will occasion no pang at the South. Under his generalship war became rapine. His march to the sea could be traced by ruins of buildings to which he applied the torch, and he left in his track hundreds of violated women and deflowered maidens. . . . There is something noble in war that is conducted on chivalrous principles. No such spirit actuated Sherman. . . . Sherman excited the hate of the South.[54]

For the most part, the obituaries followed the custom and convention of extravagant praise for the deceased. But, for Sherman, press accounts often added great detail about the mourners themselves, which would not be so unusual except that in this case the mourners were old soldiers, not celebrities. And the descriptions often included stark depictions of tearful, elderly men, many of them missing limbs. It was a Shermanesque touch of realism, stripped of florid language, an exercise in facticity, unintentionally appropriate for the general who conducted war without chivalric delusions.

Animosities endured, cast and recast in the fires of public memory. No national consensus of Sherman ever emerged from the press and popular opinion. Newspaper accounts, in effect, had offered the templates of the various Sherman stories, ones that placed different emphasis on individualism versus tradition, and on innovation versus violation of norms. Competing interpretations emerged. It was never an issue of what he accomplished, but only of the meaning of his deeds. Tradition's betrayer was modernism's escort.

Notes

1. Cited in Marion B. Lucas, *Sherman and the Burning of Columbia* (College Station: Texas A&M University Press, 1976), 34.

2. Sean Dennis Cashman, *America in the Gilded Age: From the Death of Lincoln to the Rise of Theodore Roosevelt*, 3rd edition (New York: New York University Press, 1993), 3, 30–35.

3. Debra Reddin van Tuyll, "Journalists First, Rebels Second: An Examination of Editorial Reaction to the President's Proposed Conscription of Newspapermen," in David B. Sachsman, S. Kittrell Rushing, and Debra Reddin van Tuyll, editors, *The Civil War and the Press* (New Brunswick, NJ: Transaction, 2000), 437–50.

4. Brayton Harris, *Blue and Gray in Black and White* (Washington, DC: Brassey's, 1999), 97–115; Paul Ashdown, *A Cold Mountain Companion* (Gettysburg, PA: Thomas Publications, 2004), 50–51.

5. Lorman A. Ratner and Dwight L. Teeter, Jr., *Fanatics and Fire-Eaters: Newspapers and the Coming of the Civil War* (Urbana: University of Illinois Press, 2003). Chapter 1, "The Emergence of a Democratic Press," discusses the rise and character of the prewar newspapers.

6. John F. Marszalek, *Sherman's Other War: The General and the Civil War Press* (Kent, OH: Kent State University Press, 1982), 78–83.

7. Ibid., 109–13, 117–20, 126–27.

8. Ibid., 132–62.

9. Cited in Hartwell T. Bynum, "Sherman's Expulsion of the Roswell Women in 1864," *Georgia Historical Quarterly* 54 (1970), 178.

10. New York *Herald*, June 6, 1864.

11. Ibid.

12. New York *Herald*, July 18, 1864.

13. New York *Herald*, Aug. 5, 1864.

14. New York *Herald*, Sept. 3, 1864.

15. Cited in Washington *Chronicle*, Sept. 23, 1864.

16. Ibid.

17. New York *Herald*, Sept. 25, 1864.

18. Ibid.

19. Marszalek, *Sherman's Other War*, 181, 188.

20. *Countryman*, Aug. 2, 1864; Dec. 6, 1864, cited in Lawrence Huff, "'A Bitter Draught We Have Had to Quaff': Sherman's March through the Eyes of Joseph Addison Turner," *Georgia Historical Quarterly* 72 (1988), 314–24.

21. *Countryman*, Dec. 6, 1864, cited in Huff, "'A Bitter Draught We Have Had to Quaff,'" 325. On the resistance by Southern women, and their willingness to fight, see Jacqueline Glass Campbell, *When Sherman Marched North from the Sea: Resistance on the Confederate Home Front* (Chapel Hill: University of North Carolina Press, 2003); see also Nina Silver, "The Northern Myth of the Rebel Girl," in Christie Ann Farnham, *Women of the American South: A Multiracial Reader* (New York: New York University Press, 1997), 120–32.

22. *Countryman*, Jan. 10, 1865, cited in Huff, "'A Bitter Draught We Have Had to Quaff,'" 326.

23. Cincinnati *Daily Gazette*, Jan. 2, 1865.

24. Lee B. Kennett, *Marching through Georgia: The Story of Soldiers and Civilians during Sherman's Campaign* (New York: Harper Perennial, 2001), 312–13.

25. Ibid., 313.

26. New York *Times*, Jan. 6, 1865.

27. *Frank Leslie's Illustrated Newspaper*, Feb. 25, 1865.

28. Cited in Lucas, *Sherman and the Burning of Columbia*, 33.

29. Cited in Lucas, *Sherman and the Burning of Columbia*, 34.

30. John F. Marszalek, *Sherman: A Soldier's Passion for Order* (New York: Free Press, 1993), 321–26.

31. Jay Winik, *April 1865: The Month That Saved America* (New York: HarperCollins, 2001) 291–98; Marszalek, *Sherman*, 349.

32. Michael Kammen, *Mystic Chords of Memory: The Transformation of Tradition in American Culture* (New York: Vintage Books, 1993), 101–4, 111.

33. Gary W. Gallagher, "Shaping Public Memory of the Civil War: Robert E. Lee, Jubal A. Early, and Douglas Southall Freeman," in Alice Fahs and Joan Waugh, editors, *The Memory of the Civil War in American Culture* (Chapel Hill: University of North Carolina Press, 2004), 44–45.

34. Atlanta *Constitution*, July 16, 1868.

35. Atlanta *Constitution*, Sept. 2, 1868; June 27, 1875; Jan. 10, 1875.

36. Atlanta *Constitution*, May 25, 1875.

37. Marszalek, *Sherman*, 461, 369.

38. John Marszalek, "Celebrity in Dixie: Sherman Tours the South, 1879," *Georgia Historical Quarterly*, 66 (Fall 1982), 376–77; Chicago *Tribune*, Feb. 11, 1879.

39. Atlanta *Constitution*, Feb. 13, 1879. See also Charleston *News & Courier*, Feb. 13, 1879.

40. Atlanta *Constitution*, Jan. 31, 1879.

41. Ted Curtis Smythe and Paulette Kilmer, "The Press and Industrial America, 1865–1883," in William David Sloan, editor, *The Media in America: A History*, 5th edition (Northport, AL: Vision Press, 2002), 219–20.

42. Chattanooga *Daily News*, Jan. 29, 1879; Jan. 28, 1879.

43. Marszalek, *Sherman*, 476–77.

44. New York *Times*, Aug. 19, 1880.

45. Ibid.

46. Atlanta *Constitution*, Aug. 18, 1880.

47. E. Merton Coulter, "Sherman and the South," *North Carolina Historical Review* 8:1 (January 1931), 28.

48. Raymond B. Nixon, *Henry W. Grady: Spokesman of the New South* (New York: Knopf, 1943), 239–45; Henry Grady Woodfin, editor, *The New South Writings and Speeches of Henry Grady* (Savannah, GA: Beehive Press, 1971), 7–8.

49. Atlanta *Constitution*, Oct. 14, 1888; Sept. 28, 1889.

50. New York *Times*, Feb. 18, 1891; Feb. 21, 1891; Chicago *Herald*, Feb. 13, 15, 1891; New York *World*, Feb. 15, 1891, cited in *Literary Digest*, Feb. 21, 1891, 20–21; Atlanta *Constitution*, Feb. 15, 1891.

51. Atlanta *Constitution*, March 2, 1891.

52. Knoxville *Sentinel*, Feb. 14, 1891, cited in *Literary Digest*, Feb. 21, 1891, 21.

53. Richmond *Times*, Feb. 15, 1891, cited in *Literary Digest*, Feb. 21, 1891, 21.

54. Louisville *Times*, Feb. 12, 1891, cited in *Literary Digest*, Feb. 21, 1891, 20.

CHAPTER THREE

~~

Sherman among the Historians

He was, in short, a general who did not like to fight.

Albert Castel, *Decision in the West*.[1]

The voices of envy and criticism faded before the timelessness and magnitude of his achievement.

Victor Davis Hanson, *The Soul of Battle*.[2]

The March was a masterwork of psychological warfare that helped bring a bloody, tragic conflict to a quicker end. Or perhaps it was terrorism against Southern civilians, all the while a cowardly avoidance of confrontation with enemy forces. Johnston and Hood evaded Sherman. Sherman eludes historians. In 2000, Marion B. Lucas, author of *Sherman and the Burning of Columbia*, said in an overview of Sherman biographies that the general was a difficult figure to unravel. For one thing, "Words spewed from Sherman's mouth like barbed wire." He often was brash and impolitic, and made threats that were either not carried out or not nearly so severely as he promised. Like the larger culture, historians have discovered a number of Shermans, and the evidence to support the multitude of personalities and the varieties of competence. Historians remain divided as to whether his *Memoirs* is a braggart's chronicle or a factual account from an individual unafflicted with ideas of romantic war. Lucas attributed the image of a heroic Sherman, a strategic genius, to the accounts of his early twentieth-century biographers: B. H. Liddell

Hart's *Sherman: Soldier, Realist, American* (1929), and Lloyd Lewis's *Sherman: Fighting Prophet* (1932).[3]

Liddell Hart and Lewis are emblematic of a pattern in the writing of Civil War history that continues. In Liddell Hart, one sees the scholarly or professional historian, and in Lewis the amateur or journalistic tradition in the writing of history. The latter tends to focus on the story, the dramatic narrative, the popular audience. The former also is dedicated to narrative, but it serves the analytic function of the professional historian, who develops an understanding of the circumstances and individuals on the historical stage and their larger roles in shaping the story. Many of the best-known Civil War historians have had journalistic backgrounds, including Bruce Catton, Shelby Foote, and Carl Sandburg. The disparate groups wrote of the same story, but the scholarly historians eventually brought a higher standard of evidence to the profession. The earliest histories and biographies of the Civil War were by journalists and by the warriors themselves, as evidenced by the memoirs published in the years following the war. Sherman was among those writing such history—his own history of the war. And his first big fight over the issue was with a journalist, Henry Van Ness Boynton, who published in 1875 *Sherman's Historical Raid: The Memoirs in Light of the Record*, a critical attack on Sherman's *Memoirs*. It was appropriate, of course, that Sherman's first major fight over his history would be with a journalist. The journalists understood how to write for a large audience, and they created themes to which subsequent historians referred, even if to disagree. Journalists helped create not just the historical first draft, but the mythology of Sherman and the March. History was professionalized in the late nineteenth century with the creation of the American Historical Association in 1884, and further established with the founding in 1907 of the Mississippi Valley Historical Association, which changed its name to the Organization of American Historians in 1965.

Born in 1895, Liddell Hart was a bit of both worlds, having studied history at Cambridge and having served as a military correspondent for several newspapers. He was commissioned as an infantry officer in the British army at the start of the First World War, rising to the rank of captain. After he was wounded in 1916 he began writing books on military history and strategy, and he also wrote for newspapers. His more than thirty books became highly influential, especially in Europe. He had many critics as well, and not surprisingly, since he often was considered an arrogant upstart by the generals he criticized. Liddell Hart argued against the conventional wisdom that forces should be concentrated for a frontal assault, a strategy that had so often brought disaster in France. Instead he argued for indirect movement, flank attacks, mechanized warfare, and a purposeful defense. Liddell Hart chose exotic metaphors to express his theories, such as spreading out armies in formations like the "waving tentacles of an octopus," and catchphrases that expressed complex ideas in a few words: *alternative objectives*; *threatening the enemy simultaneously at several points*; *the baited gambit*; *enticing the enemy into an attack he doesn't want to make*; *strategic net*; *advancing in a wide and irregular front to keep the enemy off balance*. None of these were particularly original ideas, but Liddell Hart's pen had made the concepts fresh and interesting. When he turned to Sherman, he found a commander who had anticipated most of his principles of warfare, and who knew how to move an army. He called Sherman the "most original genius of the American Civil War," and saw in his mode of warfare lessons to be learned by the generals in the war's Eastern theater, with their "battle-lusting strategy." Sherman's success, he believed, had been lost on First World War commanders as they "faithfully imitated [Eastern theater tactics] with ever greater lavishness and ineffectiveness on the battlefields of France."[4]

According to historian Jay Luvaas, who studied the military impact of the Civil War on European armies, Sherman was more influential than any other Civil War general. Other military scholars before Liddell Hart had high praise for Sherman as well. Field Marshal Sir Garnet Wolseley, who served as the British army's commander in chief from 1895 to 1900, admired Sherman as a strategist. Captain Charles Cornwallis Chesney, a military historian at the army Staff College at Sandhurst, while critical of Sherman in some respects, hailed him as an original genius. The Marquis Adolphe de Chambrun, a French lawyer, journalist, and military analyst, called Sherman's campaign a work of genius, and F. P. Vigo-Roussillon, a French professor of military administration, praised Sherman's logistics in the Atlanta campaign. In Germany, Colonel F. von Meerheimb wrote and lectured about Sherman's operations in Georgia, praising his use of communications and logistics as well as his flanking maneuvers. But opinion was not unanimous. Justus Scheibert, a Prussian engineering officer who served with the Confederate forces and later became a leading military authority and writer, was critical of Sherman's leadership during the March, perhaps because his sympathies were with the South. While all these observers, and others, amplified Sherman's legacy to some extent, it was Liddell Hart who most successfully explained Sherman in terms of modern military theory, and made him famous.[5]

Lewis, a columnist and managing editor of the Chicago *Daily News*, meticulously researched Sherman and his military exploits, and credited him with conducting the first "modern" war. He admired Sherman and his generalship, and portrayed him as something of a raging barbarian, comparing him to the

Goths in his devastation. But Sherman was raging righteously for Lewis, who repeatedly drew on biblical imagery, not just in the title, but in a parallel to the plague of locusts, and even a chapter titled "Angel of the Lord." Though Lewis tended to cast things in apocalyptic terms, he simultaneously provided a fairly balanced reportorial treatment where debate existed, such as with regard to the burning of Columbia, or how much rape and looting actually occurred. Atlanta, he wrote, was of use to the enemy, and Sherman's treatment of the city and its people was within the rules of war. Lewis documented the debate over the burning of Columbia, and gave Hampton credit for it. For Northerners, though, the March was the most dramatic event of the war, not only in its results but also in the drama of Sherman's "disappearance" and resurfacing in Savannah. For Lewis, Sherman was like an Old Testament God, who is sometimes brutal, but always is heroic and just.[6]

Another substantial impact that journalists had was in the form of their presence among groups of enthusiasts dedicated to the study of the Civil War. Started in Chicago in 1940, the first Civil War Round Table began as a study of Lincoln and the war, and included Lewis, Bruce Catton, and Carl Sandburg among its members. Some two hundred Round Tables around the nation are active, and some are active outside the United States. Open to individuals with an interest in the war, the groups are decidedly popular in nature, though commonly calling on scholars and professional historians as their speakers.

A Great General

One of the first books about Sherman and the March was a paean to the general by a midwestern clergyman, Faunt LeRoy Senour. *Major General William T. Sherman and His Campaigns* (1865) called the Savannah campaign the "most remarkable march in the annals of history." The hero was a magnanimous conquerer, beneficent to those defeated, so much so that residents of Savannah and Charleston celebrated his arrival, according to Senour. Such a suspect finding was made more incredible by Senour's revelation that Southerners actually hated Davis. More recently, historians' views of Sherman have ranged from merchant of terror to workmanlike soldier going about his job, or from being raging bull to soldier obsessed with imposing order. Some have challenged themes of Sherman the destroyer/barbarian, and have documented the relatively small amount of rape, pillage, and murder of civilians by soldiers under his command. John Marszalek's *Sherman: A Soldier's Passion for Order* (1993) is one of the most complete and exhaustive biographies of Sherman. Marszalek, a professor of history emeritus at Mississippi State University, explains many of Sherman's lifetime actions as resulting from a near-compulsion to impose order and stability. Severe disruptions and disorder in Sherman's early life, compounded by failures in his business ventures, left him with a lifelong intolerance of disorder. Marszalek finds in Sherman a great general, but one whose legacy may have been shaped more by carelessness of expression, to which he was quite susceptible, than by historical fact. Unlike some others, Marszalek believes Sherman's strategy of avoiding the bloody frontal attacks ensured the success of the Atlanta campaign. The March was a major event, both militarily and psychologically, as well as creating for the next generation the villain for the Lost Cause myth.[7]

Stephen Davis, author of *Atlanta Will Fall*, sums up the reasons for the city's fall in his book's subtitle: *Sherman, Joe Johnston, and the Yankee Heavy Battalions*. Johnston's performance was less than admirable: "Rarely if ever has a military commander striven harder to persuade the head of his government that he [was] incapable of defeating by his own efforts the army he [opposed]." In a careful, detailed critique of the leadership of Sherman, Johnston, and Hood, Davis concludes that Hood and Sherman should be commended for their generalship, and Johnston should not. In fact, he states, Johnston rather than Hood should be blamed for the Confederate failure in the campaign. Davis is convincing in his argument that Johnston came to Atlanta with a well-earned reputation for being overly cautious, even timid; uncooperative with his commander-in-chief; and uncommunicative. In Atlanta, he lived up to the reputation. Hood had a good plan, even if a bit too bold, but it succumbed to "luck . . . war friction and war fog." Unlike Johnston, Hood at least was attacking. Davis praises Sherman for not being bound by convention, and for disciplined and careful preparation, confidence, and a drive to succeed. He knew his forces were superior, and he was willing to use them.[8]

Steven E. Woodworth finds Sherman skilled as both a strategist and a manager. In his definitive *Nothing but Victory: The Army of the Tennessee, 1861–1865*, Woodworth notes that Sherman had great combat power but could ill afford to confront a Confederate force of similar strength, "since his army's daily food supply depended on a steady, rapid advance. Sherman's excellent strategy and skillful management made the march look easy, almost as if his army might have wandered effortlessly to any point in the Confederacy." Woodworth alludes to the March's myths, which, he notes, were being created "almost before the march itself and grew apace while Sherman's men made their first few days of advance southeastward from Atlanta." He cites the stories of women abused and houses burned. But crimes against people were almost unheard of, and no matter how well behaved Sherman's men may have been, they were going to be despised. Woodworth discounts the myths, by which he generally means anything that lacks a factual basis, such as the legends of rampant plunder that came from later, enduringly embittered Southerners. Crimes against people, including rape, were rare.[9]

In an earlier article, Woodworth enumerates numerous falsehoods and half-truths about the March, as well as facts or logic that work against the legends. He writes that in spite of the supposed wholesale appropriation of food, there is no evidence of a subsequent case of starvation of people in the area. And while tales of rape and murder adorned the Southern press, people in Sherman's path acted on a different set of assumptions. Men would take in the livestock and leave the house to be occupied by the women. An occupied house was less likely to be ransacked. Myths of burnings actually grew over the years, Woodworth notes, as folk tales emerged to explain how a residence escaped firing. "In fact, no town between Atlanta and the sea was completely burned." The destruction rendered was within the limits of rules of war of the day. "[B]ut it was the atrocity that latter-day legend has painted and many Americans still believe it to have been."[10]

Even classicists have gotten into the fray over the March's place in military history. Victor Davis Hanson, in *The Soul of Battle: From Ancient Times to the Present Day, How Three Great Liberators Vanquished Tyranny*, puts Sherman in the company of Epaminondas, who in the fourth century B.C. dismantled the legendary Spartan military with an army of yeomen, and George S. Patton. "Sherman's Federal army rent the fabric of Georgian society. . . . Sherman's three-hundred-mile march had changed the entire psychological and material course of the Civil War," Hanson writes. Noting Sherman's depression, sickness, and common appearance, Hanson believes Sherman's legacy was that "his mob of burners and ravagers saved far more lives than they took, helped to free an enslaved people when others more liberal could not, and in a few months disgraced the notion of militarism without fighting a major battle." He finds Sherman a "strange mix of abstract genius and pragmatic acumen." The Southerners, he concludes, despised Sherman not because he defeated them, but because he humiliated them. "Sherman realized that the old chivalrous code and aristocratic gallantry were both outmoded and obscene in a modern war of railroads, repeating rifles, and high-velocity cannon."[11]

Sherman is in illustrious historical company again in *How Great Generals Win*. Bevin Alexander puts Sherman alongside Napoleon, Genghis Khan, Hannibal, Erwin Rommel, Douglas MacArthur, and Stonewall Jackson. Alexander gives Sherman credit for nothing less than winning the Civil War by cutting the heart out of the South with his marches to Savannah and through the Carolinas. Alexander says letters of desperation and despair, sent from home to Confederate soldiers in the Eastern theater, were the primary reason for the disintegration of Lee's army, as soldiers deserted in order to protect families. Sherman also acted more wisely than Grant, according to Alexander, in avoiding frontal assaults, which resulted in horrendous casualties for Grant in May–June 1864 in the Wilderness, at Spotsylvania, and at Cold Harbor. Sherman's flanking maneuvers consistently outwitted Johnston, who failed to grasp that fortifications and entrenchments were not an antidote to the threat to Atlanta. Ultimately, Alexander puts Sherman in the "hard war" camp, calling his campaign a "vendetta of organized ruination that had no parallel in modern history," his soldiers plundering and burning as they went. The evacuation of Atlanta was a "vindictive act against the entire population." Alexander believes the March sowed seeds of hatred that lived more than a century after the war: "Sherman's march evoked an enduring folk memory of wanton havoc that embittered the Southern people against the North, the Republican party, and the national government for generations."[12]

Burke Davis's readable narrative *Sherman's March* follows the general from Atlanta to the review in Washington after the South's surrender. His account is neither critical nor analytical, but the story of movements and battles, including accounts of looting and the success of foragers. Davis calls it an "epic march" that would bring Sherman "military immortality." Davis judges the Atlanta campaign "one of the war's most brilliant campaigns." At times, Davis may have fueled the legends of Sherman and the March, as he notes "Sherman's sentinels" (the chimneys left standing after houses were burned), the "vast region scorched and plundered," millions of dollars in damages, and how the war was taken to women and children.[13]

In contemporary U.S. culture, which ranks its accomplishments ad nauseam, it is entirely appropriate that historical judgment would eventually find its way to a "top 10" list. Sherman was there. In a *North and South* article, a panel of six leading Civil War historians tackled the issues of "Who Were the Top Ten Generals?" Sherman made all lists, ranking number three on half the lists, and from four to ten on the remainder. Grant and Lee claimed spots one and two, respectively, on all but one list. But for those disgruntled with the ranking, those who might find their favorite general omitted, or those who might be dismayed by "improper" rankings, it was not so unlike the perennial battle cry for America's favorite statistical sport, baseball: Wait 'til next year. Just wait 'til the next generation of historians, in this case.[14]

The Grant-Sherman friendship has been noted in numerous biographies and histories. Historian Charles Bracelen Flood argues that their friendship won the Civil War. Many generals were able to build good working relationships during the war, but these rarely were considered friendships. For example, Lee and Jackson worked in concert not because they were personal friends but because Jackson followed and even anticipated Lee's orders, and Lee recognized Jackson's operational brilliance. The friendship between Grant and Sherman was of a different order altogether, and there are many reasons. First of all, they were both midwesterners, each having been born in Ohio, a little more than two years apart. Each was a bit of a contrarian, a loner with a penchant for brooding, casual in bearing and accoutrement. Each could be direct to the point of bluntness. Most importantly, they genuinely enjoyed each other's company and trusted one another. Sherman comfortably accepted the role of junior partner. They were alike but also different: Grant the more intuitive, stolid, and laconic; Sherman the intellectual, garrulous, and excitable. They complemented one another, their differences adding up to something greater than either of them. Because of the special friendship, the March to the Sea had a special authority, a joint authorship. "Grant needed a gifted and effective subordinate, and at first Sherman needed a man to give him orders and then stand by him, no matter what," according to Flood. "And each needed a friend. They worked together for twenty-three months, planning, consuming countless cigars, learning the lessons taught them by their battles and campaigns."[15]

A Competent General

Richard M. McMurray's detailed, insightful military history of the Atlanta campaign is critical of Sherman, Johnston, and Hood at various points. In *Atlanta 1864: Last Chance for the Confederacy*, McMurray offers the possibility that Thomas might have ended the war in the West more quickly than Sherman. He acknowledges Sherman's high ranking as a general, but believes that reputation would be poorer if it relied solely on his ability in field operations. But McMurray gives credit to Sherman for something that few others could match by 1864, and that is his grasp of the "geopolitical-psychological grand strategy of the war." McMurray believes any assessment of Sherman has to be tempered by a consideration of his advantages at the time: He had more troops, he had ample supplies, he could wage a coordinated campaign by virtue of his command over Union forces in the West, and he had the support of his commanders, Grant and Lincoln. All of this was in contrast to conditions for Johnston, then Hood. In addition, Sherman was a brilliant logistician. His shortcomings were highlighted, in McMurray's opinion, on at least two occasions—Snake Creek Gap and Jonesboro. McMurray says Sherman was aware of the opportunity in both instances to destroy the enemy army, but made only a limited effort. While Sherman was brilliant in his attention to and grasp of the grand strategy, he proved only competent as a field commander and appeared to lack the "killer instinct" of great battle-field commanders. Johnston, on the other hand, appeared to be obsessed with the details of field operations without regard to a larger strategy, and he rarely thought above the level of day-to-day operations. Hood, McMurray says, probably does not get high enough marks because his command in Atlanta was so short, and he came to it burdened with Johnston's mistakes.[16]

A Poor General

Albert Castel may be foremost among historians who find Sherman lacking. In *Decision in the West: The Atlanta Campaign of 1864*, Castel admits to being tough on Sherman. A number of factors resulted in the loss of Atlanta, he says, including lapses in Southern leadership, and the superiority of Federal numbers and materiel. But he finds Sherman an overly methodical, low-risk commander who avoided tactical offense. Castel rejects Liddell Hart's asser-tion of Sherman's "strategic artistry" because Sherman's success was based on a number of flanking maneuvers:

> Again and again, from Dalton to Lovejoy's Station, he overlooked, ignored, and even rejected opportunities to crush or fatally cripple the Confederate forces in Georgia or at the very least drive them from the state. . . . He was, in short, a general who did not like to fight. Had Thomas's personal relationship with Grant permitted him to command in Georgia in 1864, almost surely the Union victory would have been easier, quicker, and more complete.[17]

Castel agrees with the terror thesis, citing Northern soldiers who "terror-ized" the Southern populace, a tactic that he says was the policy of Northern leaders, including Sherman. Sherman found himself in fall 1864

> a victor who cannot exploit his victory, a conqueror who is unable to continue conquering. All he can do is remain in Atlanta—he spends much of the time sitting on the porch of his mansion headquarters, wearing slippers, smoking ci-gars, and reading newspapers. . . . Such was the consequence of his having failed to smash Hood's army or, at the very least, to drive it out of the state, when he had had the opportunity.

In contrast, James W. Merrill, in *William Tecumseh Sherman*, finds that same methodical style admirable. He sees Sherman as something of a prototypical

American, going about his job in a commendably efficient fashion, an idea with its origins in Liddell Hart.[18]

Castel criticizes Sherman not only as a general but also as a memoirist. In a debate with Marszalek in *Civil War History*, Castel argues that Sherman's *Memoirs* were "filled with exaggerations and dubious assertions, omissions, and distortions of facts and with deliberate and sometimes malicious prevarications, fabrications, and falsifications." He compares the chapters on the Atlanta campaign to the *Official Records of the Union and Confederate Armies* and other primary sources. Castel cites several incidents to support his charges, such as Sherman's statement that he consulted generals Thomas, McPherson, and Schofield before his failed attack on Kennesaw Mountain, and that they all agreed with the attack. Not so, Castel states, because other sources show there was little support for the attack—including Schofield's biography, which states that all three opposed the plan. He demonstrates that the *Memoirs* are often very much at odds with other accounts or histories. The lies and distortions were, Castel concludes, "the offenses that Sherman perpetrated against historical truth and fairness in writing about the Atlanta campaign in his *Memoirs*." Marszalek acknowledges that Sherman was "notoriously careless about detail," and agrees that memoirs, not just Sherman's, are often inaccurate in detail. Marszalek challenges Castel's assertion that Sherman never admitted making a major mistake. "On the contrary, he admitted mistakes many times." Instead, Sherman wrote the *Memoirs* "to tell his version of the war the only way he knew it," according to Marszalek. "Castel sees Sherman as a prevaricator; I see him as a blunt chronicler of his own view of the Civil War."[19]

Castel's frontal assault continues in *North and South* magazine, where he engages Woodworth on Sherman's generalship. Castel concedes that his critical view is a minority opinion, "albeit a growing one." Liddell Hart's 1929 biography, he believes, "seduced" historians with its "epigrammatic prose and superficial profundity." Castel cites Sherman performances that ranged from poor to uninspired in Kentucky, Missouri, Shiloh, Chickasaw Bluffs, Vicksburg, and Chattanooga. He admits that the capture of Atlanta in September 1864 was one of the three most decisive military events of the war. Of course, he also wrote an authoritative history of the campaign. "But does Sherman's great contribution to the Union victory make him a great commander?" The logistics and flanking maneuvers were commendable, Castel says, but Sherman failed at four different times to take advantage of opportunities to crush the opposition's army. Doing so could have ended the war much earlier. The March itself and the Carolinas campaign did not demonstrate great military leadership, according to Castel, who gives Hood credit for Sherman's success.

The March was possible, Castel asserts, because Hood attacked Sherman's rear rather than getting in front of him, and because Grant allowed Sherman to come to Virginia via the Carolinas rather than by sea. In addition, he believes that if Sherman and Hood had fought it out in Georgia, it would have had no effect on the outcome of the war. Sherman was only one of many factors in Lee's surrender.

Woodworth takes sharp exception to such an argument, which he says minimizes the logistics and turning maneuvers involved in the Atlanta campaign: "[I]t was operational wizardry of a high order that enabled Sherman to turn Johnston again and again." The Georgia and Carolina marches were "masterpieces," and he finds Castel's criticisms linked to Hood "absurd." Castel, Woodworth says, takes Sherman to task based on standards of knowledge current more than a century later. By Castel's standards, according to Woodworth, "nothing short of omniscience qualifies a general for greatness." He rebukes Castel for employing "what-might-have-been history."[20]

A Barbarian General

John Bennett Walters, in a 1948 article in the *Journal of Southern History*, "General William T. Sherman and Total War," may have been the first historian to apply the idea of total war to Sherman and the Civil War. Walters claimed that "it was generally understood that the noncombatants or civilian population should be free from all violence or constraint other than that required by military necessity." He cited general field order no. 100, in which the federal government said unarmed citizens and private property were in general to be spared. Sherman's views on the issue evolved with the war. After Bull Run, Walters found Sherman's attitude to be orthodox in that it was a "game" between two armies. In Kentucky, Sherman wrote his brother John that civilians in the South would have to be reckoned with. After Shiloh, he appeared to see civilians retarding Halleck around Corinth. In Memphis and West Tennessee, he began to equate with guerrilla warfare the civilian cooperation with Confederates. In September 1862, the general erupted over the firing on steamboats bringing supplies to Memphis. His order to burn the town of Randolph put into practice the theory of collective responsibility. Fall 1862 in Memphis, Walters argued, was a rehearsal for Mississippi, Georgia, and South Carolina. Ten square miles of Memphis eventually became the sixty-mile swath across Georgia. Walters called the actions in Memphis Sherman's "first full-dress performance in total war." Sherman's orders for the March across Georgia were in concert with accepted rules of war. But, Walters concluded, "it is difficult to escape the conclusion that these orders were formulated more for the record than for the guidance of his troops." Furthermore:

> The suddenness with which this orgy of destruction came to an end as the army moved into North Carolina early in March provided striking evidence of the deliberate vengeance which had determined its character in South Carolina, and indicated also that it might have been kept under control had there been any real desire to do so in earlier stages of the campaign.[21]

Walters stated that Sherman ultimately justified his actions on the basis that civilians brought it upon themselves, quoting the general himself: "They have sowed the wind and must reap the whirlwind. Until they . . . submit to the rightful authority of the government they must not appeal to me for mercy or favors." Walters put a sharper edge to the same thesis in his 1973 book *Merchant of Terror: General Sherman and Total War*. He accused Sherman of a "strange hatred" of Southern people, an idea at odds with other historians and biographers. In recounting outrages of Sherman and his troops, Walters charged the general with waging "a war almost of annihilation against those whom he professed he was bringing back into the Union of States." He portrayed Sherman as maniacal in his contempt for Southerners and near sadistic in measures used in his campaigns.[22]

Mark Grimsley takes the Walters thesis to task in *The Hard Hand of War: Union Military Policy Toward Southern Civilians, 1861–1865*. Grimsley studies both how the North came to adopt such a policy and the policy in action. He arrives at the conclusion that Walters's work was "as much polemical as analytical." But Grimsley concedes that Walters did strike a chord with subsequent historians. He believes the "hard war" approach, which he differentiates from "total war," was essentially adopted in September 1862, with the issuance of the Emancipation Proclamation. It signaled less regard for the impact of war on Southern society, as the military would act against civilians and private property as part of a campaign to cripple the Southern war machine and demoralize Southerners. Sherman did not conduct a campaign of indiscriminate war—total war—contrary to Walters's claims. Instead, Grimsley finds a pattern of "directed severity," differentiating among secessionists, those who were neutral, and loyalists. This was illustrated particularly by the change in behavior once the Union troops entered South Carolina, with accelerated destruction, and then crossed into North Carolina, when destruction decelerated. The slaveholding aristocracy was burdened with a presumption of guilt in this case. It was never clear, Grimsley points out, that Sherman and his generals intended the troops to show great restraint in dealing with the civilian population, not could they have enforced such restraint.

As for the hard war, crops and livestock were the primary losses in Georgia, although looting undoubtedly took place; but personal crimes, including rape and murder, were rare. Among whites, no murders were known, and reports of rape were few and sketchy. In addition, the burnings of houses and towns appear to have been much exaggerated. The myth of Sherman's hard war, Grimsley says, is a result of its usefulness to Southerners in the postwar South. It supported the idea that a gross injustice had been committed against the region; it appealed to those believing brute force had beaten the South, not military art or a failure of will; and tales of atrocities helped explain the economic disaster of the postwar South. In the latter case, Grimsley blames the worthlessness of Confederate scrip, bonds, and promissory notes, and the emancipation of slaves, both of which could be traced to the Southern decision to go to war, and would place responsibility for the consequences on Southerners themselves.[23]

Charles Royster calls his book, *The Destructive War: William Tecumseh Sherman, Stonewall Jackson, and the Americans*, a long essay "in an effort to understand Americans' ways of making their war destructive." Royster recognizes that Sherman was not the outrageous barbarian and vandal that myth has proclaimed. But, still, he gives Sherman a special place in "destructive" war. Royster sees the difference, as many others have, between Sherman's words and actions, and believes ideas about the nature of modern war have been influenced heavily by Sherman's rhetoric. So for Royster, the warrior who created "modern war" did so more rhetorically rather than in reality. It would be difficult, he concludes, to show Sherman's direct influence on war in the twentieth century. Royster acknowledges the mythology that has grown up around Sherman, so much so that his name has become a "talisman, a folk word standing for the means by which the Southern Cause had died." In a similar vein, sociologist Charles Edmund Vetter, in *Sherman: Merchant of Terror, Advocate of Peace*, explores Sherman's tactics as a campaign to disrupt Southern society. Such an assault was part of the "total war" philosophy and brought the war to a quicker end, according to Vetter.[24]

Mark E. Neely, Jr., also points to the very large gap between Sherman's words and actions. But he takes issue with the idea that Sherman invented total war. In "Was the Civil War a Total War?" Neely begins with the problem of even defining "total war" or "modern war." Citing Walters's 1948 *Journal of Southern History* article as the first application of "total war" to the March, Neely states that Walters was a Southerner and "saw in Sherman's doctrines the breeding ground of a counter-productive hatred at odds with the North's mission to heal the nation after the war." Historians may have paid too much attention to Sherman's words, as opposed to his actions, according to Neely. "In fact, [Sherman] said many things and when gathered together they do not add up to any coherent 'total war philosophy.'" Neely cites historians' use of the famous quote about making "Georgia howl." In context it is "much less vivid and scorching," and Sherman went on to speak of statesmanship, and how people in the South would reasonably reach the conclusion that the North would prevail. Neely states that "total war . . . breaks down the distinction between soldiers and civilians, combatants and non-combatants, and this no one in the Civil War did systemically, including William T. Sherman. He and his fellow generals waged war the same way most Victorian gentlemen did."[25]

Lance Janda, writing in the *Journal of Military History*, argues persuasively that total war was nothing new in the Civil War. The practice had been around for centuries. But the Civil War was a "watershed" for the concept because Union generals—especially Grant, Sherman, and Sheridan—were the first to use such tactics on a widespread scale. So they did not invent total war, but "they did rediscover [total war tactics] in their own time, and lent them vigorous prosecution and eloquent justification." Sherman's writing, Janda notes, outlined the general's three tenets of total war: *military necessity*, which meant destroying civilian property in order to deprive the military of support; *psychological war*, conducted in order to smother Southern enthusiasm for the war; and *collective responsibility*, which basically meant the South deserved its fate. Hanson is in concert with Janda on Sherman and total war, but Hanson puts the idea into Sherman following his horrific experience at Shiloh. Janda views Sherman's conception of total war in a longer military tradition that was rekindled in war.[26]

Anne J. Bailey, in *War and Ruin: William T. Sherman and the Savannah Campaign*, states that Sherman's idea of depopulating an area was not unique to him and that he had been tough on civilians in earlier campaigns, too. In addition, she says, Sherman's actions did not really compare to later war. If he had pursued such a course of true total war, Bailey believes the result would have been an irreparable schism. Physical hardships, she finds, were visited upon civilians, but Sherman's words were more severe than actual events.[27]

Jacqueline Glass Campbell differs from most Sherman historians in two respects. In *When Sherman Marched North from the Sea*, she focuses on the march through the Carolinas rather than the March to the Sea. Second, her focus is on the impact on civilians, rather than military history. She argues persuasively that the Carolinas campaign did not crush Southern resistance.

Instead, Southern white women on the home front were steeled by the pres-ence of Northern troops, and their resolve hardened. Their audacious resist-ance, both verbal and physical, surprised the Union troops. Campbell also observes that Sherman's soldiers were less than magnanimous liberators in re-spect to the slave population. Campbell is not the first to point out that Sherman saw the freed slaves as a burden. He had neither the supplies nor the inclination to assist them. In addressing the impact of these women on memory of the war, Campbell cites the writings of Southern women as con-taining images in which the seeds of the Lost Cause mythology resided. For many women, Sherman became the "personification of Yankee atrocities." Campbell says, however, that the actual destruction in Georgia fell short of what people believed it to be, and people appeared to suffer as much at the hand of Wheeler and his cavalry as they did from Sherman and his foragers.[28]

Joseph T. Glatthaar's social history is unique among Sherman studies be-cause he looks at the March from the perspective of the soldiers. In *The March to the Sea and Beyond: Sherman's Troops in the Savannah and Carolinas Campaigns*, Glatthaar would be among those who see Sherman as a practi-tioner of "total war," but Glatthaar sets out to "explore the attitudes of the men toward their comrades, blacks, Southern whites, the war, destruction, and reconstruction." He finds the soldiers quite willing to conduct war harshly, at times vengefully. They saw foraging as a weapon against the South, much the same way their leader did. There were even cases of the sol-diers propagating myths of their own barbarism, such as two who told women in Barnswell, South Carolina, that their fighting forces consisted entirely of convicts released for the purpose of subjugating the South. A guard in Co-lumbia told a woman the Union troops would take all food, burn the city to cinders, then let the soldiers loose on the community. In spite of such threats, Glatthaar writes, the army treated Southern civilians well. Like their gen-eral, the soldiers waged hard war in order to end it.[29]

Tormented General

With book titles ranging from Sherman as prophet to terrorist, perhaps the most engaging title belongs to Earl Schenck Miers, *The General Who Marched to Hell: William Tecumseh Sherman and His March to Fame and Infamy*. The book is restricted to the war years, from Louisiana to Bentonville. The introduction states that the book attempts to capture "moods and motivations of one of the unique episodes in American history," and tries to "see into the minds" of sol-diers and civilians on both sides. The intriguing discoveries in the psychohis-tory include the fact that as the general prepared to leave Atlanta for the coast,

"Sherman's mind fondled each detail" as the officers and men around him assumed a "devil-may-care" attitude, which made him even more conscious of his responsibility. Miers's work is a heroic rendition of the general, the soldiers, and the March. Sherman's troops "must march to the sea or perish." Moods were divined during the magnificent vengeance:

> From the Savannah River to the Peedee every home shrank from the stored-up fury that Sherman's swaggering, triumphant mood threatened; tight-lipped, nervous, and unhappy, South Carolinians believed that no family or no principle of decency would be secure under the reign of the redheaded, redbearded general who once had gloated that he would "bring every Southern woman to the washtub."[30]

Miers goes to the writings and mind of Hampton to ignite the mythic fires of Sherman's savagery:

> Who but Sherman and his "Hellhounds" would have watched indifferently while old men, women, and children, "the flames . . . rolling and raging around them," were "driven out headlong by pistols clapped to their heads, violent hands laid on their throats and collars"? . . . Who but the dastardly Sherman and his "rascals" would have permitted "a lady undergoing the pains of labor to be borne out on a mattress into the open air" while "they beheld the situation of the sufferer and laughed to scorn the prayer of safety"? Who but Sherman and his mob of "demons" would have broken into the room of a woman recently confined and whose "life hung on a hair," snatching rings from her fingers, the watch from beneath her pillow, and so overwhelming "her with terror that she sank under the treatment, surviving but a day or two"?[31]

Miers, whose book was published in 1951, reflected something of the enduring mix of contempt and admiration that Sherman still evoked. He even raised the question of whether—like the Hiroshima bomb—the inevitable suffering of the day shortened the bloodshed and conflict.

Michael Fellman finds Sherman to be a conflicted individual, angry with the world, brutal and racist. He ultimately made the South pay for his rage. In *Citizen Sherman*, Fellman sets out to understand the origins of the warrior, not just social, but also emotional. He finds a man motivated time and again by rage, an unstable and disappointed person with tragedy and failure defining his early life and early career, an individual subject to erratic mood swings from depression to elation. Fellman, in his introduction to Sherman's *Memoirs*, alludes to a "lifelong sense of abandonment and betrayal" that would "underpin his brilliantly articulated, destructive wartime role as a psychological warrior against the South." He allows that Sherman was a good general, citing Atlanta as a "textbook case of maneuver and flanking," but gives much of the credit to Johnston, whose timidity supported Sherman's tactics. Though Sherman may have been brilliant at times, Fellman insists that he conducted a "measured campaign of terror," warning Southerners of what he planned to do with "sadistic anticipation." Fellman admits that Sherman did not do all he threatened and did not destroy everything, and that the men did not rape and kill civilians. "His was the energy of mass violence, and yet it was channeled, calculated, and effective."[32]

Stanley P. Hirshson disagrees completely with Fellman, Marszalek, and Lewis. Unlike Fellman, Hirshson finds that Sherman was not a racist, a philanderer, or an anti-semite. He accuses Marszalek of failing to support his thesis that Sherman spent a lifetime developing a passion for order (which Stephen Bower thinks is a misreading of Marszalek's thesis), and says Lewis's assessment of Sherman as the forerunner of modern war was an exaggeration. Hirshson says Fellman is amiss in targeting an inner rage that drove the general. Instead, Hirshson finds the psychological key to be Sherman's "realization that mental instability plagued his mother's family." He appeared to be tormented in all aspects of life—domestic life, the struggle to make a living, the breakdown in Kentucky during the war, the death of son Willy, his destruction of Southern property, and even the squabbles with his army associates. But Hirshson admits that there were many Shermans. Although he finds assessing him as a general difficult, he believes Sherman to be a commendable general, one whose careful actions did not always match his extreme language. His marches made him unique, however. And the multitude of Shermans remains evident: "To Georgians and South Carolinians he remains a beast, intent on destroying not soldiers but civilians, genius and madman . . . exemplifying the contradictions and strengths of the country that produced him."[33]

The popular historian Stephen Ambrose also contemplates Sherman's psyche and finds the general "unique," but not manic-depressive. "The manic-depressive goes into a mood for no reason at all; Sherman became exhilarated or depressed for excellent reasons." Ambrose praises Sherman for his grasp of strategy and insight into tactics. He was, admittedly, "intensely emotional," but the "quickness of mind . . . eventually led to greatness."[34]

Nassir Ghaemi, a psychiatry professor at Emory University in Atlanta, entered the long-running debate about Sherman's mental state in a 2006 magazine article. Citing the conclusions of historians and examining statements made by and about Sherman, Ghaemi offers a qualified diagnosis. According to Ghaemi, Sherman possibly exhibited the classic symptoms of "manic depressive illness, or bipolar disorder, characterized by extreme shifts of mood, energy, and ability to function." But, he adds, Sherman's likely mental illness doesn't mean he was manic or insane in Georgia, because mental illness can be marked by periods of stability, and Sherman seemed very much in control during the March. Furthermore, Ghaemi suggests, Sherman may have prevailed decisively in Georgia "not despite but because of his mental illness. Sherman knew the depths of human fear. He knew the paralyzing power of terror."

Evidence of Sherman's mental state is, of course, circumstantial at best, and historians who put generals, presidents, and even other historians on the couch are speculating at very long range. Sherman's madness, if that is what it was, has become a trope that explains more about the effect than the cause. Sherman knew that war itself was insanity. He put the war on the couch. Its effect on the warrior is profound, yet difficult to unravel.[35]

The Moral Warrior

With Sherman having been deconstructed tactically, strategically, and even psychologically, it is not surprising that theological and moral judgment also have been passed. The moral issues surrounding Sherman's March are confronted from a more philosophically informed perspective in Harry S. Stout's *Upon the Altar of Nation: A Moral History of the Civil War*. Stout studies the actions of North and South on the basis of Just War theory, an idea that began with Saint Augustine's *Summa Theaologic* nearly 2,000 years ago. Stout sees the March as a testament to Sherman's organizational skill. "Moral genius was another matter." In Savannah, Sherman authorized seizure of private property with the idea of maximizing the discomfort of Southerners. The March itself "represented a new chapter in the history of war." Because he was cut off from Grant and Lincoln, "[Sherman] was effectively the reigning deity wherever he went, with no higher accountability to check his martial impulses. . . . A sort of madness enveloped him and his soldiers as they marched into the heart of darkness, destroying without resistance." Stout deems him a "virtual dictator of his army," operating "free from all moral, no less than military, reviews." Sherman was not alone in believing there to be no innocents in the war, an idea shared by Grant, Lincoln, and Halleck. After the war, neither Grant nor Sherman made a moral commentary on the level of destruction. Stout says Sherman was almost alone among Civil War generals in forsaking God:

> For Sherman, God had long ceased to be the governor of this war. The cause was just and indeed holy, but the conduct profane and disconnected to God

and the Suffering Savior. Sherman's religion was America, and America's God was a jealous God of law and order, such that all those who resisted were reprobates who deserved death. . . . Sherman could blame the enemy for anything and everything that happened to them. They deserved it.[36]

Stout's observation on America as Sherman's "religion" is congruent with another historian's theological approach to Sherman. Stephen E. Bower takes issue with Fellman's assessment that Sherman was unstable and angry. He believes Fellman has misread the evidence. Instead, Bower finds, in "The Theology of the Battlefield: William Tecumseh Sherman and the U.S. Civil War," that it was a religious war for the general. This derived from the general's "civil religion," which meant Sherman believed in the divine origins and destiny of the nation, and "representative government, having replaced the divine rule of monarchs, was sacred." Though Sherman found no evidence of God on the battlefield, according to Bower, "the cause of the war remained sacred." For Sherman, the brutal prosecution of war demonstrated for the Southern transgressors a life without social order. In this respect, Bower is very much in concert with the thesis of Marszalek's biography, and Bower admits to being at odds with Fellman's view of Sherman as a practitioner of unjustifiable violence and virulent racism. Bower cites the famous exchange with Hood as evidence of this civil religion. Sherman believed Hood hypocritical and sacrilegious to find God close to the battle of Atlanta: "The war itself was God's judgment upon his people, and the judgment was just. . . . In short it did not matter to Sherman whether the evacuation of Atlanta was unprecedented, cruel or kind, moral or immoral; it was simply what war had wrought, and the people of Atlanta would have to live with it." For Sherman, the "great object of the war was to mend the sacred cloth of American nationhood."[37]

Unlike many others, Lee B. Kennett finds little atrocity on the part of Sherman and his soldiers. *Marching Through Georgia: The Story of Soldiers and Civilians During Sherman's Campaign* is a broader history of the March. As the title indicates, it is less a military history and more a history of both soldiers and civilians caught in the war, and the March's impact on both groups. Kennett finds that fire, though the primary means of destruction for the soldiers, was applied to only a minority of houses in the path of the March. The foraging system he judges inefficient and wasteful, with 10–20 percent of the army roaming about the country, sometimes over the same areas, seizing far more food, mules, and horses than they could use. But he believes the soldiers behaved no worse on the March than soldiers at other times and places during the war. However, the March differed dramatically in a significant respect from other events during the war in that it put more soldiers and civilians into contact with one another, by virtue of the number of soldiers, the length of the campaign, and the miles covered. Rape was rare, but legend was not. Acknowledging that much of what people "know" of Sherman is wrapped up in folklore and legend, Kennett notes such things as the popularity of the song "Marching through Georgia," to which he gives deference in his book title; the inflation of Sherman's misdeeds with the passage of time; and tales of Sherman's personal application of the torch to residences, and his collection of white horses along the path of the March.[38]

Folk Hero

Books written for young readers may not carry much historical heft, but they are important transmitters of historical knowledge for future generations. Many such books have been written about Sherman. Two titles, written eighty-two years apart, illustrate how the genre functions.

Gen'l Wm. T. Sherman, His Life and Battles, or From Boy-Hood, to His "March to the Sea," Mostly in One Syllable Words was written in 1886 by Ida B. Forbes. Sherman grows up in Ohio hunting and fishing, a precocious frontier boy not much interested in wars and serious about his schoolwork. Each experience in his life seems to prepare him for greater challenges. Forbes instructs her young readers about the "great blot that had for years been on our land. The men of the South owned black men as slaves, and bought and sold them like beasts." Sherman speaks out against slavery, and when war comes he reluctantly leaves the South and fights to preserve the Union. The March to the Sea is covered in only a few pages, with slaves treated kindly, and much of the damage attributed to the retreating Confederates. The great general, still living at the time the book was written, "is as fond of the woods as when a boy, and rides on horse-back, or walks, as the mood takes him." Still a child at heart, in other words. The book ends with a benediction for "the brave man who has done so much for us."[39]

Charles P. Graves's *William Tecumseh Sherman: Champion of the Union* (1968) begins with young Cump being teased by schoolchildren at the age of nine. "Ha, ha! Who ever heard of a redheaded Indian?" asks a bully. Young readers got the message: even a boy who grows up to be a famous general once had to endure ridicule. But Sherman grows up, shows his mettle at West Point, in the Seminole War, and in California, and finds himself in the midst of an unwanted Civil War. During the March, although Sherman "was sometimes harsh, he could be kind too." Sherman's orders to forage liberally were misconstrued. "Unfortunately some of his men took everything they wanted from Georgia homes. Sometimes they burned barns and houses, leaving many innocent people homeless." Sherman's racism is ignored, and he is depicted as a kindly liberator. He brushes off the cruel names he is called by angry Southerners and does all he can to help them. After the war, he makes treaties with the Western Indians and helps unify the country. Sherman, ultimately, is an American boy who makes good and helps save the nation.[40]

These stories, and others like them, don't deal with complexity, and are intended to impart moral lessons in the Horatio Alger tradition. They are a reminder that historical facts are contested territory, and that the various reassessments proposed by historians might come as a shock to those weaned on childhood folklore. Conditioned to expect simple explanations, grown-up readers often are stunned to find historians in less agreement than Forbes implied.

Although not a historian, English professor Mark Coburn wrote a popular biographical study of Sherman the soldier, in which he gets at some important truths. His *Terrible Innocence: General Sherman at War* takes exception to the folkloric view that Sherman was "like Attila the Hun, but less cuddly." The trouble with turning Sherman into a cartoonish barbarian, Coburn writes, is that it "*matters* that Georgia and the Carolinas were devastated not by Lucifer or the Bogeyman, but by an intelligent, often witty general." He declines to get into the business of writing a "moral Pageant," opting instead to come to terms with a Sherman who was "brilliant and pigheaded, farsighted and foolish, cruel and tender, a friendly soul and a porcupine, prophetic and naïve, a lousy politician and a splendid writer. And more. Whittle him down to fit some pet interpretation, and he'll keep squiggling away."

Coburn, in other words, tries to separate Sherman and his March from myth, so Sherman can be dealt with honestly. If we dismiss him as some kind of moral aberration, maniac, or superman, or look for some single explanation to define him, he ceases to be like others, like us, and we cannot understand him. Coburn's Sherman sometimes becomes a fully developed literary character who might have stepped out of a novel by William Faulkner. Coburn uses as an epigraph a quotation from Faulkner's *Absalom, Absalom!* regarding "that innocence which believed that the ingredients of morality were like the ingredients of pie or cake and once you had measured them and balanced them and mixed them and put them into the oven it was all finished and nothing but pie or cake could ever come out." Sherman's "terrible innocence" was neither pie nor cake. The moral recipe was too complex to produce anything so predictable.[41]

Just as in life, in death Sherman appears to remain a master of the flanking maneuver, as he consistently moves around historians who would confront and corner the "real" Sherman. Whether in word, action, or both,

Sherman appears unknowable and remote, but familiar and immediate—like a myth. To varying degrees, historians have found him brilliant, but sometimes just lucky, barbaric in war but magnanimous in peace.

Notes

1. Albert Castel, *Decision in the West: The Atlanta Campaign of 1864* (Lawrence: University Press of Kansas, 1992), 565.

2. Victor Davis Hanson, *The Soul of Battle: From Ancient Times to the Present Day, How Three Great Liberators Vanquished Tyranny* (New York: Anchor Books, 2001), 259.

3. Lloyd Lewis, *Sherman: Fighting Prophet* (New York: Harcourt, Brace, 1932); B. H. Liddell Hart, *Sherman: Soldier, Realist, American* (New York: Dodd, Mead, 1929).

4. Liddell Hart, vii.

5. Jay Luvaas, *The Military Legacy of the Civil War: The European Inheritance* (Chicago: University of Chicago Press, 1959), 64, 71, 97, 102–5, 124, 145, 222–24; B. H. Liddell Hart, *Sherman: Soldier, Realist, American* (New York: Praeger, second printing, 1958), vii–viii; Garnet Wolseley, "General Sherman," *United Service Magazine* N.S. 3 (May–July, 1891), 99–103; Charles Chesney, "Sherman's Campaigns in Georgia," *Journal of the R.U.S.I.*, 9 (1866), 205–6; F. P. Vigo-Roussillon, "Puissance militaire des Etats-Unis d'Amerique d'apres la guerre de la secession, 1861–1865" (Paris, 1866), cited in Luvaas, *The Military Legacy of the Civil War*, 63, 157–88, 309, 411; Jacques Aldebert de Chambrun, "Impressions of Lincoln and the Civil War: A Foreigner's Account" (New York, 1952), cited in Luvaas, *The Military Legacy of the Civil War*, 6–7, 31, 62; F. von Meerheimb, "Sherman's Feldzug in Georgien" (Berlin, 1869), cited in Luvaas, *The Military Legacy of the Civil War*, 123–24.

6. Lewis, *Sherman*, 501–2, 418, 443, 457.

7. F. (Faunt LeRoy) Senour, *Major General William T. Sherman and His Campaigns* (Chicago: Henry M. Sherwood, 1865), 318, 350, 395; John F. Marszalek, *Sherman: A Soldier's Passion for Order* (New York: Free Press, 1993), 283, 316.

8. Stephen Davis, *Atlanta Will Fall: Sherman, Joe Johnston, and the Yankee Heavy Battalions* (Wilmington, DE: Scholarly Resources, 2001), 7, 92, 136, 147, 197–200.

9. Steven E. Woodworth, *Nothing But Victory: The Army of the Tennessee, 1861–1865* (New York: Knopf, 2005), 590–95.

10. Steven E. Woodworth, "November 1864: The March to the Sea," in *1864: Grinding, Relentless War* (Leesburg, VA: Primedia Enthusiast Group, 2004), 70–78.

11. Hanson, *The Soul of Battle*, 7, 230, 252, 259.

12. Bevin Alexander, *How Great Generals Win* (New York: Norton, 1993), 144–69.

13. Burke Davis, *Sherman's March* (New York: Vintage Books, 1988), 4–13, 289.

14. Steven E. Woodworth, Reid Mitchell, Gordon C. Rhea, John Y. Simon, Steven H. Newton, and Keith Poulter, "Who Were the Top Ten Generals? A Panel of Historians Discusses the Strengths and Weaknesses of Leading Civil War Commanders," *North and South* 6:4 (May 2003), 14–22.

15. Charles Bracelin Flood, *Grant and Sherman: The Friendship That Won the Civil War* (New York: Farrar, Straus and Giroux, 2005), 4–5.

16. Richard M. McMurray, *Atlanta 1864: Last Chance for the Confederacy* (Lincoln: University of Nebraska Press, 2000), 49, 74, 181–87.

17. Castel, *Decision in the West*, 565.

18 Ibid., 549–50; James M. Merrill, *William Tecumseh Sherman* (Chicago: Rand McNally, 1971).

19. Albert Castel, "Prevaricating through Georgia: Sherman's Memoirs as a Source on the Atlanta Campaign," *Civil War History* 40:1 (March 1994), 48–71; John Marszalek, "Sherman Called It the Way He Saw It," *Civil War History* 40:1 (March 1994), 73–78.

20. Albert Castel and Steven E. Woodworth, "How Good a General Was Sherman?" *North and South*, 7:2 (March 2004), 62–73.

21. John Bennett Walters, "General William T. Sherman and Total War," *Journal of Southern History* 14:4 (November 1948), 447–80.

22. John Bennett Walters, *Merchant of Terror: General Sherman and Total War* (New York: Bobbs-Merrill, 1973), xi, 82, 204.

23. Mark Grimsley, *The Hard Hand of War: Union Military Policy Toward Southern Civilians, 1861–1865* (New York: Cambridge University Press, 1995), 3–5, 174, 193, 199, 201, 221–22.

24. Charles Royster, *The Destructive War: William Tecumseh Sherman, Stonewall Jackson, and the Americans* (New York: Knopf, 1991), xi, 355–56; Charles Edmund Vetter, *Sherman: Merchant of Terror, Advocate of Peace* (Gretna, LA: Pelican Publishing, 1992).

25. Mark E. Neely, Jr., "Was the Civil War a Total War?" *Civil War History* 50:4 (December 2004), 434–58.

26. Lance Janda, "Shutting the Gates of Mercy: The American Origins of Total War, 1860–1880," *Journal of Military History* 59:1 (January 1995), 7–26.

27. Anne J. Bailey, *War and Ruin: William T. Sherman and the Savannah Campaign* (Wilmington, DE: Scholarly Resources, 2003), xii–xiv, 133–38.

28. Jacqueline Glass Campbell, *When Sherman Marched North from the Sea: Resistance on the Confederate Home Front* (Chapel Hill: University of North Carolina Press, 2003), 10, 103.

29. Joseph Glatthaar, *The March to the Sea and Beyond: Sherman's Troops in the Savannah and Carolinas Campaigns* (Baton Rouge: Louisiana State University Press, 1985), xiii, 71, 79, 133.

30. Earl Schenck Miers, *The General Who Marched to Hell: William Tecumseh Sherman and His March to Fame and Infamy* (New York: Knopf, 1951), 215–16, 285.

31. Ibid., 315.

32. Michael Fellman, *Citizen Sherman: A Life of William Tecumseh Sherman* (New York: Random House, 1995), ix, 5; Michael Fellman, introduction to *Memoirs of General W. T. Sherman* (New York: Penguin, 2000), xi-xiv.

33. Stanley P. Hirshson, *The White Tecumseh: A Biography of William T. Sherman* (New York: Wiley, 1997), ix–x, 391–92.

34. Stephen E. Ambrose, "William T. Sherman: A Personality Profile," *American History Illustrated* 1 (January 1967), 5–12, 54–57.

35. Nassir Ghaemi, "Sherman's Demons," *Atlanta* (November 2006), 76–82; see also Joshua Wolf Shenk, *Lincoln's Melancholy: How Depression Challenged a President and Fueled His Greatness* (Boston: Houghton Mifflin, 2005).

36. Harry S. Stout, *Upon the Altar of the Nation: A Moral History of the Civil War* (New York: Viking, 2006), 415, 419, 371.

37. Stephen E. Bower, "The Theology of the Battlefield: William Tecumseh Sherman and the U.S. Civil War," *Journal of Military History* 64:4 (October 2000), 1005–34.

38. Lee B. Kennett, *Marching through Georgia: The Story of Soldiers and Civilians during Sherman's Campaign* (New York: Harper Perennial, 2001), 269–77, 320–23.

39. Ida B. Forbes, *Gen'l Wm. T. Sherman, His Life and Battles, or From Boy-Hood, to His "March to the Sea," Mostly in One Syllable Words* (New York: McLoughlin, 1886), 12, 157.

40. Charles P. Graves, *William Tecumseh Sherman: Champion of the Union* (Champaign, IL: Garrard, 1968), 7, 91, 94.

41. Mark Coburn, *Terrible Innocence: General Sherman at War* (New York: Hippocrene Books, 1993), 11–12.

CHAPTER FOUR

⌒

Still Marching
Sherman in Literature

For it is still marching, that legendary Army. It was never anything but
a great myth marching to Savannah on the Sea!

Ross Lockridge, Jr., *Raintree County*, 1948[1]

Even before the war ended writers already were at work shaping the memory
of the conflict, and publishers were eager to meet the demand for rousing stories. The public wanted heroes and villains, and Sherman could be construed
as both. As different testaments about the war were propagated by witnesses,
including combatants, politicians, journalists, and civilians caught up in the
fighting, fictions were already part of the shrapnel of memory. The writers became the first Civil War reenactors, dressing up their characters in period cos-
tumes and animating them with authentic speech and action. Fiction became
an alternative commentary about the war, an imaginative enhancement of
the never-ending blast of battle books and biographies of Lee, Jackson, Grant,
Sherman, and the lesser commanders. In time, these "great man" biographies
devolved to stories about ever more minor figures, down to the final forgotten
captain, the littlest drummer boy, the last hapless widow. Fiction trotted right
along as the war receded into the past. Even Lee's horse had the chance to tell
his story to a stable cat in Richard Adams's novel *Traveller*.[2]

The story of Sherman's March gave some fiction writers the chance to try
to make sense of the war, much as Sherman himself had attempted to do.
Those writers, many of them journalists, often reflected the concerns of the
times, some seeking to continue fighting the war in fiction, some hoping to

hasten reconciliation. Sherman and the March became symbols for larger is-sues and causes. Journalism was still in a period of transition between En-lightenment rationalism and scientific positivism, different approaches to pursuing the slippery concept of truth. Newspapers still published fiction and highly personal interpretations of the news. In attempting to tell the larger story of the war, many journalists found imagination a surer path through the inner meaning of the war, as they avoided straying too far from the evidence gleaned through personal observation, reports, and the testimony of others. Journalists were still not far from the lofty ideals that inspired the Revolution and the creation of the United States and American myths. During and af-ter the Civil War, large ideas still mattered, and facts mattered, but in differ-ent ways. In the Enlightenment era, the existence of truth was assumed, but the ability to find it was as often doubted. In the emerging scientific and in-dustrial era, facts and truth were converging, especially if facts were reliable and had utility. Journalists writing about the war had reason to be skeptical of both the absolute "truths" advanced to justify the war and the "facts" about what actually happened. Evaluating the morality of events such as Sherman's March could not be a matter of weighing competing abstractions or sorting through contradictory interpretations of the movement of armies and the hazy recollections of soldiers who saw only pieces of the battles in which they fought. Unraveling the complexity of moral judgments was be-yond purely objective journalism, which in any event hardly existed.

As a character in fiction, Sherman presented a challenge. Like many of the journalists who wrote about him, he too was a transitional figure shaped both by abstract ideas and concrete solutions. His personality was erratic and opaque, however. He seemed daunting, less accessible imaginatively than other notable figures of the war. His involvement in the Atlanta campaign and the March, however, turned him into a force, a monster, a machine plowing up not just the Old South but the soil in which so many American myths had flourished as well, and announcing the arrival of a new industrial age. The story of the March, like so much American fiction, also became a story of the road, a journey toward and away from something, with the road itself a central character. Sherman's March was a familiar American story, a crossing of barriers just to show it could be done. One version of the story would complement perfectly the emerging myth of American industry as a moral, progressive, and continental force.

But armies on the move leave few monuments, and once it left Atlanta, Sherman's army left fewer than most. If Sherman was the vandal Southern mythology claimed he was, then everything along the route of the March went up in smoke. There were no real battles, so there are no real battlefields, only skirmishes denoted by the odd historical marker along a highway. Fiction writers provided the missing monuments, most of them mere curiosities attracting only a few visitors on the back roads of literature. Although the literary memory of the March has sometimes crackled and burned as fast as Georgia pine, not every book has been part of the bonfire.

Uncle Billy's Boys

From the Union point of view the literary March begins with Lieutenant Colonel George Ward Nichols, a journalist who served as an aide-de-camp on Sherman's staff from the fall of Atlanta to the end of the war. *The Story of the Great March*, published in 1865, was one of the earliest factual accounts of Sherman's army. Some 60,000 copies were sold within a year, and on the strength of this success Nichols turned to fiction, publishing *The Sanctuary* the next year. The novel features a swoon of romantic scenarios that would be cloyingly repeated in much subsequent Civil War fiction. There is a Union officer from Georgia who is estranged from, and finally reunited with, the Savannah girl whom he loves but who has scorned him as a recreant. There is the noble Boston girl, who fends off the advances of an amorous Yankee war profiteer while her true love fights with Sherman. And there is the evil plantation master who seduces a slave. Their offspring winds up choking his white half brother, a Confederate general named Ralph Buford. Sherman is less a character in the novel than the author's former boss, a modest and unselfish soldier who preserves the republic as the "sanctuary" of a reunited people.[3]

Next came Ambrose Bierce, an eighteen-year-old Indiana farm boy who enlisted in a volunteer regiment early in the war and was with Sherman during the Atlanta campaign as an infantryman and mapmaker. After he was shot at Kennesaw Mountain, he was sent home to recover, later returning to serve at Franklin and Nashville, rejoining Sherman in the Carolinas. In 1867 he began writing journalism and short fiction. His stories would eventually include "An Occurrence at Owl Creek Bridge" and "Chickamauga," two of the best known tales to come out of the conflict, and accounts of Georgia battles, such as "Killed at Resaca." Bierce's fiction is psychological, surreal, allegorical, sardonic, and morbid, and as a journalist he earned the sobriquet "Bitter" Bierce. He was skeptical both about moral absolutes and about the efficacy of facts alone for making sense of the war. Gordon Berg writes that in an era extolling "the myth of the good war to save the Union and free the slaves, Bierce cried out that war is about wasted lives, mutilation, disease, decay and death." The Civil War stories appeared in book form as *Tales of Soldiers and Civilians* in 1891, the year Sherman died, and in later collections. Edmund Wilson gives Bierce a chapter in his study of Civil War literature, commenting that his short stories "are often distinguished from the hackwork of the shudder magazines only by the fact that the shudder is an emotion that for the author is genuine." Bierce's disappearance in Mexico late in 1913, shortly after he toured the Civil War battlefields where he had fought, only added to the mystique of the March.[4]

Sherman's death inspired other former soldiers to write about him also. Edward G. Bird, one of Sherman's lieutenants, wrote a dime novel titled *Sherman's "March to the Sea," or Fighting His Way through Georgia*. The story turned up in print little more than two weeks after the general's death and follows the pattern of much early Civil War fiction. Sherman befriends Harry Clinton, an impoverished young lieutenant from New York, and sends him on a mission to find out how General Hood is getting information about where to attack Sherman's lines during the siege of Atlanta. A local Union sympathizer with a beautiful niece switches sides, and is in cahoots with a renegade Union officer peddling secrets to Hood, who wants to kidnap Sherman. Clinton is captured and taken to Hood. He escapes, engages in swordfights with an old friend serving with the Confederates, foils the plot, marches to Savannah, and marries the niece, who not only is true to the Union but also has a large inheritance that her evil uncle was trying to steal. The general promotes Clinton to colonel and attends his wedding. Years later, the couple witnesses Sherman's funeral procession in New York. And all that in twenty-nine pages.[5]

Warren Lee Goss was born in Massachusetts in 1835, attended Harvard Law School, became a teacher, and enlisted in the Union army early in the war. He was captured—twice—and incarcerated at Andersonville and other notorious Confederate prisons. After the war he wrote bitter accounts of his prison experiences and moralistic, autobiographical fiction for young people, including *Tom Clifton, or Western Boys with Grant and Sherman's Army, '61–'65*, published in 1892. Tom Clifton goes from Massachusetts to Minnesota with his family before the war, has boyhood adventures on the frontier, and then joins the army when the war breaks out. He first sees Sherman at Shiloh, serves with him during the Atlanta campaign, is captured, escapes, is recaptured, and eventually paroled. Sherman is "quick and nervous" but approachable. A "common soldier could address him without rebuff, although he was sometimes distant to others." Goss continued writing and lived until 1925.[6]

William Henry Shelton, best known for his military paintings and illustrations, wrote "Uncle Obadiah's Uncle Billy," a story that appeared in the

Century in 1893. Obadiah Brown, an eighty-year-old veteran of Sherman's army, wounded during the Battle of Atlanta and personally decorated by Sherman, comes to an Ohio town in February 1891 to repair the town clock. "Uncle Obadiah" continues to search for his son, who was among the missing at Missionary Ridge. He encounters other veterans at a tavern, where they swap tales about "Uncle Billy." Uncle Obadiah is sure Uncle Billy will be able to help him find his son, and he has saved money for a journey to New York to see the general. But Sherman has died, and his funeral train will soon pass through the town on its way to St. Louis. The old soldiers march to the station during a nighttime storm, but Uncle Obadiah loses his senses and imagines he is under special orders to wait for Uncle Billy. The veterans build shelters and huddle around campfires along the tracks, as they had during the March. Uncle Obadiah falls asleep "with a childish trust in his great commander." Soon the train approaches and the soldiers stand to attention. "As if it were the passing spirit of their great commander, the fierce light flashes along the ranks of his old veterans, gleaming for an instant on bared heads and tearful faces, and gilding once more the fragmentary names of his battles on their ragged standards, and then leaves the old line in redoubled darkness." Meanwhile, Uncle Obadiah has died.

Another soldier-turned-journalist, Byron A. Dunn, used his wartime experiences to create fact-based, turn-of-the-century stories about Sherman's March. His "Young Kentuckians" series features the daring adventures of a captain who serves as Sherman's scout and chief intelligence officer. He manages to escape from Andersonville in *Battling for Atlanta* and then gets the girl and the glory in *From Atlanta to the Sea*.[7]

The American journalist, essayist, and novelist Winston Churchill was among the most widely read authors from 1899 to 1916. Interest in historical romances was at its peak in the years between 1896 and 1902. In 1901, Churchill's *The Crisis* resonated with readers who saw American history as a romance and a progression toward greatness. Churchill grounded the novel in his research into the Civil War period in his native St. Louis, where Sherman had lived before the war, and where the memory of the war was still vigorous. The protagonist is based on Sherman's aide during the March, Henry Hitchcock, who provided background information for the novel. Sherman is a godlike figure, a man of the West, indefatigable, decisive, one of history's great commanders. The Northern view of the general was fulfilled in this novel, but would not go unchallenged.[8]

Goldie's Inheritance: A Story of the Siege of Atlanta, published in 1903, was an unusual addition to the war literature, as well as a scholarly detective story. Thomas G. Dyer, a University of Georgia professor, rooted through archives and linked the novel to "Miss Abby's Diary," a document kept during the siege by an anonymous Union sympathizer. More sleuthing identified Cyrena Bailey Stone, a Vermont woman living in Atlanta, as the probable diarist. When Sherman entered the city he tried to protect its Unionists, most of whom, including Stone, eventually left and went north. Louisa M. Whitney, born in 1844, was Stone's younger half sister, and she drew on the diary as well as the experiences of another sister in writing the novel. Its significance, according to Dyer, is that it offers a different perspective on Civil War Atlanta from Margaret Mitchell's *Gone with the Wind*. Rather than heroic Confederates, the heroes in this book are Unionists, and Sherman is a deliverer rather than a destroyer. "We who look calmly back and see all the results of that wonderful march through Georgia can little realize the living, torturing suspense of those summer days," Whitney wrote. But the story she told would soon be forgotten. Mitchell's story would endure.[9]

Fire Warriors

The Southern literary rebuke of Sherman began soon after the war, simmered for several decades, then intensified. William Henry Peck, a journalist, novelist, and teacher, published *The M'Donalds, or The Ashes of Southern Homes* in 1867. Born in 1830, Peck had grown up in Georgia and Florida, graduated from Harvard, and written for New York publications. For a time he was a professor of history and literature in New Orleans; then he returned to Georgia to start a literary journal, the *Georgia Weekly*. At the time of Sherman's March, Peck was teaching in Talbotton, Georgia, safely removed from the fighting, but close enough to inhale some literary smoke from the smoldering mansions in Sherman's path. Nothing much escapes the "fire-warriors of Shermanic conquest" while the "world is aghast with horror and rebuke." The mother and daughter of the title flee burning Atlanta, but wherever they lodge Sherman and his minions burn them out again. The women are hounded by an evil Atlanta peddler and a sleazy Union captain, a former Boston rummy, out for loot, while a good Yankee tries to protect them. Peck wrote in a documentary style, liberally quoting passages from Sherman's reports to underscore the general's nefarious intentions, and setting the pattern for much subsequent Southern fiction. Because Sherman was notorious for using language that was much harsher than his actions, his own words came back to haunt him as he was demonized in Southern myth.[10]

Sara Beaumont Kennedy's *Cicely: A Tale of the Georgia March*, published in 1911, is a Lost Cause romance, with the sweetheart of a Confederate soldier being driven from her Georgia home by Sherman's army. "If General

Sherman persists in making exiles of these homeless, defenceless people, he will earn for himself the abiding bitterness of the South," cries Cicely. "No number of years will ever win him forgiveness." But a good Yankee comes to Cicely's rescue and all is well, although Sherman is unredeemed. In 1912, Mary Johnston, a Virginian and a cousin to General Joseph Johnston, published *Cease Firing*. The novel includes chapters on Sherman and the "swathe of misery, horror, and destruction" resulting from the March, defends the author's relative, and offers a melancholy lament for the sullied South. Margaret Mitchell's mother was a schoolmate of Mary Johnston's and read the novel to her daughter. Mitchell said she considered *Cease Firing* "the best documented novel ever written," and consulted it to get the correct weather details when she was writing *Gone with the Wind*. Just where Johnston found the information isn't clear, because Mitchell said she was unable to find what she was looking for in primary sources. In any case, Civil War fiction was shaped by earlier fiction, perpetuating and amplifying errors and interpretations with each succeeding version of an old story.[11]

The Agrarians: Dixie Looks Back

The 1920s witnessed a peculiar, resurgent interest in the Civil War. The last living links to the conflict were dying, as postwar industrialism recalibrated the scales for weighing cultural progress. The decade saw reactions to the industrial ethic, such as the eugenics movement, an absolute embrace of the Social Darwinist view of life. Like a good assembly line, the goal was the production of fitter individuals who would make the social engine run stronger and more efficiently. Among the most eloquent reactions against such pseudoscientific doctrines, and against modernism in general, were the Southern Agrarians, who found in a mythical Dixie the elixir to cure the contemporary South of its social and economic ills.

The Agrarians were a regional reaction, uniquely Southern and intimately tied to the past. The group grew out of a literary enclave, the Fugitives, at Vanderbilt University around 1915, and over the next decade eventually centered on sixteen individuals, including John Crowe Ranson, Allen Tate, Andrew Lytle, Robert Penn Warren, Donald Davidson, and Stark Young. Their literary output included poetry, novels, history, criticism, and essays. It was never a formal organization, and it had begun to lose its energy by the mid-1920s. The 1925 Scopes spectacle in Dayton, Tennessee, revitalized the group, which in 1930 published *I'll Take My Stand*, a series of loosely connected essays in defense of agrarian life and values, of traditional Southern values and heritage. It became their manifesto, a reaction to the national insult represented in the trial. Baltimore journalist H. L. Mencken was the most bitter of the South-baiters, making South-bashing a national sport. The Agrarians took exception in their reaction against modernism. They preached the salvation of traditional religion and an imagined, Edenic farm community. Ransom, in the introduction to *I'll Take My Stand*, assailed the "cult of science," which the Agrarians saw as presumptuously pretending to have answers to everything, while being blind to the mysteries of nature. They celebrated a mythology of frontier and Garden, of yeoman and cavalier. They imagined an Old South apart from and above the rest of the country in both its myth and history, where rebuke and slavery were in fact manifestations of strength and benevolence that had been lost in the gross misrepresentations of Reconstruction and the Gilded Age. Their South was defined as much by its opposition to modernism as by its allegiance to agrarian life, real or imagined. The Agrarians were radically conservative in their defense of nineteenth-century proprietary capitalism, and in seeing science and liberalism as undercutting the Victorian morality that was their social gospel.[12]

Sherman was critical for the Agrarians, but they never gave him the attention that they did his Tennessee nemesis, Forrest, whom Lytle idealized as an example of Old South values. Like the serpent in Genesis, Sherman was an absolute necessity to the story and its teachings. As the Agrarian antithesis, Sherman exemplified that which they abhorred, demonstrating for them the emptiness of unheroic war and the abandonment of chivalric notions about the conduct of war. Davidson did set Sherman directly against Forrest, casting them as antihero and hero. In the second volume of his history of the Tennessee River Valley, Davidson wrote:

> Among Confederate commanders, only General Forrest saw clearly what needed to be done and had the genius and the will to do it. . . . [He] had achieved tremendous results on land with limited means. . . . Sherman, in desperation, vowed to punish the people of the Confederacy for Forrest's audacity. In 1864, Sherman wrote to McPherson: ". . . If we do not punish Forrest and the people now, the whole effect of our vast conquest will be lost."[13]

Davidson gave unique status to Forrest by virtue of the fact that Sherman supposedly offered a promotion to anyone who killed him. Davidson also aggrandized Tennessee in the obverse by making it the place where Sherman could not do his March without supply lines, which were being ripped up by "that devil Forrest." Therefore, it was easier and more spectacular to march through Georgia and the Carolinas. The Federals, he said, reverted to "classic forms of sack and pillage," taking hostages and, when attacked by guerrillas, making reprisals against local communities. "[T]he Federal invasion . . . could hardly be distinguished from the inroads of a Genghis Khan or an Attila. In April, 1864, Confederate General [James Holt] Clanton reported that 'the Yankees spared neither age, sex, nor condition.'" According to Davidson, the Tennessee Valley was a training ground for the March to the Sea:

> Grant and Sherman had evolved in the Tennessee Valley what is known today as total war. . . . From end to end the Tennessee Valley was a wasteland—a ruin cloaked only by the indomitable wilderness, which again put forth its seasonal green in the bitter spring of 1865 and advanced its fringe of sprouts and saplings a little farther over deserted farms and untilled fields. . . . Across the bruised earth, the track of the armies was plainly discernible. In future years it would be veiled, but never completely obliterated.[14]

Sherman was especially significant for Davidson because of the latter's provincialism. Fred Hobson points out that Davidson was doubly provincial, preaching a special South only in the Tennessee River Valley and Middle Georgia. Other parts of the South, especially the coastal and traditional Old South, he believed to have been corrupted by Northeastern industrialism and modernism. His exceptions to a corrupted South correlated well with the prelude to and culmination of Sherman's March. By giving Tennessee a special place in the story, as a sort of genesis to the great March, he gave Tennessee (and, by extension, Middle Georgia) a special place in the myth of destruction and redemption. The serpent Sherman strikes first and most severely in Tennessee, refines his tactics, and marches off to Georgia. The Tennessee Valley was the first to be destroyed, as Eden was destroyed, and so it would be the first to be redeemed. It was the place, after all, where the new prophets of the Old South gathered and codified their history-laden faith in *I'll Take My Stand*.[15]

By the 1930s, the Agrarians had waned, but not their ideas. Their mythic vision resonated across the South and the nation. Paul V. Murphy believes the Agrarians' intellectual will was sapped by demands of allegiance to a Southern past. It didn't work the same for popular culture, however, which in a newly invented Old South found morality tales that confirmed redemption of the vanquished, and wrapped it in a story of opportunism, romance, and bravery.[16]

So Red the Rose

So Red the Rose, Stark Young's best-selling 1934 novel about the Bedfords and the McGehees, two interrelated families living on plantations near Natchez,

Mississippi, during the Civil War era, features Sherman in a revealing role that anticipates the March. Young was born in Mississippi in 1881, and became a prominent theater critic in New York, writing regular reviews for the *New Republic*, poems, plays, and novels. Although Young remained somewhat of a fringe figure among the Agrarians, distancing himself from their political entanglements, he, too, saw the South in conflict with modernity. Laying the philosophical groundwork for the novel in "Not in Memoriam, But in Defense," the concluding essay in *I'll Take My Stand*, Young lamented the collective national thinking that was paving over the South's agrarian roots. "It would be childish and dangerous for the South to be stampeded and betrayed out of its own character by the noise, force, and glittering narrowness of the industrialism and progress spreading everywhere, with varying degrees, from one region to another," he wrote. Young urged aristocratic resistance to corrupting trends that were compromising manners and civility, and "a less democratic, mobbed, and imitative course of things" in matters of education and culture.[17]

In *So Red the Rose*, Sherman visits Montrose, the home of the McGehee clan, on March 1, 1864, to pay his respects to the parents of Edward McGehee, a Confederate soldier killed at Shiloh. Edward had been a student at the Louisiana Military Academy when Sherman was superintendent, and Sherman is distressed to learn of his death. Hugh and Agnes McGehee had been Unionists until Mississippi seceded, and they politely welcome Sherman, seeing in him "a kind of rough cleanness of soul. His remarks had the authority of impetuous people who feel with the clarity, if not the finality, of logic." They are touched by him, sensing an emotionally dependent, "pathetic, strong child, full of impetuous integrity."[18]

And yet, they wonder, could the courtly general in their parlor be "the Sherman with the looting, burning, and wreck behind him—around Jackson for twenty miles the country stripped and burnt to a cinder?" Their daughter Lucy cares little for Sherman's psyche, complaining that "everybody's got to be explaining him instead of knocking his head off." Sherman, having wrestled with himself and lost, is soon off to make Georgia howl, leaving Montrose to be burned by black troops, an act which in itself is symbolic of the reversal of the South's fortunes and the inversion of order.[19]

When the war ends, Hugh McGehee ruminates on the future of the South, now sullied by Northern chicanery and looted by carpetbaggers who "seemed to him to have no conception at all of a civilization." Sherman's victory not only put the Old South to the torch but also built the smelter in which the industrial monster would be forged. The eager, impatient, rapacious newcomers talk of statistics, opportunities, energy, "competent

both to think without knowing and to know without thinking, a temperament sustained by innocence, emptied by shallow choice, and run by
steam." In their view

> society was actually a state of war. Competition without social principles. This
> would lead to a legalistic attitude, law as the letter, the strategic game; and this
> meant the debasement of the social sense. It meant secretiveness. Not lies, but
> a system of moving secretly, which ends in being only deceit and suspicion.
> Hiding the hen-nests, the prudence of white trash.[20]

Davidson, in an introduction to the 1953 edition of *So Red the Rose*, interpreted Sherman as representing all that was alien to Southern tradition.
The real enemy, however, was science. The scientist, like Sherman, was a divided self, indifferent to "affections" and committed to materialism. This was
the burden of the Enlightenment, when "we are always being drawn into desperate choices between the truth of our feelings, which is intuitive and traditional, and the scientist's purely logical dicta, which abhor intuitive and
traditional knowledge." Sherman became "the Enemy in military fact as well
as in fully rationalized intent." Mississippi was yet another pre–March to the
Sea laboratory for total war. What Sherman intruded upon and destroyed was
the Southern "culture of the whole personality." He, in turn, was "a grand
apotheosis and cataclysmic realization of the cult of the divided personality."
The logical, unsympathetic part of his mind could justify any means to
achieve his ends.

According to Davidson, Agnes McGehee realizes that Sherman

> knew he had entered on a new stage or policy toward the invaded territory,
> that he went back and forth between the first attitude and this later harsher
> one, that this conflict of policy had become a conflict in his own nature, and
> that the story that was building up of him as a ruthless monster did at the same
> time both serve him and his purposes as a picture of war, and antagonize,
> grieve, and enrage him as a picture of himself.[21]

So while Young offered a somewhat Shakespearian portrait of the historical
Sherman as he became the mythic Sherman the Barbarian, Davidson implied even more. Not content just to let the bipolar Sherman struggle with
his demons like Othello or Macbeth, he transformed him into the mad scientist Frankenstein blowing fuses in the Agrarian laboratory. The Union that
Sherman resurrected was a monster in Sherman's own image, a schizophrenic
two-headed Yankee grafted onto a decapitated Confederate body with a
warm heart.[22]

The War Was All Around Her

Margaret Mitchell's husband John Marsh didn't want his wife to read *So Red the Rose* when it was published, for fear that she might give up writing her own epic novel about the Civil War. He need not have worried. Mitchell's role in creating myths about the Civil War and Sherman's March can hardly be overstated. Indeed, her book is said to have outsold everything but the Bible. It is unlikely that any work of American fiction is better known outside the United States, and, thanks to Mitchell and the movie, Sherman ranks among the great pyromaniacs in popular history.[23]

Mitchell was born in Atlanta in 1900 in her grandmother's antebellum home, which had survived the fire of 1864. Annie Fitzgerald Stephens had been raised on a modest plantation in nearby Jonesboro, and had come to Atlanta with her husband James just a year before Sherman's arrival. They had remained in their home during the battle, within sight of a line of Confederate entrenchments, and they hadn't joined the refugees fleeing the city after the fire. Mitchell absorbed her grandmother's stories about antebellum Georgia, the war, and Reconstruction, and listened to veterans' tales of battles, the fall of Atlanta, and the March to the Sea. As a child, Mitchell read the Thomas Dixon novels that became the basis for D. W. Griffith's *Birth of a Nation*. Inspired by the novels, and too young to understand them, she and her friends dressed up as Klansmen and performed in plays, complete with mock lynchings. But real horrors were part of her early life. She witnessed one of the South's worst race riots in Atlanta in 1906, shortly before her sixth birthday.[24]

Mitchell spent summers in Jonesboro and learned how her grandmother had allegedly persuaded one of Sherman's generals to post a guard at the Fitzgerald farmhouse, which spared the structure but didn't prevent looting. On the road to Jonesboro, Mitchell's mother pointed out the ruins of much grander plantations that she said were destroyed by Sherman's army. For the precocious daughter, the Civil War wasn't merely a romance in which living relatives had played a part. The war was all around her. After a year at Smith College in Massachusetts, Mitchell took a job as a feature writer for the *Atlanta Journal Sunday Magazine* in 1922. She was a good interviewer and fit in easily among the hard-drinking journalists and genteel scribblers who comprised the Atlanta literary scene. She dabbled at writing short fiction for a few years but was unable to interest any magazines in her work. She left the *Journal* for good, and in 1926 she started writing the story that had been on her mind since she was a child.[25]

By April 1935 she had enough of the novel completed to interest Harold Latham, a Macmillan Company executive who was in Atlanta looking for manuscripts. He had been tipped that Mitchell had been working on a novel, although no one but her husband had seen it. A meeting was arranged. Mitchell was diffident about discussing her unfinished, untitled work. He persisted, she resisted, he insisted, she relented, and soon Latham was stuffing pages into a suitcase and boarding a train for New Orleans. Somewhere west of Atlanta, he knew he had the makings of a book that just might have a chance to sell out a first printing of 10,000 copies, and then maybe more. Mitchell finished the book by February 1936, and even before it was published it was a Book of the Month Club selection and film studios were wrangling for movie rights. When the novel reached the bookstores in June, 50,000 copies were sold in one day and a million within six months.[26]

Gone with the Wind has rarely been regarded as great literature, yet its enormous success suggests a powerful story that many people wanted, and perhaps needed, to hear. Nothing about the novel is too complicated, so its accessibility alone gave it a potentially far larger audience than better novelists like Faulkner or Young could have attracted. Breathless with stereotypes pulled from minstrel shows, Dixon novels, *Uncle Remus*, *The Birth of a Nation*, Lost Cause apologetics, and the Atlanta newspapers, the novel charmed and beguiled a vast readership. And yet Civil War potboilers had been churned out for more than seven decades before *Gone with the Wind* appeared. What made the difference?[27]

Several seemingly minor changes in the manuscript may have been crucial. Mitchell originally called her heroine *Pansy* O'Hara, which lacks the rouged insouciance of *Scarlett*. The O'Hara plantation inspired by the Fitzgerald family's Jonesboro farm, which was simply called Rural Home, was upgraded to a stuffy-sounding Fontenoy Hall in early drafts before Mitchell thought of "Tara." The title itself was an afterthought. Mitchell had considered *There's Always Tomorrow*, *Another Day*, *Milestones*, *Bugles Sang True*, and *Ba! Ba! Black Sheep*, clinkers that might have consigned the novel to obscurity. She found the title in a poem written by Ernest Dowson, a fin-de-siecle English decadent. The melancholy lines "I have forgot much, Cynara! gone with the wind" have more to do with unrequited love and absinthe than with lost causes in Georgia, but it was a congenial choice, and even better than other lines from Dowson she might have chosen, like "the days of wine and roses" or "the weeping and the laughter." Mitchell told Latham the title could mean lost times in a metaphysical sense or refer to "things that passed with the winds of war, or to a person who went with the wind rather than standing against it." Readers could make what they wished out of the metaphor, and fill in the blanks as to *what* had gone and *where*, and *who* or *what* was doing the blowing. Even better, each subtraction added strength to a myth that explained it. If the Confederacy was gone, it was resurrected by the Lost Cause myth. If the Old South had died, the Plantation myth had arisen to justify slavery. Cavaliers mutated into Klansmen. Destruction begat Reconstruction. If innocence had been sullied, the Garden myth was as pure as a field of cotton.[28]

The book's success had much to do with the Depression. Scarlett is a survivor in a time of economic ruin. Her pluck and self-reliance pull her through hard times, and that appealed to readers, as did the portrayal of a strong female character. At the same time, war clouds were scudding across Europe and Asia, and young men and women again would be called upon to make sacrifices. Causes again would matter. Meanwhile, the living memory of the Civil War was coming to an end. The last significant gathering of veterans took place at Gettysburg in 1938. Each death of one of the few remaining veterans was another reminder that the precious past was gone with the wind, intensifying the nostalgia evoked by the novel. Edmund Wilson, in *Patriotic Gore*, suggests that as Northern cities began to lose their charm after the war due to rapid industrial development, Northerners co-opted Southern myths and reveled in them. Sentimental tales of the Old South softened Northern animosities, inclining Northerners to want to recompense the South for its destruction. The commercial success of *Gone with the Wind* as novel and film was the culmination of Northern penance. If so, Sherman was destined to be the fall guy.[29]

A Force beyond Evil

Sherman doesn't arrive as a character in *Gone with the Wind* for a couple of hundred pages, and he doesn't tarry long; but he is the force that compels and animates the action. He rises in the north like a sirocco in May 1864, "a hot dry May that wilted the flowers in the buds," as if the natural order is submitting to the force that is coming. Sherman, according to news reports, is in Georgia, above Dalton. At first, no one in Atlanta is much concerned, for Dalton is near Tennessee, where fighting has raged for three years. Moreover, Johnston stands like an "iron rampart in the mountains" and "so bitterly did he contest Sherman's desire to pass down the valley toward Atlanta that finally the Yankees drew back and took counsel with themselves."[30]

Sherman flanks Johnston's lines, and with reports of Johnston's retreat to Resaca, Atlanta is "surprised and a little disturbed. It is as though a small, dark cloud had appeared in the northwest, the first cloud of a summer storm." Sherman "inexorably advanced step by step," giving Johnston no rest. Sherman's army moves relentlessly "like a monster serpent, coiling, striking venomously, drawing its injured lengths back but always striking again." As the wounded are brought into Atlanta the town is "appalled. . . . The small cloud on the horizon had blown up swiftly into a large, sullen storm cloud and it was as though a faint, chilling wind blew from it." Hope is momentarily restored at Kennesaw Mountain, and then Sherman quickens his advance. The slaughter increases as the new Confederate commander, Hood, launches aggressive assaults. Atlanta—besieged, overwhelmed, immolated, and vanquished—is in the hands of the conquerer.[31]

"Sherman! The name of Satan himself did not frighten her half so much," writes Mitchell, describing Scarlett's thoughts as she flees to find out if Tara has withstood the invaders. Sherman evolves from an impersonal force of nature to a willful force beyond evil. His army is a merciless pack of grave robbers gnawing the bones of the defeated South. The wind that blew down the edifice so swiftly had come, from Scarlett's point of view, at a time when

> she and everyone else had thought that Atlanta could never fall, that Georgia could never be invaded. But the small cloud which appeared in the northwest four months ago had blown up into a mighty storm and then into a screaming tornado, sweeping away her world, whirling her out of her sheltered life, and dropping her down in the midst of this still, haunted desolation. Was Tara still standing? Or was Tara also gone with the wind which had swept through Georgia?

Tara has been spared. Ironically, Sherman has used it as a headquarters, preserving the house while defiling it.[32]

Four months later, cut off from news about the war, Scarlett finally learns the fate of Atlanta, "acres and acres of chimneys standing blackly above ashes, piles of half-burned rubbish and tumbled heaps of brick clogging the streets, old trees dying from fire, their charred limbs tumbling to the ground in the cold wind." Yankee soldiers have desecrated cemeteries, looting graves and scattering bones and corpses. Packs of starving animals roam the city as "buzzards splotched the wintery sky with graceful, sinister bodies." Sherman, meanwhile, has reached Savannah practically unmolested. The March is almost an afterthought. Once Atlanta has fallen, the South is doomed. Metaphoric winds have been sweeping through literature from the *Odyssey* to *The Wizard of Oz*. Scarlett's "wind" is Sherman, and while the Old South, the mythic Garden, may be "gone," Tara, the mythic Plantation, still stands. Scarlett herself becomes the South Triumphant. Her innocence lost, chastened and expelled from the Garden, she learns, like the South, to survive by cunning and guile.[33]

Gone with the Wind is, of course, also a love story. Scarlett O'Hara, a symbol of the South, longs for Ashley Wilkes (the Old South cavalier) and learns she really loves Rhett Butler (the materialist, gunrunning critic of the Old South, the New South grifter). She gets neither, as she is torn between the romance of gentility and the material reward of business success. And unlike the heroines in many another Southern romance, she doesn't get to live happily ever after. Nor does the South. But the road to national reconciliation was paved with Lost Cause gold. Gilding defeat pointed the way to a better country ready to face the future. As David W. Blight explains, one of the primary ideas the Lost Cause instilled into the national culture is that "even when Americans lose, they win. Such was the message, the indomitable spirit, that Margaret Mitchell infused into her character Scarlett O'Hara." *Gone with the Wind* is American mythology. Jim Cullen asserts that if a "shared national culture can be said to exist GWTW would have to be at the heart of it."[34]

Paradise Lost

Neither Sherman nor his March were sighted often in fiction for a decade after *Gone with the Wind*. Occasional stories appeared in magazines during the Second World War, but perhaps that wider conflict had displaced interest in a destructive, divisive invasion of Georgia, or perhaps after Mitchell's novel and the film there seemed little else to say about the general. One exception was in the form of the Captain Little Ax stories written by Mississippi journalist and novelist James Street. Captain Alexander Xerxes Trowbridge, called Little Ax, "the arrogant gamecock of the Confederacy," is the bantam-size teenage guerrilla leader of the ruthless "Cradle Company," boy soldiers who take on Sherman with the tacit approval of generals Johnston and Forrest. In "All Out with Sherman," published in *Collier's* a week before Christmas in 1942, Sherman advances across Mississippi after the fall of Vicksburg "in a dress rehearsal for the march through Georgia." Little Ax knows Sherman has to be stopped before his strategy destroys the Confederacy:

> Sherman is fighting this war to win. He can't beat our armies, but he can beat our homefolks and that'll beat our armies. We ain't seen nothing yet. Both sides are mean mad now, and when Americans get mean mad they're the bloodiest, killin'est folks in the world. Sherman is a whole-hawg soldier and he's going all the way out to break our backs first, then our necks. I wish my company could get one more crack at him.

Little Ax's martial speech no doubt was what "mean mad" *Collier's* readers wanted to hear in 1942, with American soldiers in combat in North Africa and the Pacific—even though the Cradle Company is almost wiped out after briefly stalling Sherman's advance across the Pearl River. Outnumbered, the bantlings have fought almost to the last boy, and that showed American, and especially Southern, pluck, courage, and determination. Little Ax and a few survivors then head for Georgia to fight on.[35]

Raintree County by Ross Lockridge, Jr., was largely written during the Second World War and was published in January 1948. Two months after its publication, and with the novel atop the best seller lists, the thirty-three-year-old Indiana author committed suicide. Accordingly, the author and his sprawling, 1,066-page opus were given a certain literary mystique. Lockridge attempted to write a grand epic that placed the Civil War, and Sherman's March, at the heart of the national experience. The action is compressed into a single day, July 4, 1892, when Johnny Shawnessy, poet, journalist, and teacher on a mission "to record in stone the eternal verities of the Republic," recalls his life. Shawnessy had come of age in the mythical Raintree County, Indiana, an American Eden. His noble ambitions, idealism, and innocence had been compromised when he was seduced, like the North, by Susanna Drake, a sultry young psychopath from New Orleans whose childhood was clouded by the fear of miscegenation. Their tormented marriage became a tragedy, and during the war she wound up, like the South, in a madhouse. The grieving Shawnessy joined the army and marched through Georgia with Sherman. The industrial North defeated the agrarian South because it had "too many engines on too many tracks, too many factories in too many cities, too many determined generals juggling sheets of supplies and railroad timetables, too many corps of engineers, too many whirring, remorseless machines," and Sherman's indomitable army, "a strong tide, a swift river, which must somewhere come to the sea."

The war brought an end to Paradise and ushered in the Gilded Age. *Raintree County* is mulched with myth and allegory, as a battalion of characters, including Sherman and Lincoln, struts through American history. Each major character stands for Something Big—the Sinful South; American Innocence; Big Business; the serpent in the Garden; or one of many folk heroes, legends, and martyrs from Johnny Appleseed to John Brown and from Uncle Sam to Uncle Tom. Had the novel been written a decade earlier, it might have stood as a more cerebral and metaphysical Midwestern counterpart to *Gone with the Wind*. But *Raintree County* didn't quite seem to fit the jaded Cold War spirit, which hoped for less arduously overwrought national narratives. [36]

Rescues and Rotten Apples

The approaching Civil War Centennial rekindled an interest in fiction. Street's *Captain Little Ax*, collected stories about his diminutive soldier, appeared in

1956, as did John Brick's *Jubilee*, in which a hardened New York soldier rises through the ranks to become a general in Sherman's army during the March. The actual process of "bumming" gets more attention in Brick's novel than any other, as soldiers discuss the morality and ethics of what has become "a picnic, an outing, a traveling carnival." Sherman is more benevolent "Uncle Billy" to his own men than scourge of the South in *Jubilee*. Richard O'Connor's *Company Q* came out in 1957 and is one of the more imaginative Civil War novels. Company Q is a Union punishment battalion made up of cashiered officers who are used as cannon fodder for their crimes. Major Frank Archer, unjustly punished for exposing the sacking of a Tennessee town, is reduced to the rank of private and fights his way back to respectability. Colonel Alan Farquhar, his former commanding officer in a prewar cavalry company, fights for the Confederacy and woos the Southern girl Archer loves. Archer slinks into Atlanta on a secret mission to blow up a bridge and restore his honor. He kills Farquhar, rescues the girl, and survives a bullet wound. Sherman is "excitable as a terrier, irascible, argumentative, with a fine brusque command of the language," but erratic and less the strategist than his dour, phlegmatic subordinate Thomas. The Rebels charge again and again into the maw of the Union army, carrying their "dark red battle flags, the Confederate Stars and Bars, and the embroidered silk banners presented by the ladies of their home towns." O'Connor continues the description: "[B]ugles still issued their rallying cries, swords still flashed in the sun, but all these ancient talismans of battle were revealed as frippery. This was not fighting, it was killing. There was no more chivalry about it than in a slaughterhouse." The novel is especially good at explaining the duplicity, corruption, and cynicism on both sides and exposing the civilians who exploited the conflict and were the ultimate victors.[37]

In 1959, the prolific physician-author Frank G. Slaughter added *Lorena* to his long list of best-selling doctor novels. In this tale, Dr. Yancey is an aging Georgia plantation doctor full of wit, wisdom, and whiskey. Lorena, the childless chatelaine of the plantation, is married to the scoundrel Bradfield Selby, who commands the Cray County Crusaders, an elite Confederate cavalry unit that sings its way into battle. In this unhappy feudal kingdom, the laird lacks an heir, and blames Lorena. While Captain Selby either seduces or whips his slaves and drinks himself comatose, Lorena uses enlightened and humane management techniques to run the plantation profitably. She is assisted by the good doctor (when he is sober) and by her brother, Quenten Rowley, a blockade-runner and sleazy speculator worthy of Rhett Butler. Finally, Selby rides to expel Sherman's invaders as they set off on the March from Atlanta, but he manages to lead his merry minstrels into an ambush set by Union Major Dan Carroll. The entire command is wiped out, save the sword-wielding cockerel, who rides off to fight again. Carroll soon arrives at the plantation and consummates the predictable tryst with Lorena, who produces the Selby heir. After the war, Selby goes to Mexico to try to help reestablish a slave empire and is reportedly killed. Meanwhile, Carroll returns to Cray County, secretly bankrolls the Selby plantation in collaboration with Rowley, buys adjacent properties, continues his courtship of Lorena, and fights the Ku Klux Klan, which is led by the Kleagle, who is Selby in disguise. The Kleagle is crippled in the final battle, and Lorena, ever loyal to the feudal code, cares for him while raising Carroll's child as the legatee of the Selby plantation, which is worked by loyal, intelligent freedmen.

Slaughter uses just about every Southern stereotype and cliche possible to tell the story. Even Yancey seems to weary of its predictabilities, noting that the "Quenten Rowleys in the South would always move a bit faster than history—sidestepping its debacles neatly, since they could guess the outcome of the next chapter before it was written. The Lorenas (who were no less wise) were born to face the music." Lorena would have no difficulty swapping secrets with Scarlett O'Hara, and Rowley's spirit survives in thousands of Georgia shopping malls and residential developments. Where the novel differs from *Gone with the Wind* is in its portrayal of Selby as the symbol of antebellum Southern manhood. Selby was the kind of arrogant, frothing racist who embarrassed the South in the 1960s during the Civil Rights era. While Carroll, Lorena, and Yancey represent a valiant New South ethos, Selby, significantly impotent and unable to replicate himself by siring an heir, is the fallen South, cuckolded by the North, and the better for it. Yancey knows him to be "the atavism, the destroyer of all he touched. Representing only an infinitesimal part of the South and its culture, he and his kind were the rotten apples that had ruined the barrel." Lorena even suspects that Sherman is not "the two-headed dragon people claim," probably because the only two-headed dragon she has to worry about is her husband and what he represents.[38]

"The Great Scrim of History!"

Civil War fiction flourished during and immediately after the Centennial, but Sherman didn't stage a true comeback for another thirty years; then he seemed to be everywhere. Perhaps the times were right for another look at the scourge of the South, repeating the pattern that each new generation has to rediscover Sherman and make of him what it will. Allan Gurganus's *Oldest Living Confederate Widow Tells All*, both a commercial and critical success, called attention to the fading memory of the Civil War. While in fact a few more widows survived, the story of the fictional ninety-nine-year-old Lucy Marsden, who at age fifteen had married a fifty-year-old former Confederate child soldier, served its purpose. Lucy's "Captain" Marsden, who lives on to become the war's last survivor, mythologizes his war service, which his widow recalls through her own haze of memory. Her mother-in-law had been disfigured in a fire set by Sherman's "patriotic firebugs" as they swept through North Carolina. The cruelty of the burnings, according to Lucy, was manifest in the ordinariness of their efficiency as "the terrible becomes routine. We've all got this dangerous built-in talent: for turning horrors into errands. You hear folks wonder how the Germans could've *done* it? I believe part of the answer is: They made extermination be a nine-to-five activity." But a teacher had cautioned Lucy and her classmates against taking a one-sided view of Sherman, because there is "always more to know, especially about the villains. Perhaps you all have sensed this from your earliest fairy-tale readings. . . . Is Sherman our enemy? You decide. Once we depreciate others as being wholly unlike ourselves, we've succumbed to the same flattening they've practiced on us. We cannot have enemies if we choose not to."[39]

Just what Gurganus may have meant became clearer when he wrote an essay for the *New York Times Magazine* in 2001, shortly after the September 11 attacks. Recalling the ruins of buildings burned by Sherman in his native North Carolina, Gurganus suggested that Sherman left them as a moral lesson,

> payback to our arrogant country that'd forgot its kindnesses, its professed gentility, its obligations to all other nations. . . . And yet, they failed to teach us the lessons that Marse Sherman intended. We vilified not our own slave-owning culture, but Sherman himself. We romanticized our loss. . . . Invaded, aggrieved, we felt nobler, almost Roman. Homes overrun, our elders vowed to make their kin warriors forever. We could match them blow for blow, fire for fire.

Insular and materialistic, forgetting the lessons of its own history, the United States "lately seems so cut off, so arrogant, we did not even *know* we could be hurt." This was not the first, or the last, time that Sherman's March would be seen as a parable for contemporary events.[40]

Sherman's March, a 1994 novel by Cynthia Bass, is composed of a preface, an afterword, and four parts, the first three of which offer in succession the voices of Sherman, a Union captain, and a Southern widow. In the final section, each speaks as their stories converge. Sherman has the first and last word, framing the March by explaining, in the preface, his intentions in the present tense in 1864 and then, in the afterword, assessing his achievement for history. Sherman speaks in the style of his *Memoirs*, but with greater candor and a longer view, as if he speaks from history itself. History, for Sherman, is not to be trusted, however. History "has so garbled and huckstered and gilded the March that by now it's the single most pervasive image in the war's bleak iconography." History has become myth, "the great scrim of history!"

Sherman admits he no longer fully remembers what happened, and damns journalists, "literary whores . . . always panting to pump up the empty barrels of their pens with somebody else's blood," prostituting the truth for profit under the banner of the First Amendment. "What actually happened may have been different. What actually happened may have been worse. What really happened may have been terrible. If we remember the past as it really happened, we'd probably kill ourselves." Rape, he believes and hopes, did not occur literally. "Metaphorically, I hope we *did* rape," he says. "For metaphorically we had every right to." He fought to end the war, and in so doing has "become not a general in a particular war, but eternal—the eternal destroyer in an ageless, eternal war. It's hard to become immortal without being misunderstood. Look at Christ." Sherman's egomaniacal, Caesar-like commentary on his war is in contrast to the other two speakers, who appear to move within history as Sherman transcends history. There are, then, at least two stories here: the March itself, what really happened; and the March in memory, as it may have happened. In the end, history can only be mystery, and for Sherman, "those who revere me and those who abhor me revere and abhor for the same illusion."

Captain Nicholas Whiteman, too, thinks about history, but on the March he learns that history is interesting "because historians do good laundry: they twist out the water of every life." War, for the captain, becomes a living thing that transcends and absorbs its actors, mostly bored but then possessing "an extramilitary character more lethal than actual combat. Nothing was legal but everything was permitted—which wound up meaning everyone did what he felt like and no one was responsible for any of it. . . . War is the last thing you should ever think about while serving in one." And, of course, that's what he's doing. He's nearly killed for thinking later on, when the widow shoots him. The ironically named Whiteman is logical. War is not. And so he suffers, both mentally and physically.

Annie Saunders Baker, a refugee swept up by the March, changes radically. It is hard to say whether the change is evolution or devolution, but she survives. In many respects she becomes less human, wanting to kill. But she becomes more human when she begins the "exodus" with the refugees, freed, like her slaves, from the plantation for the first time in her life, and freed to witness the raw strength and stark vulnerability of life. Biblical allusions are thick as locusts as the refugees cross their metaphoric desert, scavenging from the dead to stay alive. Annie is befriended by Sarah Jackson, the sort of woman she would have shunned before the March. Sarah gives her a bartered Revolutionary War British soldier's uniform topcoat to keep her from freezing to death. "Ain't that a hoot?" Sarah says. "The good old days, when we both were fighting the same enemy! But it's thick and it's whole and at least nobody'll mistake you for being on whatever side they aren't." So it is a very "American" garment, captured booty from the war when all were rebels. Sarah tells Annie she will need to rip and soil the coat so no one will want to take it from her.

The dispossessed, then, symbolically despoil the finery and the ideals of revolution. The less property stake one—such as Annie—has in either the Southern revolution or the myth of *the* Revolution, the less one saves its trappings for posterity, and the more one puts them to use for immediate, practical purposes. Annie's transformation is complete when she shoots Whiteman. Now she is cold and emotionless, and has to be talked out of finishing him off by a "Confederate archangel," Major Lindley Holland, who knows the difference between a soldier's duty and murder. Holland, a teacher who doesn't enjoy teaching history, is practically the only character in the book who is moral and practices restraint in the war; yet he is murdered by Union renegades. This unsparing story is one of the best novels yet written about Sherman's March.[41]

Comet Dust and Crushed Ice

Toss history into a blender; add some alternative flavors; mix in some anachronisms; garnish generously with sorcerers or vampires, satire, puns, pastiche, and parody; agitate vigorously; sprinkle liberally with comet dust; pour the resulting literary julep over crushed ice and enjoy.

MacKinlay Kantor's *If the South Had Won the Civil War* was alternative history that speculated about how events might have turned out differently. Kantor originally wrote *If the South Had Won the Civil War* for *Look* magazine in 1960. The North loses the war after Grant is crushed to death by his horse and Sherman is killed by a sniper during the abortive Vicksburg campaign. The March, of course, never happens. Lee wins at Gettysburg, the Confederates take Washington, and Lincoln resigns. Three countries, including Texas, emerge, and eventually are reunited in 1960 to fight communism, after rumblings in Soviet Alaska. Southerners reading Kantor's article may not have realized they were being persuaded to put aside regional squabbles about civil rights and to join with their Northern brethren to save the world.[42]

Any fantasy inspired by *Gone with the Wind* is sure to attract the interest of romance readers smitten by bodice-ripping love stories perfumed with magnolia blossoms. Karen White tells readers that when she read Margaret Mitchell's novel she knew she wanted to grow up to be a writer. White's time-travel romance, *In the Shadow of the Moon*, sends a modern-day suburban Atlanta woman tumbling back through time in comet dust to Civil War Georgia. In between fighting an evil time-traveling Shadow Warrior plotting to save the South by murdering Sherman, and dallying with a wounded Confederate soldier who becomes her husband, she manages to protect her family plantation from the Union Army, reap a fortune on Coca-Cola stock, become Bill Clinton's ancestor, and create her twentieth-century self in I'm-my-own-great-great-grandma fashion. She is befriended by Sherman, who passes up an opportunity to compromise the lady's virtue and takes her along on the first leg of the March so she can save her husband and rescue her daughter. This fictional Sherman is not such a bad fellow, even as he metaphorically sullies Georgia—if not the modern-day Scarlett caught in a time warp.[43]

Sherman meets another time traveler—this time an erotic French vampire—in Chelsea Quinn Yarbro's *In the Face of Death*. Madelaine de Montalia, a scholar and protégé of the legendary Count Saint-Germain, comes to San Francisco in 1855 to begin work on a study of American Indian tribes. As the senior officer of the Lucas and Turner Bank, Sherman takes charge of her financial affairs, and they soon become lovers. Although professing loyalty to his absent wife and their children, Sherman finds Madame de Montalia irresistible, even when she tells him that although she looks barely 20 she was born more than 130 years earlier and died in 1744, only to be reborn as a vampire. Madame de Montalia is more healer than bloodsucker, a good vampire nourished by love and wisdom. Sherman struggles with his conscience, his humanity, and his overheated libido throughout the novel. They meet again during the Civil War, when Madame de Montalia uses her curative powers to treat wounded soldiers. She accompanies Sherman on the March, becoming the source of the rumor that he had a mistress during the campaign, and then sails from Savannah to Europe, where they meet for the last time seven years after the war. She offers Sherman, now world famous, the chance to become a vampire and gain immortality if he will "taste my blood," but Sherman declines, saying it is "not fitting for an officer of the United States Army to . . . bite women." But by symbolically biting the South in the neck, and tasting its blood, he already had gained another kind of immortality and would live on as a military vampire in the embrace of the Lost Cause.[44]

Harry Turtledove's upside-down history of the Civil War reimagines the Atlanta campaign in a playful way, although the real March, by all accounts, wasn't all that funny. *Marching through Peachtree* is the second book in the War between the Provinces series, preceding *Advance and Retreat*. *Sentry Peak* opens the series, which ostensibly is about the secession of the northern provinces of Detina and the ensuing conflict. The gimmick is that the war takes place in a mythical feudal age. Events generally correspond to the American Civil War, but in a funhouse mirror. The South under King Avram invades the North under Grand Duke Geoffrey to free the serfs (blond) and restore the kingdom. General Hesmucet (Sherman, with Tecumseh spelled backward) leads his Army of Franklin (Army of the Tennessee) from Sentry Peak (Lookout Mountain) through Peachtree Province (Georgia), against Joseph the Gamecock (Joseph Johnston). In case readers don't get it, Turtledove, who has a doctorate in history, provides a summary of the actual campaign in a "hysterical note" at the end of the book. The intent in this kind of fantasy literature is not to speculate about the potential outcome of a different course of historical events, but to see what we do know in a different light. Hesmucet's comic march through Peachtree is more *Gone with the Wind* meets Harry Potter than a new look at a brutal campaign.[45]

A very different alternative history series comes from veteran science fiction writer Harry Harrison. His trilogy, *Stars and Stripes Forever*, *Stars and Stripes in Peril*, and *Stars and Stripes Triumphant*, speculates about a British invasion of North America during the American Civil War; an alliance between the Union and the Confederacy; and American invasions of Canada, Ireland, and England. Sherman is the mastermind who directs this improbable world war, which involves everything from Russian spies to Gurkhas and Sepoys fighting in Mexico, and he even gets the chance to skewer John Wilkes Booth when the actor tries to assassinate Lincoln. In this war it is the British, not the Confederates, who must learn that "war is all hell" and who must "lose so badly that they will no longer consider these kinds of military adventures." Sherman insists he is fighting a new kind of war backed by a military-industrial complex that supplies experimental rifles and canons, prototypes of internal combustion engines, rotating gun turrets, ironclads, and even tanks developed by inventors such as Gatling, Parrott, and Ericsson. In this alternative scenario, the Sherman tank of World War II has its origins in Sherman's tank in 1865. Says Sherman: "The faster the attack, the quicker the end of the conflict. . . . The tiger of machine warfare has been loosed and we must ride it." A final confrontation looms when the British herd the Irish into concentration camps, seize cargos from American ships, and then fire on an American convoy. After scouting the English coast disguised as a Russian

SITE OF THE BANK OF
LUCAS, TURNER & CO.
(SHERMAN'S BANK)

WILLIAM TECUMSEH SHERMAN ESTABLISHED THE BRANCH
BANK OF LUCAS, TURNER & CO. IN SAN FRANCISCO
IN 1853. HE SETTLED THE FIRM IN THEIR OWN BUILDING
ON THE NORTHEAST CORNER OF JACKSON AND MONT-
GOMERY STREETS IN THE SPRING OF 1854. SHERMAN
SUCCESSFULLY CARRIED THE BANK THROUGH THE
FINANCIAL CRISIS OF 1855, AND REMAINED UNTIL THEY
DISCONTINUED BUSINESS IN 1857.

STATE REGISTERED LANDMARK NO. 453

TABLET PLACED BY CALIFORNIA CENTENNIALS COMMISSION
WITH THE COOPERATION OF THE SOCIETY OF CALIFORNIA PIONEERS
DEDICATED JANUARY 17, 1950

Sherman's service as a San Francisco bank manager lasted about as long as his military service in the Civil War. Under his leadership the Lucas, Turner and Co. bank weathered several financial crises in the rough and tumble California business and political environment. While his destiny lay elsewhere, Sherman would come to symbolize for many Southerners the counting houses and industrial might of Northern capital. Jennifer Ashdown

QUITE THE REVERSE.

"JOHNSTON has SHERMAN just where he wants him."—*Richmond Enquirer.*

After a Richmond newspaper claimed, during the Atlanta campaign, that "Johnston has Sherman just where he wants him," a Harper's Weekly artist turns the tables. Sherman is shown grabbing the Confederate general instead. Courtesy of Special Collections/ Musselman Library, Gettysburg College, Gettysburg, Pennsylvania

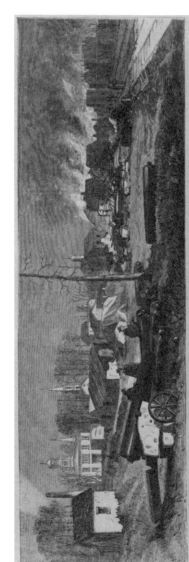

DESTRUCTION OF THE DEPOTS, PUBLIC BUILDINGS, AND MANUFACTORIES AT ATLANTA, GEORGIA, November 15, 1864.

Sherman's army destroys depots, arsenals, factories, and weapons while leaving Atlanta in ruins on November 15, 1864. This engraving appeared in Harper's Weekly on January 7, 1865, as Sherman was preparing to continue his march through the Carolinas. Library of Congress

THE FOURTEENTH AND TWENTIETH CORPS MOVING OUT OF ATLANTA, November 15, 1864.

A conquered Atlanta behind them, an unrepentant South before them, Sherman's soldiers leave Atlanta on the morning of November 16, 1864. "Behind us lay Atlanta, smouldering and in ruins," he later wrote in his Memoirs, recalling black smoke "hanging like a pall over the ruined city." Library of Congress

XIII.—LEAV-ING AT-LAN-TA.

Sherman takes command of a column of cheering troops leaving the burning city of Atlanta as the March to the Sea begins. Ida B. Forbes, General William T. Sherman, His Life and Battles *(1886)*

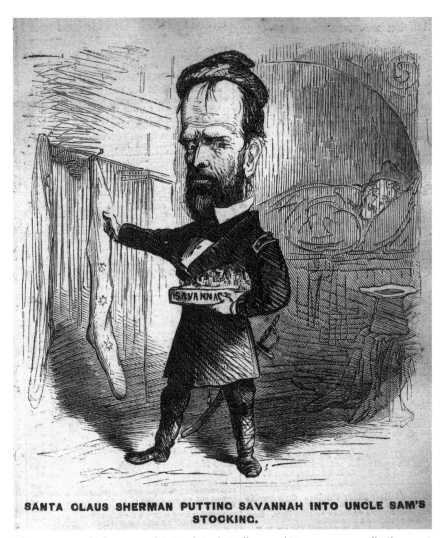

SANTA CLAUS SHERMAN PUTTING SAVANNAH INTO UNCLE SAM'S STOCKING.

This cartoon, which appeared in Frank Leslie's Illustrated Newspaper, *recalls Sherman's telegram to Lincoln offering the city of Savannah as a Christmas present. The timing of the city's occupation was fortuitous, and added a joyful flourish to the conclusion of Sherman's March to the Sea.* Courtesy of Special Collections/Musselman Library, Gettysburg College, Gettysburg, Pennsylvania

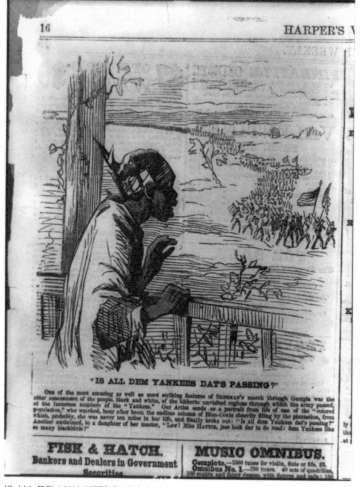

"IS ALL DEM YANKEES DAT'S PASSING?"

One of the most amusing as well as most striking features of Sherman's march through Georgia was the utter amazement of the people, black and white, of the hitherto unvisited regions through which the army passed, at the immense numbers of the "Yankees." Our Artist sends us a portrait from life of one of the "colored population," who watched, hour after hour, the endless column of Blue-Coats cheerily filing by the plantation, from which, probably, she was never ten miles in her life, and finally broke out: "Is all dem Yankees dat's passing?" Another exclaimed, to a daughter of her master, "Law! Miss Hattie, jess look dar in de road: dem Yankees like so many blackbirds!"

IS ALL DEM YANKEES DAT'S PASSING? A Harper's Weekly *artist observed "the utter amazement of the people, black and white, of the hitherto unvisited regions through which the army passed." Harper's speculated that the bewildered slave who sees Sherman's passing troops probably had not journeyed more than 10 miles from the plantation in her life. The crude racial stereotype mocks both the innocence and credulity of the slave and the general provincialism of the rural Georgia counties through which Sherman passed virtually unmolested. The March became a mere spectacle to be gawked at and to be held in awe as if it were a force of nature.* Library of Congress

Sherman's soldiers wreak havoc on a Georgia homestead in this woodcut. Their energy and attention are devoted entirely to slaughtering animals, while the slaves—who should be the focus of their moral mandate—are ignored. The artist even puts the soldier in the foreground on the same level as the swine, wallowing on the ground with it as an officer approaches, perhaps to skewer the pig with his sword or wrest it from the soldier for his own supper. The scene becomes a comic parody of battle. Battles and Leaders of the Civil War *(1887)*

Thomas Nast renders a scene from the Georgia campaign that is subject to multiple interpretations. A Georgia woman has a home and several children to protect while her husband is away. The Yankee invaders seem friendly, but she appears unconvinced that they are to be trusted. The drawing appeared in Harper's Weekly on June 30, 1866, and reflects a memory of the war, perhaps intended as a corrective to the charges that Sherman's troops callously destroyed property and terrorized civilians. Library of Congress

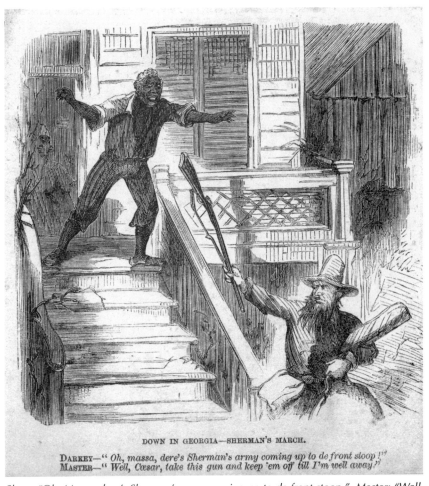

DOWN IN GEORGIA—SHERMAN'S MARCH.

DARKEY—" *Oh, massa, dere's Sherman's army coming up to de front stoop!*"
MASTER—" *Well, Cæsar, take this gun and keep 'em off till I'm well away.*"

Slave: "Oh, Massa, dere's Sherman's army coming up to de front stoop." Master: "Well, Caesar, take this gun and keep 'em off till I'm well away." This cartoon from Frank Leslie's Illustrated Newspaper *makes sport of one of the cherished myths of the Lost Cause—that slaves would remain loyal. It also mocks the planters who would rather flee than fight.* Courtesy of Special Collections/Musselman Library, Gettysburg College, Gettysburg, Pennsylvania

A well-stocked Union commissary enabled the ladies of occupied Savannah to replenish their depleted larders. Sherman wrote in his Memoirs that while the residents of the city "had no special claims to our favor," they nonetheless were well provided for. He even helped organize a relief mission that returned from Boston with supplies "for gratuitous distribution." Frank & Marie-Therese Wood Print Collections, Alexandria, Virginia

When one of his officers was injured by a sunken torpedo, or land mine, Sherman was furious. "I immediately ordered a lot of rebel prisoners to be brought from the provost-guard, armed with picks and spades, and made them march in close order along the road, so as to explode their own torpedoes, or to discover and dig them up. They begged hard. . . ." The Union guards curiously seem oblivious to their own fate should one of the torpedoes explode. Frank & Marie-Therese Wood Print Collections, Alexandria, Virginia

Sherman's army has put an abandoned schoolhouse to the torch in this scene from D. W. Griffith's The Birth of a Nation. *The scene is shot from the perspective of a family cowering in the hills as soldiers sweep through the valley below. The victims, claiming the moral high ground, are powerless to stop the invaders, who wantonly attack not only civilians but civilization.* Photofest

Character actor Paul Hurst portrays a Union deserter about to be shot dead by Vivian Leigh's Scarlett O'Hara in this enduring scene from Gone With the Wind. *Audiences might have recognized Hurst as the heavy from many crime dramas. Here, however, he is really the surrogate for Sherman, who metaphorically ravishes the South as the deserter criminally violates Tara. Scarlett, like the South, strikes to preserve her virtue even in defeat. But virtue in the fallen South is pragmatic. Scarlett loots the looter's pack, finding enough money to feed her household.* Photofest

John Wayne played a grizzled General Sherman in How the West Was Won. *Wayne's swagger may have fit the public perception of Sherman, but the general lacked the actor's broad appeal as an American icon.* Photofest

Motorists can follow the path taken by each wing of Sherman's army as it approached Savannah. But the occasional rural roadside historical markers only point to landscapes engulfed by the past. Although the woods, fields, and streams may yet yield a few more bullets, buckles, and bayonets, the detritus left by passing soldiers on their way to the sea, the March has left few other traces. Edward Caudill

His battles behind him, the old general put on his uniform for a final portrait four years after he retired from the army, and only a few years before his death. His famous scowl has softened into a beatific gaze.
Library of Congress

naval officer, Sherman develops an elaborate surprise invasion plan involving a fleet, landing craft, armies, secret weapons, railroads, and an attack on Buckingham Palace. By the end of the trilogy, the Americans are triumphant everywhere, Sherman is a military dictator imposing martial law, Queen Victoria abdicates, the Scots, Irish, Canadians, and Mexicans all gain their independence, and the English form a new American-style government approved by John Stuart Mill. Harrison explains in an afterword that the fictional Sherman's "lightning war" anticipates German blitzkrieg tactics used in World War II. But this Sherman is really a comic book hero fit for a twenty-first-century superpower.[46]

Leonard Palmer's *The Sherman Letter* is a murder mystery mixed with a historical detective story, but with a twist that might have changed history. A washed-up, hard-drinking, tough guy reporter known only as Moon stumbles into a murder case involving Elaine Haskell, a small-town historical society's alcoholic archivist, who had some letters written by a Wisconsin captain who served on Sherman's staff during the March. Seeking to protect the impulsive general, the captain had swiped an intemperate letter that Sherman had written to Stanton after the war secretary had reprimanded him for offering Johnston generous peace terms. Sherman had threatened to march his army to Washington and take over the government unless Stanton resigned. The captain was murdered by a soldier who wanted the letter so he could sell it, but it wound up back in Wisconsin in the custody of the captain's father, with his son's other papers. Moon finds out who killed the archivist and two other people to get the letter, which is worth a fortune, and has to decide what to do with it when he finds it. He realizes the captain had stolen the letter "out of a moral obligation to both his country and his general. If Stanton had gotten hold of the letter, it would have been the final nail in Sherman's coffin, ending a glorious career in disgrace and probably a hangman's noose," not to mention touching off another civil war. "Think about it," a historian tells Moon. "Sherman moves on Washington. Grant moves to intercept. The north divides along lines of loyalty to the two generals. In the south, there are still a hundred and fifty thousand men at arms in the field. It boggles the mind." Indeed. Moon decides he owes more to the captain than to history, and burns the letter. All this takes place in 1991 during the first Gulf War. Sherman's hatred of the press is a descant that plays throughout the novel, as Moon rages against the current media scene, yet ironically buries his biggest story to protect Sherman and the courageous captain.[47]

Sherman's fourteen-year-old drummer boy Bucksaw Hooper has quite an adventure in Richard L. Hawk's novel *Moonstalker*. Sherman sends Bucksaw from Louisville, Kentucky, on a secret mission to scout the Confederate works at Corinth, Mississippi. The general advises the boy, who comes from Lancaster, Ohio, his hometown, to "stalk the moon" by traveling at night to avoid capture. Equipped with some of Sherman's cigars, Bucksaw gets to Corinth, joins the Confederate Army, sneaks around mapping terrain, deserts, gets captured, escapes, outwits a relentless pursuer, and delivers his sketches of the fortifications to Sherman back in Louisville. The information could not have been of any use to Sherman because the Rebels already had evacuated the town by the time he got there; but at least Bucksaw avoids getting himself hanged for spying and presumably resumes his former job as regimental drummer.[48]

A Kick in the Shins

Miriam Freeman Rawl's *From the Ashes of Ruin* (1999) is another Union-officer-meets-distressed-but-tough-Southern-belle romance. Sherman sends Major John Arledge to find out who killed three of his foragers near a South Carolina plantation. Ellen Heyward knows something, but she and the lusty Arledge spark while Columbia burns. Sherman revels in his reputation as "Lincoln's most successful general" and, mistrusting reporters, writes "his own accounts of the march through the South." Arledge thinks Sherman will end the war "and all future wars, it seems."[49]

Savannah, by James Reasoner, is the ninth volume in a series that chronicles the adventures and misfortunes of a Virginia family, the Brannons, who are caught up in the war. The book, published in 2003, seems to confuse Savannah with Stalingrad. Sherman's army callously sweeps toward Savannah "destroying everything in its path like a horde of ravening locusts. . . . Across a swath of Georgia sixty miles wide, hardly a building was left standing. They had all been burned, as had the fields on every farm and plantation." John Jakes's *Savannah, or A Gift for Mr. Lincoln* is a romance set in its namesake city in December 1864 and January 1865. Told through the eyes of a Confederate war widow and her twelve-year-old daughter, the story employs war and Sherman as stage props for the woman's trials and triumphs, which closely parallel those of the most famous fictional belle in the path of the March. Like Scarlett, the widow's first love is a Confederate officer, though Ashley in *Gone with the Wind* does not die in war. And then the first love's antithesis appears, with Yankee dash and a bit of vulgarity about him. Whereas Rhett Butler is a gunrunner, out to make money, the widow's Yankee captain in *Savannah* is an accredited New York reporter who plays piano in a brothel when he gets the chance. But both men are charming and opportunistic, and have something that appeals to a Southern woman. *Savannah*'s captain is also very much the Yankee myth and stereotype, in that he worked his way up from more humble origins to newspapers and brothels—a satire on the Alger myth.

Jakes, like Reasoner, employs historical and regional stereotypes and myths. The Union bummers in Jakes' *Savannah* are ugly, stupid, corrupt, and don't follow orders. Sherman himself is a rather one-dimensional character, showing up on occasion to assist the ladies or salvage some gallantry for the North. In one unlikely scene, the twelve-year-old girl, in a fit of belligerence, actually kicks Sherman in the shins, but the general appears charmed by her grit and ultimately calls the child to his headquarters. So, again, a pugnacious magnolia is the real heart of an intransigent South. Jakes acknowledges in the afterword his use of what he calls the contemporary image of Sherman in the South: "Sherman is largely excoriated in the modern South, although this doesn't prevent his familiar bearded face from being used freely to advertise many a commercial tour in Savannah and elsewhere in Georgia." It is in many respects a theme from *Gone with the Wind* and *Savannah*, in which the Yankee is despised, but eventually and willingly submitted to by the South, with the promise of financial bliss. The finest historical irony may have been any use of Sherman, of all war figures, as a romantic in time of war. Jakes is, of course, not ignorant of Sherman's views of war, and even quotes him accurately on it: "War is cruel. You can't make it anything else." Jakes demonstrates the subtle contradictions in the historical myth and the contemporary imagination.[50]

A more literary novel about the Atlanta campaign, *A Distant Flame*, appeared in the same year, 2004, as *Savannah*. Philip Lee Williams imagines the Atlanta campaign from the point of view of Charlie Merrill, a young sharpshooter who has joined the Confederate army in time to fight at Chickamauga. Once again Sherman is the unseen hand who forces all the action. Wounded and disillusioned, Merrill finally deserts and returns to his home as Atlanta is destroyed and the March begins. Fifty years later, on the anniversary of the battle, Merrill, who has been a journalist and novelist since the war, gives a speech in which he says he "cannot bring you a victory that it was ordained we should never have in the Battle of Atlanta. I cannot touch mythologies that we construct to explain such loss, and I dare not. We invent the past to suit our present, but there is no truth in the present, for with each breath it is drawn backward into history."[51]

A legend that Sherman had a love affair with a Georgia woman whom he met long before the war, and then spared her home later, served as the basis for another memory story, Diane Haeger's *My Dearest Cecelia: A Novel of the Southern Belle Who Stole General Sherman's Heart*. Cecelia Stovall visits her brother at a West Point ball in 1837 and meets Sherman. Their love affair is thwarted by family intrigues, lost letters, misunderstandings, and coincidences. They are briefly reunited when Cecelia, now married to a Confederate general, helps slaves escape on the Underground Railroad, spies for the Union, and delivers secret information that saves Sherman's army. The novel plays fast and loose with history and biography. In one scene before the war, Sherman finds his old West Point friend Grant passed out from drink in a San Francisco street. The novel's central conceit is that Cecelia is the key to Sherman's unpredictable character. As one Southerner puts it, the newspapers say Sherman "had some mysterious Southern weakness—likely a woman if you ask me—that has driven him to the edge of lunacy befo', and, general or not, no one is ever quite certain what he will do next!" Cecelia lives on until the 1890s, and refuses to tell the story of her love affair to her nephew, who is the editor of the Augusta *Chronicle*.[52]

Sherman's brass cigar case becomes a talisman in Margaret Erhart's *Crossing Bully Creek*, a novel about the waning days of the segregated Deep South in the 1960s, when the Vietnam War and the Civil Rights movement are intensifying. The wealthy Henry Detroit and his wife Rowena, both Northerners, own the Longbrow Plantation on the Georgia-Florida border. Henry's death in 1969 heralds the end of an era as various characters, black and white, move back and forth through time over four decades in hazy vignettes. "He's going to empty this place right out when he goes. A whole way of life," says Rowena. Born in 1895, she is the granddaughter of Sherman, a man "she'd never known. She'd seen the last portraits, stood in the room where he died and imagined him, and did not understand how the gaunt old thin-haired figure, blue-lipped and smelling of cardboard, spittle on his collar, asleep in his padded chair, added up to the Civil War general astride his mount. She guessed the photographs lied." Rowena has the letters Sherman wrote to his wife during the March, "a neat yellowed packet tied with thin brown twine, and she threw herself at them, into them, asking of her grandfather, What is this? What is war? and at that moment he came alive in her hands, leaping from one century to the next with the effortless grace of a ghost fulfilled." When Henry dies Rowena fills Sherman's battered canister with her husband's ashes. It is an arresting image, the ashes of the plantation South usurped by the conquerors mixing with the ghostly dottle left over by the March, Sherman's legacy protected by a latter-day Sherman.[53]

The Worm Turns

Readers who picked up the *New York Times Book Review* on Sunday, September 25, 2005, must have been shocked by the arresting front-page illustration by M. K. Perker. The cartoonish drawing covered the top half of the influential tabloid section above the headline "Making War Hell" and the first paragraph of a review by Walter Kirn. The *Times* was blowing a literary bugle to announce the publication of *The March*, a novel by a major American writer, E. L. Doctorow, best known for *Ragtime*. Five days earlier, a *Times* staff critic had reviewed the book in the newspaper's Tuesday edition. The Sunday review by Kirn reinforced the attention the book was receiving following a timely publicity buildup by its publisher, Random House, and news events the publisher hardly could have anticipated.

Perker's illustration depicts what appears to be a mythical invertebrate slithering across railroad tracks traversing a barren landscape, its tail sweeping through the remains of a devastated city against the backdrop of a rouged sky. The head and torso of the beast comprise a bearded military figure, attired in a blue uniform and holding a sword in his left hand. So assembled, the beast becomes a kind of devolved centaur, a creature cast forth from the fires of Hell, half millipede, half Sherman. This image is suggested in the novel by Union army doctor Wrede Sartorius, who describes Sherman's legions as

> a nonhuman form of life. Imagine a great segmented body moving in contractions and dilations at a rate of twelve or fifteen miles a day, a creature of a hundred thousand feet. It is tubular in its being and tentacled to the roads and bridges over which it travels. It sends out as antennae its men on horses. It consumes everything in its path. It is an immense organism, this army, with a small brain. That would be General Sherman, whom I have never seen.[54]

Kirn swallows, or is swallowed by, the entire metaphor, even likening Doctorow's narrative to "peristaltic storytelling: that process by which a writer captures his audience not by creating loose ends that must be followed, but by swallowing the reader whole and then conveying him—firmly, steadily, irresistibly—toward a fated outcome." The action of the story, accordingly, takes place "in this creature's elongated gut as it traces its infamous historic course. . . . excreting smoke and rubble from its hindparts as well as thousands of indigestible skeletons." The small-brained general, then, "is most important in the novel not for what goes on inside his skull, but for the turbulent miniature cosmos alive inside his dragging, swollen belly. He's the head of a serpent, and he doesn't march at all—no more than history is said to march. It crawls along the ground with open jaws, and the world and its people pass through it and are changed."[55]

Kirn's peristaltic theory of history as a form of mastication and digestion, although it may not channel Doctorow's understanding of the March, does suggest some of the bizarre ways the March continues to be defined, explained, and remembered. The imagery is not original. Mitchell described

Sherman's army as a monster serpent almost seventy years earlier, although Doctorow's parasitic metaphor is stronger. Language and metaphor, in essence, are Doctorow's weapons in the novel. Sherman, as character, understands as much during his negotiations with Johnston:

> And so the war had come down to words. It was fought now in terminology across a table. It was contested in sentences. Entrenchments and assaults, drum taps and bugle calls, marches, ambushes, burnings, and pitched battles were transmogrified into nouns and verbs. . . . No cannonball or canister but has become the language here spoken, the words written down, Sherman thought. Language is war by other means.

And language is always contested territory.[56]

Hurricane Sherman

Just why Doctorow's novel was creating such a media buzz in 2005 had everything to do with the war in Iraq and Hurricane Katrina. Doctorow had long been identified with liberal politics, and he was not reticent about expressing his opposition to George W. Bush and the war. He was coy when asked about a connection between *The March* and the war, however, telling *U.S. News & World Report*: "I didn't write the book specifically thinking about Iraq. All I will say is I thought it was necessary to start writing it about 2 1/2 years ago." Although Doctorow ostensibly refused to be drawn, others saw the *The March* as a commentary, if not a parable.[57]

The Katrina connection in the press was far more explicit. Reviews of the book and interviews with Doctorow began appearing only days after the destructive storm struck New Orleans and the Gulf Coast. If the novel, as many reviewers interpreted it, presented Sherman as a force of nature, a natural disaster even, then a new Sherman-like force had struck the South again, invoking historical parallels. "The images of wreckage and refugees are all too familiar these days: This is Hurricane Sherman," wrote reviewer Jerome Weeks, with the general "barely in control of this storm surge. He's just riding it." Novelist John Updike, writing in the *New Yorker*, saw the March "conjured up as a human entity as large as the weather, a 'floating world' that destroys as it goes and carries along some living fragments."[58]

Interviewed for a Los Angeles *Times* article, Doctorow drew a parallel between the black victims of the storm and the plight of blacks caught up in the aftermath of the March and the war. "Right up to this moment, it's possible to say that the South won the war," said Doctorow, after quoting a passage from the novel in which he has Sherman contemplating defeated Confederates "sublimed to a righteously aggrieved state that would empower them for a century." Doctorow pointed to

> the dismal history of Reconstruction, the way it was sabotaged; the years of lynchings and poll taxes; even after the civil rights struggles of the '60s, playing the race card politically to gain strength in the South, as Reagan did, as both Bushes did. Sherman, my Sherman, is saying that the South has won the war. Very often losing is a powerful impetus to organize society.

This Sherman may have been speaking more for the author than the author realized. Doctorow told one reviewer that among other things a novel was "a system of opinions." With all those opinions, "Hurricane Sherman" was blowing up a perfect storm of publicity for the book.[59]

Stephen Matchett, writing in the *Australian*, may have come closest to explaining the novel's impact when he divined "an un-American sense in this book of a world where the best and the brightest are incapable of imposing order." The Civil War was a response to a failure to maintain order, and the restoration of order was itself messy and disorderly, as the fictional Sherman laments. Katrina and the Iraq war, too, seemed chaotic events in which American gumption and efficiency were no match for natural, moral, and political disintegration. This theme also was picked up by Vince Passaro in the *Nation*. Passaro saw Doctorow's larger message as

> the war in the end was a tragedy of high technology and bad ideas all around, a specifically American kind of tragedy full of seers and self-invented monarchs, an outburst of madness that completely destroyed the South and displaced thousands of its residents, both white and black. . . . We're still paying the price of this war, with its well-armed religiosity and its strong pull toward disintegration.[60]

Doctorow does a skillful job of wrapping up greater historical generalizations, even stereotypes, into a procession of characters who seem constantly to disguise or reinvent themselves as they come in contact during the March. Sherman's army is composed of industrialized killers, and is set in opposition to Emily Thompson, the strong Southern woman taken from the plantation by the "machine," in the person of Sartorius. He is a brilliant, foreign-born physician-scientist, seemingly indifferent to the men whose limbs he amputates in his medical factory, all the time thinking about advancing medical knowledge—but not humanity, at least not directly. Sartorius sees no place for sentimentality in war. Thompson attempts to love him, but ultimately cannot, and chooses to enlarge life to its sentiments. Her father, a Georgia Supreme Court justice, is another good symbol, the noble male of the Old South, and he dies just about as soon as Sherman's army arrives in the Georgia capital, Milledgeville.

One of the more interesting, and loathsome, characters is Arly Wilcox, a Confederate soldier, jailed for sleeping on picket duty, who escapes in Milledgeville during the confusion. He is chameleon-like as he changes sides from Confederate to Union and back again, and he believes he has some divinely sanctioned mission to play in the war. He manages to impersonate a Union photographer who has died, and he takes off with Calvin Harper, the photographer's capable black apprentice. Is Doctorow trying to point out something else about Southern masculinity, taking a leaf perhaps from Faulkner? Is Arly symbolically a creature of the moment, one without a history and without a future, contriving pretenses as they suit his circumstances, the "Southern white-trash Reb" Calvin thinks he is? In reality, Calvin is the photographer, the one who has labored and understood the chemicals and processes, who has dirtied himself. "In the guise of servitude, he, Calvin Harper, was running things." It's the old cliche about the South being a slave to slavery. Calvin thinks Arly is crazy. If not insane, Arly is absolutely unprincipled, and without apology. Interestingly, he tells Calvin that he, Arly, has the same "quality of mind" as Sherman, whom he wants to "shoot" in a photograph, a "meeting of the minds." When Arly tries to assassinate Sherman by firing a pistol through the lens, it is Calvin who sacrifices himself to save the general, by lunging for the camera. Arly is executed and Calvin recovers. So it is the degenerate element in the South that sees in Sherman an image of itself, and in trying to kill Sherman kills itself. A black man saves Sherman, gets no thanks for the deed, and eventually survives through his own initiative. Calvin is principled and moral, and no other character in the book recognizes this.[61]

Pearl Jameson, a light-skinned slave girl who is caught up in the March, is another odd character and in many ways the book's moral center. Lieutenant Clarke from Boston, who leads a foraging party, rescues Pearl from an abandoned plantation, seeing her as "a white Negro, white like white chocolate," and perhaps with "some royal African blood." About fifteen years old, she seems to be coming of age as she grasps the possibilities and challenges of freedom. She is attractive, shrewd, and strong both physically and mentally. After Clarke is killed, the girl manages to pass as a Union drummer boy, and is befriended by Sherman, who easily puts aside his racial prejudice only because Pearl is in multiple forms of disguise and reminds him of his own dead son. She "liberates" the son of her former master, her father, and gives him gold that had belonged to another ex-slave. It is a magnanimous act on her part, eliciting only sniveling ingratitude from her lustful half brother.

Pearl is a complex symbol of innocence that refuses to be sullied by the Old South but yet is part of it. Because she can so easily change races, she is a harbinger of racial change. Her very whiteness causes Stephen Walsh, a wounded Union soldier who falls in love with Pearl and takes her to New York after the war, to find a justification for the March:

> In this strange country down here, after generations of its hideous ways, slaves were no longer simply black, they were degrees of white. Yes, he thought, if the South were to prevail, theoretically there could be a time when whiteness alone would not guarantee the identity of a free man. Anyone might be indentured and shackled and sold on an auction block, the color black having been a temporary expedient, the idea of a slave class itself being the underlying premise.[62]

But what of Sherman, the worm brain, the keeper of winds, in this literary séance? Could the military Aeolus still be a transparently historical figure who, like the real Sherman, is ornery, depressive, stubborn, opaque, intellectual, emotional, tender, sorrowful, and combative? Sherman resides largely on the fringes of the various subplots of the novel, appearing every now and then to remind us that individuals are part of the greater events in history. Doctorow has the personality mostly right, but what emerges in the novel is a philosopher-general who contemplates morality, meaning, and meaninglessness in a modern framework:

> Though this march is done, and well accomplished, I think of it now, God help me, with longing—not for its blood and death but for the bestowal of meaning to the very ground trod upon, how it made every field and swamp and river and road into something of moral consequence, whereas now, as the march dissolves so does the meaning, the army strewing itself into the isolated intentions of diffuse private life, and the terrain thereby left blank and also diffuse, and ineffable, a thing once again, and victoriously, without reason, and whether diurnally lit and darkened, or sere or fruitful, or raging or calm, completely insensible and without any purpose of its own.[63]

Doctorow could not credibly have put these thoughts in the minds of many Civil War figures, and even in the mind of his Sherman they strain plausibility—he sounds more like a twentieth-century French existentialist than a nineteenth-century Union general given to blunt aphorisms and tent-talk. If the meaning of the March was the March, the sanctification of the land with high moral purpose, the birth pangs of a new, revitalized nation, what purpose could then ultimately be served? In his final words in the novel, Sherman thinks of Grant, victorious yet solemn, because "he knows this un-meaning inhuman planet will need our warring imprint to give it value, and that our civil war, the devastating manufacture of the bones of our sons, is but a war after a war, a war before a war." A dark yet not unreasonable phi-losophy for a West Point graduate who had just battered Robert E. Lee into submission; but maybe Grant was solemn and cranky because he was out of cigars. Literary license only goes so far.[64]

War So Terrible

S. C. Gylanders, a London writer, didn't produce a cosmic thriller in her 2006 novel *The Better Angels of Our Nature*. Rather, she read her military his-tory carefully, followed Sherman plausibly from the battle of Shiloh to his de-parture for Chattanooga after the Vicksburg campaign, and gave him a sin-gular companion. During a nocturnal stroll through his camp shortly before Shiloh, Sherman finds "kneeling on the wet earth with bowed red head" a small figure wearing a baggy uniform. "Who are you?" asks the general. "What are you doing here? Have you fallen out of the sky?" Those questions are never quite answered, but if the girl called Jesse isn't an angel, she is a fair substitute, complete with wings.

Sherman initially assumes Jesse is a boy soldier, and allows her to stay with the army. Here the story is similar to *The March*, and Jesse and Pearl are even about the same age. In addition to serving, and sometimes protecting, Sher-man as an orderly, Jesse also assists the cynical military surgeon Seth Cartwright, who resembles Sartorius, in the army's field hospital. Jesse has a healing touch and inexhaustible compassion, while quickly absorbing Cartwright's progressive medical techniques as the battlefield turns into an abattoir and Sherman comes "miraculously face to face with his own des-tiny." After Jesse is shot while helping a wounded Confederate soldier and her true gender is discovered, Sherman threatens to send her away, but he re-lents. He all but acknowledges her seemingly mystical powers when she re-veals she once saved him from drowning during a shipwreck. Although both Cartwright and the noble young general Thomas Ransom fall in love with Jesse, she remains devoted to Sherman. When Sherman's young son Willy becomes ill with typhoid, Sherman begs Jesse to heal him, but Jesse says she cannot, and Willy dies. War, so terrible, is beyond even the ethereal Jesse's ministrations. Sherman, the man of facts, disdaining religion, ironically ap-peals to a heavenly being, and feels rebuffed. Sherman then knows he must wage "war so terrible" to end the conflict, and the March will be the result.

Jesse knows her "mission" is to follow, or lead, Sherman, eschewing all human desires. Jesse may be a Christ figure, sacrificing herself for others while sharing in and redeeming human suffering; or she may be a moral voice in Sherman's fevered mind, or even a red-haired psychological projection of Sherman himself. She may represent what Lincoln tried to invoke, the "better angels" of human nature, the purity of conscience in confrontation with the chaos of any war. Whatever she is, few historical novels have explored the carnage of the Civil War with more empathy, or placed Sherman so provocatively at the center of the storm.[65]

Sherman has changed shape in fiction so often in the last 140 years that he has become the literary Proteus of the Civil War. Those who knew him in real life noted his restless energy and his garrulousness. Fiction writers have turned him either into wind or windbag, force of nature or moral philosopher of war and order. Often at the periphery of events he initiates and controls, Sherman is like the inventor of a great machine, which is the real change agent. He is all things to all writers because he is more myth than man, cavorting with vampires, warlocks, angels, and time travelers in some stories, or still marching through history in others.

It remains the difficult, but essential, task of historians to try to separate fiction from fact. When a historical figure like Sherman becomes a fictional character, however, there is always a danger that historians may subconsciously confuse the real and the imagined. It has happened often enough with Lincoln, Jackson, and Lee, along with Forrest, Mosby, and dozens of other Civil War icons. The problem, moreover, is common to all historical writing. The human capacity, even need, to create and remember powerful stories is, in a way, the enemy of history. And yet it is a mistake to deny what truths literature may reveal, even if those truths sometimes reveal our capacity for self-deception.

Notes

1. Ross Lockridge, Jr., *Raintree County* (Boston: Houghton Mifflin, 1948), 695.

2. Richard Adams, *Traveller* (New York: Knopf, 1988).

3. George W. Nichols, *The Story of the Great March* (New York: Harper, 1865); George W. Nichols, *The Sanctuary* (New York: Harper, 1866); Irene M. Patten, "The Civil War as Romance: Of Noble Warriors and Maidens Chaste," *American Heritage* 22:3 (April 1971), 48–53.

4. Ambrose Bierce, *Tales of Soldiers and Civilians* (New York: United States Book Co., 1891); David M. Owens, *The Devil's Topographer: Ambrose Bierce and the American War Story* (Knoxville: University of Tennessee Press, 2006); Allen Guelzo, "Bierce's Civil War: One Man's Morbid Vision," *Civil War Times* 44:4 (October

2005), 35–40, 60; Gordon Berg, "'Phantoms of a Blood-Stained Period,'" *Civil War Times* 44:4 (October 2005), 42–48; Edmund Wilson, *Patriotic Gore: Studies in the Literature of the American Civil War* (New York: Oxford University Press, 1962), 624.

5. Edward G. Bird, *Sherman's "March to the Sea," or Fighting His Way through Georgia*, Old Cap Collier Library no. 398 (New York: Old Cap Collier Library, Mar. 2, 1891).

6. Warren Lee Goss, *Tom Clifton, or Western Boys in Grant and Sherman's Army, '61–'65* (New York: Crowell, 1892), 171, 301; J. Michael Martinez, *Life and Death in Civil War Prisons: The Parallel Torments of Corporal John Wesley Minnich, C.S.A. and Sergeant Warren Lee Goss, U.S.A.* (Nashville: Rutledge Hill, 2004).

7. William Henry Shelton, "Uncle Obadiah's Uncle Billy," *Century* (June 1893), 307–12; Byron A. Dunn, *Battling for Atlanta* (Chicago: McClurg, 1900); Byron A. Dunn, *From Atlanta to the Sea* (Chicago: McClurg, 1901).

8. Warren I. Titus, *Winston Churchill* (New York: Twayne, 1963), 7, 45–51; Carl Van Doren, *The American Novel 1789–1939* (New York, 1949), cited in Titus, *Winston Churchill*, 36; Winston Churchill, *The Crisis* (New York: Macmillan, 1901), 477.

9. Louisa M. Whitney, *Goldie's Inheritance: A Story of the Siege of Atlanta* (Burlington, VT: Free Press, 1903), 240; Thomas G. Dyer, *Secret Yankees: The Union Circle in Confederate Atlanta* (Baltimore: Johns Hopkins University Press, 1999), 19, 179–212, 333.

10. William Henry Peck, *The M'Donalds, or The Ashes of Southern Homes* (New York: Metropolitan Record Office, 1867), 183, 188.

11. Sara Beaumont Kennedy, *Cicely: A Tale of the Georgia March* (Garden City, NY: Doubleday, Page, 1911), 27; Mary Johnston, *Cease Firing* (Boston: Houghton Mifflin, 1912), 406; Richard Harwell, editor, *Margaret Mitchell's "Gone with the Wind" Letters, 1936–1949* (New York: Macmillan, 1976), 8.

12. Paul V. Murphy, *The Rebuke of History: The Southern Agrarians and American Conservative Thought* (Chapel Hill: University of North Carolina Press, 2001), 30, 121–23.

13. On Forrest and the Agrarians, see Paul Ashdown and Edward Caudill, *The Myth of Nathan Bedford Forrest* (Lanham, MD: Rowman & Littlefield, 2005); Donald Davidson, *The Tennessee, Vol. 2: The New River, Civil War to TVA* (New York: Rinehart, 1948), 91.

14. Davidson, *The Tennessee*, 107, 111–12.

15. Fred Hobson, *Tell about the South: The Southern Rage to Explain* (Baton Rouge: Louisiana State University Press, 1983), 221–22.

16. Murphy, *The Rebuke of History*, 62.

17. John Crowe Ransom et al., *I'll Take My Stand* (New York: Harper, 1962; orig. pub. 1930), 328, 339.

18. Stark Young, *So Red the Rose*, with an introduction by Donald Davidson (New York: Charles Scribner's Sons, 1953; orig. pub. 1934), 303–5, 316.

19. Ibid., 303–4, 311.

20. Ibid., 383–85.

21. Donald Davidson, introduction to *So Red the Rose*, by Stark Young (New York: Charles Scribner's Sons, 1953), vi, xxiii–xxiv.

22. Writing in the *New Yorker* in 2006, critic Louis Menand noted that while the Southern point of view in Civil War fiction is often a defense of tradition and local communities, "an allegory for the defeat of the crafted by the machine-made, the hearth by the factory, the folk by the mass," the Confederate point of view is something different, "a vision of an expanding slave empire in which businessmen operate vast plantations on assembly-line principles and hold absolute power over people whose ancestors had once, on another continent, belonged to local communities, made a living in the traditional ways, and so on." The Confederate view, as Menand saw it, is "at least as techno-imperialist as the Northern agenda is frequently accused of being." Although Menand wasn't writing specifically about the Agrarians, his point could well apply to them. *So Red the Rose* and other Agrarian fiction is both Southern and, at times, Neo-Confederate, both a defense of rural tradition and an apology for one type of commercial empire in preference to another. Louis Menand, "Dispossession," *New Yorker*, Oct. 2, 2006, 92.

23. Anne Edwards, *Road to Tara: The Life of Margaret Mitchell* (New York: Dell, 1983), 159.

24. Ibid., 15–32.

25. Patrick Allen, editor, *Margaret Mitchell: Reporter* (Athens, GA: Hill Street Press, 2000).

26. Edwards, *Road to Tara*, passim; Jim Cullen, *The Civil War in Popular Culture: A Reusable Past* (Washington, DC: Smithsonian Institution Press, 1995), 67.

27. For example, Mitchell gets only a line in Richard H. King's *A Southern Renaissance: The Cultural Awakening of the American South, 1930–1955* (New York: Oxford University Press, 1980).

28. Edwards, *Road to Tara*, 182.

29. Wilson, *Patriotic Gore*, 605.

30. Margaret Mitchell, *Gone with the Wind* (New York: Macmillan, 1936), 96–201.

31. Ibid., 202–10.

32. Ibid., 251, 271.

33. Ibid., 328–29.

34. David W. Blight, *Race and Reunion: The Civil War in American Memory* (Cambridge, MA: Harvard University Press, 2001), 284; Cullen, *The Civil War in Popular Culture*, 67.

35. James Street, "All Out with Sherman," *Collier's*, Dec. 19, 1942, 72–77.

36. Lockridge, *Raintree County*, 685, 708, 1053; Daniel Aaron, "On Ross Lockridge, Jr.'s *Raintree County*," in David Madden and Peggy Bach, editors, *Classics of Civil War Fiction* (Jackson: University Press of Mississippi, 1991), 204–14.

37. James Street, *Captain Little Ax* (Philadelphia: Lippincott, 1956); John Brick, *Jubilee* (New York: Doubleday, 1956); Richard O'Connor, *Company Q* (Garden City, NY: Doubleday, 1957), 213, 222.

38. Frank G. Slaughter, *Lorena* (Garden City, NY: Doubleday, 1959), 46, 56, 59.

39. Allan Gurganus, *Oldest Living Confederate Widow Tells All* (New York: Knopf, 1989), 262–66.

40. Allan Gurganus, "Sherman's Ghost," *New York Times Magazine*, Sept. 23, 2001, 101.

41. Cynthia Bass, *Sherman's March* (New York: Villard, 1994), 8–9, 11, 58, 61, 113, 181, 193, 228.

42. MacKinlay Kantor, *If the South Had Won the Civil War* (New York: Bantam, 1961).

43. Karen White, *In the Shadow of the Moon* (New York: Dorchester, 2000).

44. Chelsea Quinn Yarbro, *In the Face of Death: An Historical Horror Novel* (Dallas, TX: BenBella Books, 2001), 311.

45. Harry Turtledove, *Marching through Peachtree* (Riverdale, NY: Baen, 2001).

46. Harry Harrison, *Stars and Stripes Forever* (New York: Del Rey, 1999); Harry Harrison, *Stars and Stripes in Peril* (New York: Del Rey, 2000), 106, 318; Harry Harrison, *Stars and Stripes Triumphant* (New York: Del Rey, 2003), 134.

47. Leonard Palmer, *The Sherman Letter* (Aurora, CO: Write Way Publishing, 1994), 144, 198.

48. Richard L. Hawk, *Moonstalker: The Adventures of Gen. Sherman's Drummer Boy* (Lancaster, OH: Beechwood Books, 1993).

49. Miriam Freeman Rawl, *From the Ashes of Ruin* (Columbia, SC: Summerhouse, 1999), 234.

50. James Reasoner, *Savannah* (Nashville, TN: Cumberland House, 2003), 317, 339; John Jakes, *Savannah, or A Gift for Mr. Lincoln* (New York: Dutton, 2004).

51. Philip Lee Williams, *A Distant Flame* (New York: St. Martin's, 2004), 295.

52. Diane Haeger, *My Dearest Cecelia: A Novel of the Southern Belle Who Stole General Sherman's Heart* (New York: St. Martin's, 2003), 284; Helen Dortch Longstreet, *In the Path of Lee's "Old War Horse"* (Atlanta: A. B. Caldwell, 1917), 21.

53. Margaret Erhart, *Crossing Bully Creek* (Minneapolis: Milkweed Editions, 2005), 26, 99.

54. E. L. Doctorow, *The March* (New York: Random House, 2005), 61–62.

55. Walter Kirn, "Making War Hell," *New York Times Book Review*, Sept. 25, 2005, 1, 14.

56. Doctorow, *The March*, 348.

57. See, for example, Doctorow's column "The Unfeeling President," in the East Hampton (NY) *Star*, Sept. 9, 2004, widely circulated on the Internet; "Doctorow Booed after Anti-Bush Speech," *USA Today*, May 26, 2004; "Doctorow Is In," *U.S. News & World Report*, Oct. 10, 2005, 22; John R. MacArthur, "Sherman's Vast Ambivalence," Providence (RI) *Journal*, Feb. 8, 2006; Mini Kapoor, "Is There a Good War?" *Sunday Indian Express* (Mumbai, India), Nov. 20, 2005; Stephen Matchett, "Power of the Patriot," *Australian* (Sydney), Sept. 30, 2006; Lloyd Sachs, "E. L. Doctorow Brilliantly Retells Sherman's March," Chicago *Sun-Times*, Sept. 18, 2005.

58. Jerome Weeks, "Gen. Sherman Marches to the Sea in Doctorow's New Novel," Lincoln (NE) *Journal Star*, Oct. 20, 2005; John Updike, "A Cloud of Dust," *New Yorker*, Sept. 12, 2005, 98; John Freeman, "Marching through Georgia," Louisville (KY) *Courier-Journal*, Sept. 18, 2005; Doctorow, *The March*, 349.

59. Lewis Beale, "History through Art's Prism," Los Angeles *Times*, Sept. 18, 2005; Janet Maslin, "Using History as a Guide, but Skipping the Details," New York *Times*, Sept. 27, 2005.

60. Matchett, "Power of the Patriot"; Vince Passaro, "Another Country," *Nation*, 36.281:14 (Oct. 31, 2005), 32–36.

61. Doctorow, *The March*, 204, 302–4.

62. Ibid., 13, 43, 188.

63. Ibid., 358–59.

64. Ibid., 359.

65. S. C. Gylanders, *The Better Angels of Our Nature* (New York: Random House, 2006), 5, 140, 433–34.

CHAPTER FIVE

Long Remember

Sherman on Stage and Screen, in Song and Poetry

They will long remember Sherman
And his streaming columns free—
They will long remember Sherman
Marching to the sea.

Herman Melville, "The March to the Sea," 1866[1]

Sherman enjoyed the theater and show business, having seen his first play in New York as a cadet on his way to West Point. He saw plays whenever he could, even during the war, preferring Shakespeare but also enjoying melodrama. He liked meeting actors, actresses, and impresarios after the war, presided over a theater group, and helped found the Players Club. His interests included spectacles such as Buffalo Bill's Wild West Show and the circuses staged by P. T. Barnum. He spoke of drama as entertaining and educational, but he was aware of its mythologizing function as well. He knew enough about military and political life to understand the way pageantry, panache, and rhetoric shaped the meaning and memory of public events. "No one who was an actor in the Grand Drama of the Civil War seems willing to risk its history," he wrote in 1874. The March to the Sea itself was a kind of performance art designed to terrify unwilling audiences herded into a smoking, military theater of the absurd. During a particularly difficult period for Sherman after the war, he told a friend that he felt like a stage actor rehearsing his lines "and yet with no heart in the play." Sherman himself would become a character, sometimes as an offstage presence, in theatrical performances as well as the newer media of film and television. His legacy and myth have been shaped by the way writers, directors, actors, and poets have interpreted both the general and the March that made him famous. But the interpretation has come with a price. Popular culture has exploited the war's entertainment value, subtracting much of the mystery from history, and turning it into a commercial product full of sentiment, romance, and adventure.[2]

Probably the earliest play featuring Sherman as a character was written in 1875 by Judson Kilpatrick, his cavalry chief during the March, and J. Owen Moore. After the war, Kilpatrick had served as ambassador to Chile, and then made money giving a lecture titled "Sherman's March to the Sea" more than four hundred times. The five-act play, titled *Allatoona*, references the battle that occurred on October 5, 1864, but is really a corny romance involving another love affair between a Yank boy and a Reb girl. Reviewers hated it; but it was performed on August 27–28, 1878, at a veteran's reunion at Kilpatrick's farm near Deckertown, New Jersey, before about 1,500 people. Kilpatrick had craftily promoted the event by announcing that Sherman, Governor McClellan, and President Hayes would attend. The best-known dignitary who actually showed up, however, was the controversial former Union general Dan Sickles. The little town's newspaper warned that streets would be overrun by pickpockets and "base women," which, given Kilpatrick's shady wartime reputation, was not unlikely. Some 40,000 people showed up for a battle reenactment that degenerated into a brawl before Kilpatrick rode into the fray carrying a white flag. Sherman stayed well clear of the affair.[3]

Sherman's army appeared in a few silent films, most notably *Hearts and Flags* (1912), in which one of Sherman's officers, shamed by the mayhem brought about by the March, intervenes to save his lover's plantation; and *When Sherman Marched to the Sea* (1913). In *The Birth of a Nation* (1915), a family of Southern refugees cowering on a Georgia hillside observes Sherman's relentless advance and his army's destruction of an abandoned schoolhouse. Griffith actually filmed the scene in the San Fernando Valley near Los Angeles, but consulted veterans of the March in order to make the scene as accurate as possible. Movie audiences of the day saw a frightening image of what an invasion may have looked like through the eyes of terrified civilians. The burning of Atlanta adds visual impact as civilians flee the city through the smoke and flames. Although Lee, Grant, and Lincoln show up in *The Birth of a Nation*, Sherman is absent, except as a title card. Sherman, played by an uncredited actor, has brief appearances in Griffith's first sound film, *Abraham Lincoln*, in 1930.[4]

Belles and Brownshirts

Sherman is not present in *Gone with the Wind* as his army sweeps toward Atlanta, although he is central to the story. As in *The Birth of a Nation*, Sherman is an invisible force rather than a personality. He is known by his deeds, by the flames, carnage, and confusion he leaves as he sweeps by. The famous scene in which Scarlett O'Hara shoots a straggler who invades Tara left an image that "will forever *be* Sherman," according to James Reston, Jr. The on-screen flames are a defining point in the movie—the cavaliers and belles in a garden of plenty, stately plantations, contented slaves at home in a benign institution; versus a devastated landscape, the grind of capitalism displacing chivalric pastures. Like the screen erupting in celluloid flame, Sherman burned his way into the memory chain, leaving a smoldering myth, just as he had left a charred landscape. [5]

The film's premiere in Atlanta on December 15, 1939, was the culmination of an immense publicity buildup that had surrounded the casting of the actress who would play Scarlett O'Hara after a nationwide talent search. Clare Boothe's successful 1938 play *Kiss the Boys Good-Bye*, a spoof of Hollywood's search for Scarlett O'Hara (called Velvet O'Toole in the play), was, according to Boothe, "a political allegory about Fascism in America." The Southern Belle, Boothe argued, is distilled emotion, decanted as intoxicating "Southernism," the "pure white race" standing firmly for tradition through a seduction of reason. The Southern Belle, in these terms, is an incipient fascist, calling forth "the dangerous nostalgia of the North for the white South's passionate and radiant acceptance of its own Supremacy." Furthermore, fascism was not something imported into the United States from abroad. Rather, Southernism was "a particular and highly matured form of Fascism with which America has lived more or less peacefully for seventy-five years." Margaret Mitchell saw the play in Atlanta before the *Gone with the Wind* premiere and, according to an interview published in the *Constitution*, enjoyed it, but doubled over with laughter when told that Boothe regarded her play as an "indictment of the south as the stronghold of Fascism."

Boothe, however, was no leftist critic of the Agrarians or the South in general. Married to *Time* and *Fortune* publisher Henry Luce, she later served as ambassador to Italy and supported the conservative wing of the Republican Party. The contretemps over her play was just another indication that much of the country was still trying to explain the South long after the Civil War. Especially after the Scopes trial, the South was under attack and mounted a spirited defense. The Agrarians had been called fascists, so Boothe's claim that the Southern Belle, in the satiric terms of her play, "is an American version of a Brown Shirt street brawler from Munich, in a swank Berlin coffee house, circa 1930," was not out of character in the nervous 1930s.[6]

Controversy was in the air even before the film was released. On the very day Hitler invaded Poland, the New York *Times* reported that the Daughters of Union Veterans, an auxiliary group of the Grand Army of the Republic (GAR), claimed the film tarnished Sherman's reputation and implied Union soldiers were rapists. After agitation by the Daughters, the GAR, meeting in Pittsburgh, passed a resolution charging that *Gone with the Wind* portrayed the Union soldier as "a hideous marauder, attacking women," and urged that members boycott the "defamatory film." The Daughters claimed the film was "an outrageous attempt" to "smirch the reputation" of General Sherman. "The war orders of the Confederate States prove conclusively the raiding and burning of the Southern homes and supplies were done by the Confederates themselves," according to the Daughters. "Were it not that young people will see the picture, it could be ignored, but it is unfair that our boys and girls should be given such a distorted view of what actually took place." In the South there were objections to the casting of English actress Vivian Leigh to play the part of Scarlett O'Hara. Leigh's portrayal of Scarlett, however, transformed the Southern Belle into an international symbol of Southern heritage that could be used for multiple purposes. Between 1939 and 1945 alone, an estimated 120 million Americans saw the film, a figure roughly equivalent to the entire adult population. Film historian Bruce Chadwick points out, however, that the "fingerprints of *The Birth of a Nation* were all over *Gone with the Wind*," beginning with the opening scrolls in both films proclaiming that the South was a separate civilization, one supported, according to the films, by the benign institution of slavery and ruthlessly destroyed by predatory Northerners led by their vulture Sherman. Reconstruction just finished what Sherman had started, and even Scarlett's business ventures in the city symbolized the price the Old South had to pay for Northern conquest and New South carpetbagger capitalism.[7]

"They Got It Coming"

William Cameron Menzies, who designed the sets for *Gone with the Wind*, directed *Drums in the Deep South*, a 1951 film about a Confederate plan to stall Sherman's advance on Atlanta. A detachment of Rebel soldiers hauls a cannon up a mountain and shells Sherman's supply trains while Union soldiers try to stop them. The opposing officers were friends at West Point before the war, and a woman is involved. In order to blow the Confederates off the mountain, the Federals bring the mountain down on top of the gorge through which the rail line passes. If something of the sort had actually occurred in 1864 it might have slowed Sherman down a bit, but it didn't, and he pressed on. The film does succeed in showing the difficulty of defending the supply lines as the army moved south, and the justification for the later strategy of severing the rail connection.

Sometimes Sherman got the blame in cinema for things he didn't do in real life. As Brian Wills points out, this was the case with the 1951 film *Red Mountain*. The script confuses Sherman with Sheridan. It was Sheridan, not Sherman, who "slashed wounds" in the Shenandoah Valley. Alan Ladd, portraying a Confederate captain whose home was in Columbia, South Carolina, tells a Northerner that war is hell. "If anyone wants peace they should listen to General Sherman's boast, 'If a crow should fly over the Shenandoah Valley it would have to carry its own rations.'" Wills observes that Sheridan's words are attributed to Sherman, but adds that Sherman "was the man movie audiences expected to say such words and commit such dire acts in the name of Union victory." Another film, *The Raid*, tells the story of the Confederate attack on St. Albans, Vermont. Slipping across the border from Canada, the raiders robbed some banks and set fires in October 1864. The preparations for the raid and the raid itself took place before the March to the Sea was in progress. The 1954 film has Richard Boone, best known for his later roll as Paladin in the television series *Have Gun, Will Travel*, playing a wounded Union captain, who hollers: "Savannah's going to get what Atlanta got. If I were General Sherman, I wouldn't leave a stick standing. They got it coming." When the Confederates quibble amongst themselves about whether to torch the town, one of them, played by Lee Marvin, says, "Sherman doesn't make any exceptions." Sherman, therefore, is the moral arbiter for both sides, an example for whoever has "got it coming." Peter Graves is also in the cast playing a Confederate captain, apparently warming up in a "hot war" Civil War film for his Cold War adventures in the long-running television drama *Mission Impossible*.[8]

Raintree County was supposed to be another *Gone with the Wind* blockbuster when it was released in 1957, but it didn't quite live up to its billing. Based on the epic, complex novel by Lockridge, the MGM film was several hours long and one of the most expensive cinema productions of its era. Johnny Shawnessy, an idealistic Indiana schoolteacher, joins the Union Army to find his deranged Southern-born wife Susanna, who has fled to a Georgia plantation with their son during the war. Shawnessy winds up marching through Georgia with Sherman, whose name, as usual, is on everyone's lips although the general is never on screen. While it features some of the best action footage of the March, the film was a box office disappointment, perhaps because Elizabeth Taylor's Susanna is the antithesis of Scarlett O'Hara and the story is told from the Union point of view. The film seemed jinxed from the beginning. Lockridge committed suicide soon after the novel was published. Montgomery Clift, who played Shawnessy, was seriously injured and disfigured in an automobile accident during production. When production resumed Clift looked different and, consequently, so did the film.[9]

Honor in Flames

Stories about Sherman and his army also were presented on television, as well as on stage. Gore Vidal wrote a television play about the Georgia campaign for the NBC series *Playwrights '56*. Broadcast on June 19, 1956, *Honor*, one of the last live television plays ever performed, featured Ralph Bellamy in the role of John Hinks, a nouveau riche planter who aspires to respectability in a feudal society facing the Civil War. Hinks believes honor demands that his two sons serve in the Confederate forces although he continues to rationalize his own profiteering. When Sherman's army approaches, Hinks encourages his neighbors to join him in burning their plantations so "we shall go down nobly with our expensive gestures. To no good purpose but our sacred honor." Colonel Tolliver arrives with a Union Army detachment and requisitions the house, and Hinks talks himself out of his pledge to burn it down. Confronted by his surviving son, who says Hinks has forgotten about his own honor while his neighbors' plantations are in flames, Hinks sets the fire.[10]

Vidal attempted to revise the play for Broadway, but still found it "faulty." In an introduction to a published version of the revised play, titled *On the March to the Sea*, Vidal explains that he

> could not make up my mind what I thought of Hinks. . . . Hinks was a new man. He longed to believe in the romantic code. He thought he did believe. But he could never resist a good deal . . . even when the deal went against his own set of values. . . . At times Hinks seemed to be a tiresome windbag; at other times he seemed admirably representative of the will to survive, a philosophy which I think to be the only reasonable one in a world as fragilely balanced as ours.

His solution was to give up on Hinks, "create a new character and deliberately divide the theme. Colonel Thayer is a creation I take a good deal of pleasure in: a man of good will and some sensibility, turned nihilist by war. We observe him in the process of being destroyed by self-knowledge; for he has found to his horror that he revels in destruction and in the deliberate in-fliction of pain." Vidal doesn't say that Thayer, who replaces the more ra-tional Tolliver, is a caricature of Sherman, but if not Sherman then Sher-man's army. Thayer is a maniac who prattles on with lines about the "mask one always wears. . . . Does it betray the monster? Or reveal the angel? Be-cause I am both. . . . the monster-angel, the sane-mad man, the wise fool." Hinks's wife just sees in Thayer "evil for its own sake." Thayer's drunken of-ficers debauch the plantation at a party. "They don't know what a long march it is from here to the sea," says Thayer, before Hinks gets some backbone and torches the house, as the mad colonel screams "Fire! Fire! Fire! Fire!"[11]

By turning his colonel into a moral nihilist, and Hinks into a New South hustler even before there was a New South, Vidal seems to be saying some-thing about the moral ambiguity of the March, the South, and the Union cause, leaving the problem of honor in flames. The new, overheated play ap-parently was performed in Hyde Park, New York, in 1960, but never made it to Broadway in time for the Centennial. It was, however, staged in Bonn, Germany, as *Flammen zum Meer*, or flames to the sea. German audiences per-haps saw the play in light of recent Germany history, with Thayer a thinly veiled Führer. The play was later revived and performed at Duke University in Durham, North Carolina, in 2005, with Chris Noth, of television's *Law & Order*, cast in the role of Thayer.

In 1976, playwright Thomas Babe's *Rebel Women* had its premier at the New York Shakespeare Festival, with David Dukes in the role of Sherman. The play deals with how a group of women respond to Sherman's arrival at their home in Vidalia, Georgia, during the March. One of the women barters her body for Sherman's help in releasing her husband. She is both repelled by, and attracted to, the general, who tries to explain himself to her in long speeches. Sherman, a tormented invader, affirms his love for the South, but recognizes its powers of seduction. Southerners "have always drawn me out," he tells her, "but I've shown you something: I'm not such an easy mark." She gets her way, though, and then tells Sherman: "I am in-clined to believe that when this is over and you are done stringing us up, in a few months, I will end up very coarse. I will be a terrible, hard bitch, unconquerable." And he replies: "Good for you, then, because I am a no-torious son of that same hard species. We'll grind it all up, you and I, and it has been, may I say, momentous." And then her retort: "It has been ex-citing and rotten and I feel quite empty. Well, you've got to march, Sher-man, so march, and I don't wish you well, I really don't: I had to try to cut you down a little. It took up the night at least." This sort of banter suggests the war is like a battle of the sexes as well as a battle of armies, each side seduced by the other, but at a cost to both. The play was revived in New York in 1999, with Mark Shelton as Sherman.[12]

James Reston, Jr.'s, play, *Sherman, the Peacemaker*, had its premier in Chapel Hill, North Carolina, in 1979, and has seldom been seen since. Five years later Reston published *Sherman's March and Vietnam*, a political and historical elaboration of some of the ideas he introduced in the play, especially regarding civilian control over the military. *Sherman, the Peacemaker* deals with Sherman's negotiations with Johnston at Bennett Place, his meeting with Lincoln at City Point, his feud with Stanton, and his supposed betrayal by Grant. The play concludes with Sherman's appearance before the Committee on the Conduct of the War, and his defense of Lincoln. Having won the war, says Sherman,

> perhaps I was too anxious for the laurels of peacemaker as well. . . . You cried out for an angel of wrath; I gave you what you wanted. . . . If there is no general in this war or any American war like me, so there is no politician now, nor ever will there be again like [Lincoln]. If I erred, it was because I tried to hold onto that spirit which was so quickly fading, as petty, vindictive, scheming conspirators took his place.

Sherman had done the nation's dirty work, and he had tried to make things right in the end, only to learn the political price of peace. A century and a decade later, perhaps the wounds had begun to heal. Vietnam, still an open wound, was the play's true subject.[13]

Cump and the Duke

John Wayne portrayed Sherman in film, and once on television. The television appearance came first. Wayne was a longtime close friend of Ward Bond, who starred in a popular television western, *Wagon Train*, which began on the NBC network in 1957. The director John Ford, a friend of both actors, had a low opinion of television, but as a favor to Bond agreed to direct an episode of the series called "The Colter Craven Story." It was broadcast on November 23, 1960, on the eve of the Civil War Centennial. *Wagon Train* was a post–Civil War *Canterbury Tales* that often involved the plight of veterans looking for a new start in the West. The series was loosely based on a 1950 film, *Wagon Master*, which also starred Bond and was directed by Ford.

"The Colter Craven Story" involves a California-bound doctor who has joined the wagon train but cannot perform surgery again, because of the trauma he experienced during the battle of Shiloh and a subsequent drinking problem. When a woman on the train needs help, it is up to Major Seth Adams, the wagonmaster played by Bond, to restore the doctor's confidence. He tells Craven about his old drinking friend Sam Grant, who put down the bottle long enough to win the battle of Shiloh and maybe save the Union. In a flashback sequence, Adams tells how he won his promotion from Grant on the battlefield. Wayne appears as Sherman at Shiloh. The actor stands in shadows in the scene, but the voice is unmistakably his, even though his name appears in the credits as Michael Morris and not as John Wayne (who was born Marion Morrison). So America's most recognizable actor, the living symbol of robust manhood, American national identity, the West, and conservative politics, is in disguise, and portrays Sherman, one of the nation's most controversial generals, in shadowy silhouette, as if something about Sherman can never quite be disclosed—that he, in effect, swaggers and sounds like John Wayne but isn't the same man in American memory. Wayne dramatizes war and conflict, but as an actor is only and always in the shadow of reality. War drama is inevitably a shadowy reality. It is, unintentionally perhaps, an eerie scene, and even eerier because Bond died of a heart attack eighteen days before the episode appeared on television. When Wayne saw the episode, he wept, just as Sherman wept when he was told of the death of McPherson.

A year later, however, Wayne was again portraying Sherman under Ford's direction in a scene for the epic blockbuster film *How the West Was Won*, which was based on a seven-part *Life* magazine series. In the scene, Sherman and a dispirited Grant (played by Harry Morgan) are conversing during a nighttime lull after the battle of Shiloh. Sherman, who has saved the day, tries to encourage Grant by reminding him of the noble purpose of the war and the grandeur of the nation's destiny. Grant has been criticized in the press for his handling of the army and his reputed boozing the night before the battle. Says Sherman, calmly: "A month ago they were saying I was crazy, *in-*sane. Now they're calling me a hero. Hero or crazy, I'm the same man. Doesn't matter what the people think. It's what you think, Grant." Lurking behind them is a Confederate deserter, who tries to assassinate the generals but is killed by a Union soldier. If Wayne's Sherman lurked in the shadows on television, he at least advanced to the foreground on the big screen.[14]

But not often. Sherman's only other screen appearance in a Wayne film— and a cameo at that—came in *The Horse Soldiers* (1959). A cigar-puffing Sherman, played by veteran character actor Richard Cutting, a regular on *Wagon Train*, joins a council of war during which Grant outlines a plan to send Wayne's Colonel John Marlowe on a raid behind enemy lines. The film was based on General Benjamin Grierson's cavalry raid in Mississippi during the Vicksburg campaign.

"It's All a Tragedy"

In keeping with the pattern of these brief, oblique appearances, Sherman was only the nominal subject of what has become a cult film, Ross McElwee's *Sherman's March: A Meditation on the Possibility of Romantic Love in the South During an Era of Nuclear Weapons Proliferation*, released in 1986. McElwee, who teaches filmmaking at Harvard, was in his thirties at the time he filmed the documentary, and recovering from a series of failed love affairs. He sets out from Boston to retrace Sherman's March and study its impact on the South, but the film's ostensible purpose quickly becomes secondary to McElwee's pursuit of various women he meets along the way. Some are women to whom he is introduced by his matchmaking family and friends in his native North Carolina and elsewhere in the South, and others are former lovers he cannot relinquish. As the journey to the Southern interior unfolds, McElwee reveals more about himself and his anxieties, which have much to do with his fear of nuclear weapons. Sherman's "total war" has now become something universal as McElwee documents the edgy concerns of both survivalists and proponents of nuclear disarmament, as well as his own nightmares. McElwee's obsessions reprise Sherman's depressions, insomnia, insecurities, and passions, along with his unrequited love affair with the South. "I'm really intrigued by William Tecumseh Sherman," says McElwee in one of the film's late night soliloquies. "I think he's one of history's tragic figures." Tragic, because he was forced to make war against the thing he loved (the South) and then was rebuked by the North for offering the South an easy peace. Sherman was destined to be "reviled in the South and still is today. I can't talk about him around here." We're not quite sure if Sherman destroyed the South or the South destroyed Sherman.

McElwee's ambivalence toward Southern women mirrors his ambivalence, and Sherman's, toward the South. The women, as McElwee's camera reveals them, metaphorically represent the idea of the South, sometimes beguiling, seductive, melodramatic, shallow, and vulgar behind a facade of gentility; sometimes spiritual, ambitious, courageous, resourceful, protective, and passionate about life. Although wary of outsiders, they either leave the South or, like Scarlett O'Hara, cunningly accept the yoke of Northern power to get by at home. In this, they are representative of the stereotypical Southern women who show up in Civil War fiction. Love and war, nurture and nature, past and present, become conflated, heightening anxiety. Everyone in the film seems to be searching for commitment, adrift in a murky historical present. Why even try to find love in a world where relationships are imperfect and where destruction may be imminent, either from Sherman's army or from nuclear weapons, and when war is all hell? "Hell, it's all a tragedy," says Charleen, McElwee's friend, former teacher, and chief matchmaker. "It's just a matter of how you get through it."

Playwright Arthur Miller, no doubt recognizing Sherman's oracular potential, lent his voice to the general's words in Ken Burns's PBS series *The Civil War* in 1990. George Dickerson played Sherman in the 1991 ABC television miniseries *Son of the Morning Star*, the story of Custer and the Little Big Horn. The part was small and the series was long. Reston had ended *Sherman, the Peacemaker* with an imagined encounter between Custer ("the tinsel hero") and Sherman ("the real hero"). But who was the hero? Each would have an enduring claim on the nation's memory, and on the myth of the West—although Custer would be better known in defeat, and on screen, than Sherman ever was in victory. In 2007 the History Channel presented a documentary, *Sherman's March*, with Bill Oberst, Jr., in the role of Sherman. The general also had a small part in the 2007 HBO film *Bury My Heart at Wounded Knee*, a rather loose interpretation of Dee Brown's popular 1970 account of the relocation of Indian tribes in the West after the Civil War. Sherman was played by Colm Feore, opposite former U.S. senator Fred Thompson in the larger role of Grant. Thompson's appearance in the film at a time when he was being touted as a presidential candidate, in addition to suggestive parallels with the Iraq war, gave the production a political spin.

Sherman's legacy remains contested. *The Court Martial of General William Tecumseh Sherman*, a 2006 play by Meredith A. Wilson and William J. Fleming, put Sherman on "trial" at Fort Jefferson in St. Louis for his conduct at Shiloh. Fleming, a South St. Paul, Minnesota, attorney who died in 2007, had been a playwright, comedian, and comedy writer with an interest in the Civil War. He and Wilson, his wife, had conceived the clever play, which is based on official records, memoirs, letters, and archival resources, as a riposte to the contention that Sherman had been surprised, and therefore negligent, at the pivotal battle. Testifying against Sherman is his old nemesis McClernand, and among the panel of three judges hearing the case is a young Oliver Wendell Holmes. Sherman is defended at the trial by Margaret Callaway, sitting in for her father, George Callaway, who has been incapacitated on the morning of the trial. Sherman is portrayed as bored, brash, and belligerent, often delivering witty lines that show the influence of Fleming's comedy writing and legal experience. As the trial progresses it becomes evident that Sherman lured the Confederates into a trap. As Holmes explains it: "Look,

Sherman knew he had to fight the Rebels sooner or later—to get to their railroad. Sherman made it 'sooner.' On his own ground. On his own battlefield all laid out just so. . . ." The case is thrown out of court, and "never happened." Sherman remains on trial in the court of public opinion, however, so the play was timely.

That Blasted Tune

A successful march needs a good song, and Henry Clay Work, a Chicago printer, inventor, and abolitionist originally from Connecticut, wrote one that Sherman, and most Southerners, came to despise. "Marching through Georgia" was published early in 1865, at a time when Sherman's March had captured the public imagination in the North. It had sold half a million copies by 1877, and many more were sold after that. Old soldiers crooned the rousing chorus of the five-stanza martial tune with vitality and pride:

> Hurrah! Hurrah! we bring the jubilee,
> Hurrah! Hurrah! the flag that makes you free!
> So we sang the chorus from Atlanta to the sea,
> While we were marching through Georgia.

Work's second verse makes the March sound more like a minstrel-show tune, with "darkeys" shouting when they hear the army, turkeys gobbling when they are liberated by the bummers, and sweet potatoes practically leaping into the cooking pots. In subsequent verses the March becomes "a thoroughfare for Freedom" as "Treason fled before us, for resistance was in vain." The song even celebrates loyal "Union men who wept with joyful tears, / When they saw the honor'd flag they had not seen for years," suggesting that the March liberated not only slaves but captive whites, however few they may have been.

The song dogged Sherman throughout the postwar years, beginning with its performance at the Grand Review in Washington on May 24, 1865. On one occasion he said: "I wish I had a dollar for every time I have had to listen to that blasted tune." On another, he said: "If I had thought when I made that march that it would have inspired anyone to compose such a piece, I would have marched around the state." While traveling on a train one evening he allegedly cursed when he heard a group of Pullman porters serenading him. After 350 bands and drum corps passed before him at a GAR encampment in Boston in 1890, he said he would never again appear at such an event unless every band in the country foreswore playing the tune again. Nevertheless,

"Marching through Georgia" was played during his funeral obsequies and at political conventions, and continued to be played by military bands of many nations, including Japan, at least through the Second World War. Princeton University adopted the tune as a football fight song, celebrating touchdowns scored against Harvard and Yale rather than burning plantations. Nevertheless, Southern loathing for the song probably contributed to Sherman's bad repute in the South long after the Civil War. It was one thing to suffer defeat, quite another to be accused of treason in a festive song making sport of Southern suffering and virtually ignoring Northern depredations. A carpetbagger sings the melody to "Marching through Georgia" in *Gone with the Wind*, as if to mock the blighted South. It is meant as a provocation and an insult, like singing "Rule Britannia" in an Irish pub. Ironically, Sherman's soldiers didn't sing "Marching through Georgia" while marching through Georgia, because it had yet to be written. It is a song of remembrance, a march through the memory of the war, and as such, reimagined.[15]

Somewhat less popular, but less annoying to Sherman, was "Sherman's March to the Sea," originally called "When Sherman Marched Down to the Sea," the five stanzas and chorus of which were written by Adjutant Samuel Byers of the Fifth Iowa Infantry. He was in a Columbia, South Carolina, prison when he heard Sherman was nearing Savannah, and he scribbled a poem celebrating the event. Another incarcerated soldier, J. C. Rockwell, added music to the lyrics. In his *Memoirs* Sherman wrote that a copy of the song had been given to him in Columbia.

> This appeared to me so good that I at once sent for Byers, attached him to my staff, provided him with horse and equipment, and took him as far as Fayetteville, North Carolina, whence he was sent to Washington as bearer of dispatches. . . . Byers said that there was an excellent glee-club among the prisoners in Columbia, who used to sing it well, with an audience often of rebel ladies.

After the war Byers wrote about Sherman, and served as the United States consul general in Zurich, Switzerland, where Sherman later visited him. Byers lived until 1933. The original copy of the lyrics supposedly was taken to the North hidden in the wooden leg of a paroled prisoner. More than a million copies of the sheet music were sold, but Byers had sold his rights for only a few dollars. Later the song was sometimes sung to a traditional Irish melody. The song's popularity may have inspired the name by which the March became best known. Sherman's generals liked the song, and sang it, accompanied by General John Logan on the violin, in South Carolina, and Sherman included the lyrics in his *Memoirs*.[16]

Modern composers also have been inspired by Sherman. Grammy-winning composer Robert Page arranged a choral work, *Sherman: Forced to War*, with a narrative by Kirk Hathaway. The score includes ten Civil War era melodies as the musical setting for Sherman's dramatic justification for his war service. Warren Michel Swenson set a dozen of Herman Melville's poems to music in a composition titled *Battle Pieces*. And Liz Lerman arranged a twenty-minute ballet with eighteen dancers, that attempts to show Sherman's compassion as well as his ruthlessness. The title, *Incidents in the Life of an Ohio Youth As He Marched to the Sea and Beyond and Was Witness to Minor and Extraordinary Events Along the Way*, was almost as long as the March.[17]

Versified Journalism

Edmund Wilson says the Civil War was not a favorable period for poetry. "An immense amount of verse was written in connection with the war itself, but today it makes barren reading," according to the critic. Sherman and the March attracted their share of poetry, some of it memorable, most of it forgettable. Wilson dismisses the poetry of Melville, author of *Moby-Dick* and one of most notable poets of the war, as "versified journalism: a chronicle of the patriotic feelings of an anxious middle-aged non-combatant as, day by day, he reads the bulletins from the front." Stanton Garner and other Melville scholars dispute that definition, contending that Melville, although a literary borrower, had a deeper engagement with the war than merely transforming newspaper articles into poems. Garner writes that Melville's mind "contained a rebellion record of its own. The newspapers he had read had followed the war in scrupulous detail. What was mere ink on their pages and pulses through telegraph wires was given life through his relationships with men who fought in many of the battles, and his own memories supplied images of the home front." Perhaps Melville also understood that journalism was a kind of poetry in itself, an evolving historical narrative of events at once quotidian and mythic. Hennig Cohen suggests that Melville drew upon many sources in writing his great poem "The March to the Sea," including Major George Ward Nichols's *The Story of the Great March* (1866), paintings by Thomas Nast, the Bible, and Milton's *Paradise Lost*. Indeed, the whole war might be looked upon as a rebellion by aggrieved angels, a pastiche of Milton's War in Heaven, with Sherman restoring order by driving the rebels into the sea.[18]

When Melville turns to Sherman, however, he is ambivalent. Avenger he might be, but at a terrible cost. "The March to the Sea" begins in high spirits, with Sherman's soldiers departing "charred Atlanta" in "glorious glad marching," their power unchallenged as they rush "Unpausing to the sea," a force of nature. The little fighting they do is "but frolic," as they "helped themselves from farmlands." But they leave famine in their wake, along with "a wailing, / A terror and a ban, / And blazing cinders sailing, / And houseless households wan." Abandoned towns "where maniacs ran" complete the horror. Was the March a military necessity or brute retribution for treason? Melville is uncertain. In any event, Georgia would "long remember Sherman" and his "streaming columns." Another poem, "The Frenzy in the Wake," takes up the March as it turns north to the Carolinas. Told in the voice of a wailing Southerner, the poem laments the "burning woods" and "pillars of dust" as Sherman passes, and promises that "even despair / Shall never our hate rescind."[19]

In a prose supplement at the end of *Battle-Pieces*, Melville worried that with the publication of his poems he "might be contributing to a bitterness which every sensible American must wish at an end." While the North was certainly justified in rejoicing in triumph, an immodest triumphalism could do nothing more than perpetuate the bitterness the war had caused. He counseled Northerners to show compassion and moderation in dealing with the South. Some good might yet come out of the war, but only if the nation could be truly reunited in a spirit of reconciliation and democratic renewal.[20]

Sherman's death inspired his friend, the journalist and poet Richard Watson Gilder, to write a eulogistic poem to the general and others like him who "fought for freedom, not glory; made war that war might cease." The ironic line anticipates the "war to end all wars" rhetoric of the First World War. In the poem, Sherman's coffin passes before "a million awe-struck faces far down the waiting street . . . the pageant of civic sorrow." This, too, seems an example of Wilson's "versified journalism," not surprisingly given Gilder's background. Gilder, the editor of the *Century* magazine, began his journalistic career with the Newark (New Jersey) *Advertiser* in 1868 and helped launch *Scribner's Monthly* in 1870, and its successor, the *Century*, in 1881. The publication began a series of war recollections, and Sherman, reluctant at first to contribute, eventually wrote an article on war strategy, which appeared in May 1888, to counter, he said, any impression that it was "only a scramble of power by mobs, and not a war of high principle." Besides Sherman's, articles by major war figures from Johnston and General James Longstreet to Grant and McClellan helped shape the memory of the war.[21]

Henry Van Dyke, a professor of English literature at Princeton University, saw the Augustus Saint-Gaudens monument to Sherman in New York and wrote these lines in 1904:

> This is the soldier brave enough to tell
> The glory-dazzled world that 'war is hell'
> Lover of peace, he looks beyond the strife
> And rides through hell to save his country's life

Perhaps Van Dyke could be forgiven the familiar abridgment of what Sherman actually did say about war. Like Gilder, Van Dyke looks at Sherman and sees a peacemaker and a savior. Van Dyke's "This" points both to the statue and to the future "beyond," where Sherman would live not only in bronze but as an idea. There would be need for an epitaph if the glory-daz-

Augustus Saint-Gaudens' bronze equestrian statue of Sherman was unveiled in New York on Memorial Day, 1903. Winged Victory's outstretched right arm points toward the sea and the American future as the general follows, cape billowing in the wind, his March relentless. After more than a century, both the statue and the March are tarnished by time, tainted by the war's contested memory, yet burnished by American power. Chloe Stuyvesant White

zled world were to forget. Perhaps his final epitaph is yet to be written, by a culture variously enamored of and repulsed by war.[22]

Notes

1. Herman Melville, *The Battle-Pieces of Herman Melville*, edited by Hennig Cohen (New York: Yoseloff, 1963), 120–22; Herman Melville, "The March to the Sea," *Harper's New Monthly* 32 (February 1866), 366–67.

2. Lloyd Lewis, *Sherman: Fighting Prophet* (New York: Harcourt, Brace, 1932), 615; John F. Marszalek, *Sherman: A Soldier's Passion for Order* (New York: Free Press, 1993), 410–11, 480–82.

3. Judson Kilpatrick and J. Owen Moore, *Allatoona: An Historical and Military Drama in Five Acts* (New York: Samuel French, 1875); Samuel J. Martin, *Kill-Cavalry: Sherman's Merchant of Terror: The Life of Union General Hugh Judson Kilpatrick* (Madison, NJ: Fairleigh Dickinson University Press, 1996), 250–56.

4. John M. Cassidy, *Civil War Cinema* (Missoula, MT: Pictorial Histories, 1986), 7–9; Bruce Chadwick, *The Reel Civil War: Mythmaking in American Film* (New York: Knopf, 2001), 74–76; Jack Spears, *The Civil War on the Screen, and Other Essays* (South Brunswick, NJ: A. S. Barnes, 1977), 84–85.

5. James Reston, Jr., *Sherman's March and Vietnam* (New York: Macmillan, 1984), 7.

6. Clare Boothe, "Introduction to *Kiss the Boys Good-Bye*," in Richard Harwell, editor, "*Gone with the Wind*" as Book and Film (Columbia: University of South Carolina Press, 1983), 90–97; Richard Harwell, editor, *Margaret Mitchell's "Gone with the Wind" Letters, 1936–1949* (New York: Macmillan, 1976), 233; Atlanta *Constitution*, Sept. 6, 1941.

7. "War Movie Scored by G.A.R. Veterans," New York *Times*, Sept. 1, 1939; Chadwick, *The Reel Civil War*, 188–98.

8. Brian Steel Wills, *Gone With the Glory: The Civil War in Cinema* (Lanham, MD: Rowman & Littlefield, 2007), 71, 111–12.

9. Cassidy, *Civil War Cinema*, 105–8.

10. Willard Welsh, "Civil War Theater: The War in Drama," *Civil War History* 2 (1955), 265; Gore Vidal, *Honor*, in A. S. Burack, editor, *Television Plays for Writers* (Boston: The Writer, 1957), 382, 390.

11. Gore Vidal, *On the March to the Sea*, in *Three Plays* (London: Heinemann, 1962), 87–88, 139, 140, 150.

12. Thomas Babe, *Rebel Women* (New York: Dramatists Play Service, 1977), 36, 48.

13. James Reston, Jr., *Sherman, the Peacemaker: A Play in Two Acts*, typescript (North Carolina Collection, University of North Carolina Library, Chapel Hill, revised September 1980), 63.

14. Randy Roberts and James S. Olson, *John Wayne, American* (New York: Free Press, 1995), 485–86, 492; Cassidy, *Civil War Cinema* 98–100, 150; Ray Kinnard, *The Blue and the Gray on the Silver Screen* (Secaucus, NJ: Birch Lane, 1996), 192–95; Allen Eyles, *John Wayne and the Movies* (South Brunswick, NJ: A. S. Barnes, 1976), 191–92.

15. Edwin Tribble, "'Marching Through Georgia,'" *Georgia Review* 21:4 (1967), 423–29; Charles Royster, *The Destructive War: William Tecumseh Sherman, Stonewall Jackson, and the Americans* (New York: Knopf, 1991), 364–65, 412; Lee B. Kennett, *Marching through Georgia: The Story of Soldiers and Civilians during Sherman's Campaign* (New York: Harper Perennial, 2001), 320; "Sherman's March to the Sea," Washington *Post*, Mar. 20, 1889; Henry Watterson, *"Marse Henry": An Autobiography*, 2 vols. (New York: Doran, 1919), 156; Marszalek, *Sherman*, 488; Kent A. Bowman, *Voice of Combat: A Century of Liberty and War Songs, 1765–1865* (Westport, CT: Greenwood Press, 1987), 136–37; Lewis, *Sherman*, 632–33; Randal W. Allred, "Marching through Georgia," in M. Paul Holsinger, editor, *War and American Popular Culture* (Westport, CT: Greenwood Press, 1999), 118; Henry Steele Commager, editor *The Blue and the Gray, Vol. 1* (Indianapolis, IN: Bobbs-Merrill, 1950), 581.

16. William Tecumseh Sherman, *Memoirs of General W. T. Sherman*, edited with an introduction by Michael Fellman (New York: Penguin, 2000), 638–40; Willard Heaps and Porter Heaps, *The Singing Sixties: The Spirit of Civil War Days down from the Music of the Times* (Norman: University of Oklahoma Press, 1960), 345; David Nevin, *Sherman's March* (Alexandria, VA: Time-Life Books, 1986), 157; Marszalek, *Sherman*, 326; S. H. M. Byers, *Twenty Years in Europe: A Consul-General's Memoirs of Noted People, with Letters from General W. T. Sherman* (Chicago: Rand, McNally, 1900).

17. Warren Michel Swenson, *Battle Pieces*, CD (Albany Records); *Michigan Today News*, February 2004, www.umich.edu/NewsE/02_04/music.html; Columbus (Ohio) *Dispatch*, March 29, 1993.

18. Edmund Wilson, *Patriotic Gore: Studies in the Literature of the American Civil War* (New York: Oxford University Press, 1962), 466, 479. Wilson may have appropriated the phrase "versified journalism" from Geoffrey Stone's *Melville* (New York: Sheed and Ward, 1949), 261. Stanton Garner, *The Civil War World of Herman Melville* (Lawrence: University Press of Kansas, 1993), 388–90; Melville, *The Battle-Pieces of Herman Melville*, 258–60. On the Miltonic interpretations of the war, see Daniel Aaron, *The Unwritten War: American Writers and the Civil War* (Madison: University of Wisconsin Press, 1987; orig. pub. 1973), 343–48.

19. Melville, *The Battle-Pieces of Herman Melville*, 120–24.

20. Ibid., 198–202; Aaron, *The Unwritten War*, 75–90.

21. Richard Watson Gilder, "Sherman," in Lois Hill, editor, *Poems and Songs of the Civil War* (New York: Gramercy Books, 1990), 95; Arthur John, *The Best Years of the Century: Richard Watson Gilder, Scribner's Monthly, and the "Century" Magazine, 1870–1909* (Urbana: University of Illinois Press, 1981), 126–27; William T. Sherman, "The Grand Strategy of the War of the Rebellion," *Century* 13 (February 1888), 582–98.

22. Henry Van Dyke, "The Statue of Sherman by St. Gaudens," *Music and Other Poems* (New York: Charles Scribner's Sons, 1904), 115.

CHAPTER SIX

◦━

In Sherman's Tracks

To realize what war is one should follow our tracks.

William Tecumseh Sherman[1]

Walking below a hill near the site of Sherman's camp at Shiloh on a cold December morning in 1865, the Boston journalist John Townsend Trowbridge came upon the makeshift graves of several Confederate soldiers killed in the April 1862 battle. "There many a poor fellow's bones lay scattered about, rooted up by swine," Trowbridge wrote. "I saw an old half-rotted shoe containing a skeleton foot. But the most hideous sight of all was a grinning skull pushed out of a hole in the ground, exposing the neck bone with a silk cravat still tied about it in a fashionable knot." In a few sentences, Trowbridge had cracked open the South's crypt. What had been lost in the war would not stay buried, but would be expelled from the tomb and picked clean by scavengers. The corpse was strangled by the silk cravat, symbol of the fallen gentry, and the skull sneered at the Northerner, as well as Sherman.[2]

Soon after the Civil War, many Northern writers like Trowbridge went to see the defeated South firsthand. Some had been war correspondents, while others were making their first visits to the former Confederacy. Their reports contributed to a body of travel literature about the South that predated the war. The South had always seemed a mysterious, exotic region to curious Northern readers, and this became even more true in the immediate aftermath of the conflict. Not surprisingly, the writers discovered abundant horrors and told gothic "tales from the crypt" worthy of Edgar Allan Poe. The

147

literary pillaging of the South's corpse also filled a need for information about the extent of the damages, the loyalty of former Confederates, the treatment of emancipated slaves, the reorganization of legislatures and financial institutions, and the prospects for safe travel, especially along the route of Sherman's March. None of these early journeys were without political consequence. At a time when the Radical Republicans were looking for evidence of treachery and intransigence in the South, stories of Southern depravity were welcome. Likewise, those who shared President Johnson's, and Sherman's, latitude toward the defeated rebels looked for evidence that the South was ruined, repentant, and reconciled to its defeat. As the Chicago *Tribune* put it, the most important question was the "temper and disposition of the Southern people."[3]

Ludicrous Impotence

One of the first Northern journalists to arrive was Whitelaw Reid, whose sensational, and partly erroneous, report about the Battle of Shiloh for the Cincinnati *Gazette* had helped make Sherman famous, although it had prompted the general to come to Grant's defense and had intensified his distrust of reporters. According to one account, Sherman later said he wished he had had Reid shot. They reconciled after the war in New York, where Reid was editor of the *Tribune*. Reid traveled to Atlanta by train from Knoxville in November of 1865 "over the track of the destroyer." South of Dalton, Georgia, "solitary chimneys and the debris of burnt buildings everywhere" told the story. Although he found that Atlanta was recovering faster than Richmond, "'Sherman, his mark,' was still written too plainly to be soon effaced, in gaping windows and roofless houses, heaps of ruins on the principal corners and traces of unsparing destruction everywhere." Moreover, Reid wrote, "traces of the bad passions and disregard of moral obligations which the war has taught, are written almost as plainly on the faces as are Sherman's marks on the houses of Atlanta." Property was not secure, and assaults on the back streets at night were so common that even a garroting drew little notice. He doubted that Southerners living in this kind of environment were thinking beyond survival, and would either cooperate or resist, depending on the needs of the moment.[4]

John Richard Dennett, a special assignment reporter for the *Nation*, arrived in Atlanta on Christmas 1865, shortly after Reid had left the city. Approaching Atlanta by train from Augusta, Dennett saw "burned buildings at the way stations, rails fantastically twisted and bent, and ruined locomotives—remembrances of Sherman and Johnston." The city was "a most cheerless and mean-looking place." Beside a stretch of track he saw "a heap of bones and skulls of animals, collected from battle-fields . . . and blackening in the wet weather." Elsewhere, a "great many rough-looking fellows hang about the numerous shops and the shanties among the ruins where liquor is sold, and a knot of them cluster at each street corner." Like Reid, Dennett saw recovery well underway as veterans and refugees streamed into the city looking for work. Atlanta was a city "full of goods; and though the number of traders seems inordinately great, new ones are pushing into business."[5]

Trowbridge, who contributed articles to the *Atlantic Monthly* and other publications, was asked by a publisher in the fall of 1865 to write a book based on a trip through the South. Well connected, and armed with letters of introduction, Trowbridge traveled for four months and produced a book of almost six hundred pages. Rich in anecdotes, interviews, and lyrical prose, his book, published in 1867, provided one of the most comprehensive impressions of the South while the wounds still were visible. He found North and Middle Georgia "ploughed with the furrows of poverty and ruin. Plantations were wasted, provisions taken, stock killed or driven away, buildings and farming implements destroyed. The people were left very poor." Railroads were mostly back in operation, and Trowbridge noted that those destroyed by Sherman "belonged to corporations which could best afford to rebuild them; and work upon them was going forward with considerable vigor."[6]

Along the route of the March, Trowbridge collected stories from former Confederate soldiers, farmers, and residents of small towns. He heard accounts of looting and thievery, hangings and burnings, mostly attributed to the bummers and to the stragglers who followed the army. Trowbridge tried to establish the magnitude of the March, emphasizing that it was not merely a raid, as some were calling it, but rather an invasion of armies "pursuing different routes, their caterpillar tracks sometimes crossing each other, braiding a belt of devastation. . . ." In the manner of Walt Whitman's war writing, Trowbridge piled up a series of imagined scenes that described armies in motion:

> bridges fired by the fugitives . . . the jubilant foraging parties sweeping the surrounding country of whatever was needful to support life and vigor in those immense crawling and bristling creatures, called army corps; the amazing quantity and variety of plunder collected. . . . the ripping up of railroads, the burning and plundering of plantations . . . such are the scenes of this most momentous expedition, which painters, historians, romancers, will in future ages labor to conceive and portray.[7]

Those future romancers, from Griffith and Mitchell to Doctorow (who appropriated the caterpillar imagery for *The March*) would have no difficulty imagining such scenes, or Trowbridge's dramatic account of "panic-stricken inhabitants" who "fled from their homes, carrying with them the most valuable of their possessions. . . . Mules, horses, cattle, sheep, hogs, were driven wildly across the country. . . . The mother caught up her infant; the father, mounting, took his terrified boy upon the back of his horse behind him. . . . not even the poultry, not even the dogs were forgotten" as property was left "to the mercies of the soldiers, whose waving banners and bright steel were already appearing on the distant hill-tops." Like Reid and Dennett, Trowbridge found Atlanta a shambles: "Everywhere were ruins and rubbish, mud and mortar and misery. The burnt streets were rapidly rebuilding; but in the mean while hundreds of the inhabitants, white and black, rendered homeless by the destruction of the city, were living in wretched hovels, which made the suburbs look like a fantastic encampment of gypsies or Indians." Atlanta was overrun with rats, and smallpox was evident among the blacks and poorer whites who had drifted into the city.[8]

Not all the writers who went to the South were Americans. Sir John Henry Kennaway, an English baronet, thought most of his countrymen had avoided the South before the war due to their disdain for slavery, and their abhorrence of heat, pestilence, and creaky railroads. After the war, however, Southern soil had become historical, the setting for "one of the grandest spectacles that the world had ever seen." He had seized, and perhaps embellished, an important truth, that the South's "dreams of a separate nationality have indeed been somewhat rudely broken, but in whatever else she may have failed, she, at least, has made herself a history." The passing comment "made . . . history" was prescient. Of course, the South always had a history, but now the South, like Ancient Greece, was "classic ground," a land where myths were made. Just how the New South would evolve, Kennaway said, was a subject of global interest. Kennaway apparently had no intention of visiting the South until he had "an unexpected interview" with Sherman in St. Louis. Sherman's portrait had only just been hung on the walls of the Royal Academy in London, and Kennaway was in awe of the gruff general who might "justly claim to have been a chief instrument" in ending the war, his "great march, sweeping like a tornado through the heart of the Confederacy, and leaving nothing but destruction and desolation in his rear."[9]

Arriving in Atlanta on November 3, 1865, slightly ahead of Reid, Kennaway found life and property "notoriously insecure," a place where "outrages are of frequent occurrence, notwithstanding that a military guard patrols the streets at night." A sullen Union colonel told Kennaway he considered "Southern people to be the laziest set upon earth, and wished that the North had given them another year of the war and driven them all into the sea." As he approached Savannah by train five days later, Kennaway saw everywhere "traces of ruin and destruction. . . . A wretched spectacle was presented by the remains of the bridge of the Savannah and Charleston Railway—an unmistakable piece of Sherman's handiwork. . . . cut in two places and the ends tilted down, in helpless, almost ludicrous impotence, into the river." Earlier, Kennaway had slighted Southern masculinity in a somewhat different fashion, in the context of Sherman's telling of the jokes Lincoln had made about the March, that the general "had been flirting with Augusta, embracing Columbia, and, now that he was making approaches to Charlotte, it was time that he should be giving some account of himself to Mrs. Sherman." Kennaway's book about his journey ultimately had little to do with Sherman. But, with marketing possibilities in mind, he or his publisher titled it *On Sherman's Track, or The South After the War.*[10]

Sergeant Bates's March

Just how these and other reports were received depended on where readers stood on the issues of the day. Reports of harsh conditions in the South convinced many people that Southerners would never repent, forgive their conquerors, or accept reunion. During a hot political discussion in Wisconsin in December 1867, a former Union artilleryman made a wager that the South would honor the flag of the United States. Sergeant Gilbert H. Bates had been challenged by a man who claimed Southerners so hated the flag that they would rip it to shreds and murder anyone who carried it. When Bates protested, pointing out that the flag flew in all the Southern states, his adversary argued that only military protection kept the banners aloft. Bates threw down a challenge to settle the dispute. He proposed to carry the flag unfurled across the South from Vicksburg to Washington, some 1,400 miles through six states, to prove the South's fidelity, if his opponent would give Bates's family one dollar for every day he was on the march. A contract was settled, and Bates had until July 4 to arrive in Washington in one piece. He agreed to walk the entire distance unarmed and carry the flag unfurled during the day. Like Sherman, he planned to live off the land, although not by stealing pigs and chickens, but rather by depending on the hospitality of people he met. He proposed to sell twenty-five-cent photos of himself for a widows and orphans' fund.

Walking long distances for publicity had been made popular by Edward Payson Weston, who had trekked from Boston to Washington in 1861. Weston had lost a bet on the 1860 presidential election, and to fulfill the terms of the wager, he had to attend Lincoln's inauguration. The walk was a made-to-order press event through a region thick with journalists, bringing national attention to so-called pedestrians. In 1867 Weston completed a 1,200-mile walk from Portland, Maine, to Chicago. No doubt Bates thought to follow Weston's example, but with a political objective. Bates arrived in Vicksburg on January 24, 1868, to an enthusiastic welcome. Some women in the city provided him with a flag and a velvet uniform. He was followed out of the city by a band, the mayor, and a long procession of officials and townspeople. The march quickly became a journalistic spectacle, with reports of Bates's progress telegraphed from towns along his route. Mark Twain got wind of it in Washington and sent a story to the Virginia City (Nevada) *Territorial Enterprise*, predicting that Bates would be thrashed by the former Rebels before he reached Washington.

> I expect to see him coming into Washington some day on one leg and with one eye out and an arm gone. He won't amount to more than an interesting relic by the time he gets here and then he will have to hire out for a sign for the Anatomical Museum. Those fellows down there have no sentiment in them. They won't buy his picture. They will be more likely to take his scalp.[11]

But they didn't. Instead he was usually greeted by large crowds and warmly received; given food, shelter, and whiskey; and serenaded and applauded. He passed safely through Jackson, Mississippi, and Montgomery, Alabama, although he knew the real test would come in Georgia and the Carolinas when he crossed Sherman's tracks. In Georgia, Bates's march could only conjure up the March to the Sea, and the idea of a Union soldier traipsing over even a portion of Sherman's route while carrying a flag had symbolic power. Sherman had gone where he wished, but at the head of a huge army. Bates was a solitary pilgrim. On March 5, the New York *Times* reported that Bates was somewhere in Georgia, but that little had been heard of him for two weeks since he had been welcomed in Columbus. The newspaper pointed out that Weston's walk had attracted more press coverage and wondered why telegraphed reports about Bates had been infrequent and meager in content. The *Times* praised the "deep moral purpose underlying the march," an attribute not shared by Weston's, and said that if those inclined to scoff at the feat would take up their own flags "they would render their country a better service than by staying at home and growling at the rebels." The *Times* did note that it had read accounts of Bates's journey in some Southern newspapers, but editors in the South may have been slow to pass the news on by telegraph, or failed to recognize its potential significance in the North. Despite the *Times*'s concern, Bates was receiving a gracious welcome across Georgia. As he later wrote:

The places in the South which, during the war, were most zealous in the rebel cause, were the larger towns and the cities. Newspapers, telegraphs, and railroads gave them greater facilities for obtaining information. Thus far, on my march, the large places had given me the most enthusiastic receptions. I believe the same sentiments of regard actuated the country people, but of course they had no facilities for making demonstrations.[12]

Bates did have some problems in Georgia. Near Milledgeville he was jumped by five "cur dogs . . . of a disagreeable size," and fended them off with his flagstaff in a fifteen-minute fracas. On March 11 he arrived in Augusta, where he learned that a group of toughs planned to attack him. But he escaped harm. These incidents were exceptions to the generally friendly reception in the state. By March 18 he was in Columbia, South Carolina, where, the *Times* reported, he was welcomed by hundreds, escorted to a hotel, and serenaded. On April 14, he entered Washington accompanied by crowds and a band. He was received by Johnson at the White House, but rebuffed by Radical Republicans at the Capitol when he tried to raise the flag over the dome. Bates had walked right into the teeth of the political controversy in Washington. For the president and his supporters, Bates's march had shown that the South was reconciled and in no need of harsh reconstruction. But for the Radicals who dominated Congress, and favored hard Reconstruction, Bates was an embarrassment. He had won the day, however. Four years later he made another good will walk, this time in Britain, and then settled in Saybrook, Illinois, where he died in 1917.[13]

Another kind of march across Georgia, both sociological and metaphoric, was made by an Atlanta University professor of history and economics, the essayist, novelist, and journalist W. E. B. Du Bois. Born in Massachusetts in 1868, Du Bois contributed articles to the Springfield *Republican* and the New York *Globe* before enrolling at Fisk University in Nashville, Tennessee, where he edited the *Fisk Herald*. After graduating in 1888 he continued his studies at Harvard, becoming the first black student to receive a doctorate. *The Souls of Black Folk*, a collection of thirteen essays, events reportage, and memoir pieces, and one brief work of fiction, appeared in 1903. "The problem of the twentieth century," Du Bois declared in the second essay, "is the problem of the color-line." Despite subsequent disclaimers and evasions, he insisted, "the question of Negro slavery was the real cause" of the Civil War. His travels through Georgia had revealed the true legacy of "that terribly picturesque march to the sea," with its thousands of untended, desperate black refugees trailing in its dust.

"Three characteristic things one might have seen in Sherman's raid through Georgia, which threw the new situation in shadowy relief: the Conqueror, the

Conquered, and the Negro," Du Bois wrote. "Some see all significance in the grim front of the destroyer, and some in the bitter sufferers of the Lost Cause. But to me neither soldier nor fugitive speaks with so deep a meaning as that dark human cloud that clung like remorse on the rear of those swift columns, swelling at times to half their size, almost engulfing and choking them," rolling onward into Savannah, "a starved and naked horde of tens of thousands." After enduring the failed promise of Emancipation and the coarse politics of Reconstruction, a million abandoned blacks had spread across the "crimson soil of Georgia," the state that had become, by the turn of the century, the very center and soul of the nation's "Negro problem." And at the heart of the tumult lay brash Atlanta, capital of the New South, a city and a culture segregated by the "Veil of Race." Du Bois, a leading figure in African American journalism and literature, would live on almost to the centennial of the Battle of Atlanta, dying in Ghana in 1963.[14]

The Strange Story of Father Tom Sherman

Sherman himself had visited Georgia in 1879, yet that visit did not cause nearly as much concern as did a "march" his son made in 1906. The general's visit had been almost blissful, according to a letter he wrote to a friend:

> If I were the devil incarnate, as many people thought me in 1865, I surely exposed myself to revenge or insult. I went to Chattanooga, Dalton, Rome, Cartersville, Atlanta, Macon, and Savannah, over which cities my army swept as a hurricane, and everywhere my coming was known . . . and the feelings of the people as manifested were respectful, not noisy—but in not a single instance was a word uttered, within my hearing, that was rude, impolitic, or offensive.[15]

The tragic story of Father Tom Sherman has fascinated biographers. Edmund Wilson, in his forty-five-page chapter on Sherman in *Patriotic Gore*, devotes fully ten pages to the son. Wilson sees in Father Sherman's story the ironic coda to the general's life. They were not opposites, but they were in opposition, the younger Sherman a religious rebel in the senior Sherman's war with himself. That a conflict had arisen between them was not unusual in many respects. The father, who had lost two sons during the war, had expectations and plans for Tom, who simply chose to follow his own star, as most sons do. The general had grudgingly accepted the reality of his wife's fervent Catholicism without joining the church himself. Nor had he very strenuously opposed their children's Catholic educations. This, too, was not exceptional. Colonel John Mosby, for example, was also married to a Catholic, and shared Sherman's aloofness toward the faith in family matters. In Sherman's case, however, Catholicism became more of an irritant in his relations with Ellen Sherman, and stresses in the marriage became entangled with religious tensions.[16]

The crisis came in 1878, at a time when Sherman was worried about his financial security and when Tom, who had graduated from both Yale and Washington University Law School in St. Louis, appeared well prepared for a legal career. Sherman saw his son as the eventual custodian and savior of the family finances. Sherman, of course, had witnessed his share of business failures and economic struggles. When Tom told his father he would enter a Jesuit seminary in Europe to become a Catholic priest, Sherman was devastated, blaming Tom and Ellen for deceiving him, although both had mentioned often enough the possibility of a clerical vocation. Ellen had hoped the news would lead to her husband's conversion, or at least soften his attitudes toward the church and religion. Wilson senses "something more than an accelerating Catholic fanaticism in her resolute and zealous devotion. She was perhaps trying to expiate a little the horrors and griefs of Georgia, and her son's dedication to the priesthood was perhaps the price paid by his father for the reckless elation of his March to the Sea."[17]

Sherman's response was not a surprise to the family, although his rage seemed out of bounds. Tom was made to feel he was a soldier who had deserted his post. Sherman even went so far as to seek an arbitrator in the decision, and he and Tom presented their cases to New York's John Cardinal McCloskey, with it apparently not occurring to Sherman that the cardinal might be inclined to side with Tom. During the crisis, Ellen lived in St. Louis with the family, while Sherman resided in Washington or traveled the country. Tom and his father were estranged for more than a year. In August 1880, Tom came home to reconcile with his father, and they did, although Sherman resented Tom's decision for the rest of his life, and never forgave the church for taking his son. His antipathy toward Catholicism had only increased.[18]

The root of the quarrel was less a difference of opinion about theology than an issue of authority—Sherman's as well as clerical authority. Sherman considered the Roman Catholic Church an outdated hierarchy and the Jesuits "an obsolete and worn out old order of priests. It has been abolished in about every Catholic country." His religion was really Americanism—not quite blind patriotism, not quite pure individualism, but rather a pragmatic belief in collective progress toward some kind of national, even cosmic, destiny. He wanted Tom to participate in the great, energetic American journey toward civilization, not to retreat into a ghostly monastic order better suited to the Middle Ages. If the key to Sherman's life was, as John F. Marszalek has claimed, a passion for order, Tom Sherman's life was a passion for a different sort of order. On the eve of his ordination in 1889, he wrote: "Order is heaven's first law and man's last, and to restore it in a few spots of earth takes greater exercise of divine power than to create a million worlds."[19]

The next phase of Father Sherman's life brought him national prominence. Wilson thinks it important that his fame should have begun just after his father's death. For in many ways Tom Sherman resembled his father. The young Jesuit was emerging as a powerful orator, as strong a champion of the faith as the general had been an apostle of union and American destiny. Father Sherman's biographer, Joseph T. Durkin, a Jesuit and professor of U.S. history at Georgetown University, claims that for some fifteen years after 1891, Tom Sherman was "with a handful of other priests, the Catholic doctrinal and apologetic voice in this country." Based at Catholic institutions in St. Louis and Chicago, Father Sherman lectured to thousands across the United States. "As he stood in the pulpit or on the lecture platform," according to Durkin, "he looked like nothing so much as a field commander addressing the troops. It was always noted that his spare, militarily erect figure of medium height, his snapping blue eyes, aggressive jaw, and decisive—almost impatient—gestures recalled his father's appearance." On some occasions he marched to the podium while a band played "Marching through Georgia," and he often appeared at gatherings of the Society of the Army of the Tennessee.[20]

At one of these meetings, in St. Louis in 1892, an incident occurred that foreshadowed problems to come. A granite shaft that was to be placed over General Sherman's tomb was being held hostage to a labor dispute. A stonecutter's strike had delayed completion of the monument, which sat in a company yard despite the Sherman family's insistence that it be delivered. Addressing the veterans, Father Sherman said, "I only know one way to get it, and that is to organize one of his old regiments and take it by force." The remark received a rousing response from the old soldiers, but Father Sherman followed it with a general attack against labor unions: "There is a power among us, then, higher and stronger than the power that you conquered, and our generation has yet to meet the problem of conquering, or in other words, of subduing to law that giant power." The rhetoric was ill-chosen and incendiary, revealing Father Sherman's dogmatic resistance to anything he considered socialism, and what may have seemed a casual acceptance of violence. Like his father, he was becoming a loose cannon. His father, after all, had warned against "embryo communists" during a strike in St. Louis in 1877. Also like his father, Father Sherman's sharp, colorful, concise language was often much more severe than his subsequent actions.[21]

On another occasion, a lecture in Chicago, Father Sherman had given a rousing speech defending the Jesuits against charges that the order opposed American liberty. Then he made the erroneous, provocative, and gratuitous claim that the order had originally been founded explicitly to fight Protestantism, adding insult to injury by affirming that the church still considered dissenters to be its enemies, and that to "condemn the Order of Jesus is not only to condemn progress and thought and culture and virtue, and all that is sweet and beautiful, but to condemn Jesus Christ Himself, with Whom and for Whom the Jesuit is crucified." Unfortunately for Father Sherman, the Chicago *Herald* had obtained a copy of the speech containing a passage he did not actually deliver. Denouncing former Catholics who had been presenting sensational accounts of convent life, Father Sherman had written "in vigorous protest against these wholesale venders of infamy the ex-priests and ex-nuns. The father who slays the corrupter of his child must be left to God Almighty, the man who shoots an anarchist at sight is a public benefactor. These ex-priests are anarchists of the worst stamp."[22]

When the offending passage about gunning down critics of Catholicism appeared in the newspaper's account of the speech, Father Sherman dissembled, explaining that he had mixed up some pages with another speech he intended to deliver, which he would probably modify. But the damage was done. Father Sherman now appeared to be a demagogue, and his quick tongue and erratic behavior troubled the Jesuits as much as his friends and family. His deepening animosity toward socialism, which he equated with Marxism and, eventually, communism, intensified. The position itself was not an unreasonable response to a controversial ideology, but the language he used to denounce it was toxic. "The American man who declares himself in favor of such Socialism is hell's lowest vomit," he declared. Speaking in Milwaukee, where socialists had a strong following, Father Sherman said, "Eight-tenths of all Socialists are atheists and therefore beasts. The system . . . they advance is . . . degrading . . . base, . . . [and] vile."[23]

In 1901, Father Sherman founded in Chicago an organization he called the Catholic Truth Society, which sponsored lectures and published pamphlets and tracts to defend the church against a variety of attacks. Operations of the society were entirely directed by Father Sherman, and the stresses of raising funds, public speaking, writing, and travel, in addition to serious tensions with his religious superiors, were beginning to take their toll. Then in 1906 Father Sherman was involved in what at first seemed a minor incident unrelated to missionary zeal, but which soon became a national sensation. The incident began innocently enough, when President Theodore Roosevelt gave a White House dinner in honor of the Sherman family on the occasion of the unveiling of a statue of the general in Washington. Father Sherman attended, dressed in a military uniform he acquired during his service as an army chaplain during the Spanish-American War. During the dinner it had been mentioned that a group of West Point cadets would ride on horseback over the route of Sherman's March to the Sea, and the president invited Father Sherman to join the group. Father Sherman and the cadets left Chattanooga a few months later, but by the time he arrived in Cartersville, Georgia, the journey, unbeknownst to the riders, had caused such a sensation that Roosevelt had ordered it stopped.[24]

Southern indignation had erupted when it was revealed that Father Sherman would be escorted by fewer than a dozen cavalrymen, who were to study the terrain of the March and prepare sketches and memoirs for the officers' school at their post. It was a double-barreled insult—that the March would be commemorated at all, and that the U.S. government implied some lingering Southern menace by providing Father Sherman with a military escort. The Atlanta Constitution ran a page-one story on Confederate veterans' outrage, quoting the president of the Confederate Veterans Association concerning "one of the most brutal marches ever made":

> There certainly is nothing to be proud of in Sherman's marching with a large army though a country undefended and then to report to his government that he had destroyed more than twice as much property as was necessary for support of his army. Sherman did this without just cause.
>
> Then again, the government can scarcely understand the temper of our people, since it is deemed necessary for the son of Sherman to have a guard as he advances through the country. Notwithstanding all that has been done, he would find himself as safe in this section as in any other section of the country.[25]

The Constitution quoted the acting mayor of Savannah as stating, "If it were left to me, I'd have him caught and hung before he reached Savannah." By recalling the military escort, Roosevelt took the federal government out of the argument. A few days later, a Constitution headline blared: "Father Sherman in Full Retreat." He was reported to be "deeply grieved at the revival of bitter feeling caused by his journey." In a separate item the same day, the Constitution snidely remarked, "Father Sherman should also have been accompanied by a military band to discourse 'Marching Through Georgia.'" The Constitution took exception to Northern newspapers that did not grasp the depth of offense. Quoting the Omaha Bee's criticism of "[n]arrow, violent and proscriptive intolerance," the Constitution changed direction slightly and declared that the offense was not in retracing the March, but in the implication of Sherman needing a military escort for protection while in the South, and in soldiers "junketing with a civilian . . . whether that civilian was the son of General Sherman or the son of nobody of note." The Atlanta paper cited the Jacksonville *Times-Union* as stating that there was no "'unreasonable excitement,' 'prejudiced outcry' or 'insane sensitiveness' over the foolish matter." A Georgia veteran was quoted in the New York *Herald* as saying, "I wish no one harm, but I would not regret at all if some one killed young Sherman should he attempt to march through Georgia."[26]

In the North, the Chicago *Daily Tribune* agreed that it was proper to abandon the march. Even though all physical traces of Sherman's March were gone, it said, "the march to the sea has left its indelible mark on the Georgia mind." It went so far as to conclude that if harmony was to be preserved "there must be no mention of Sherman's grand march to . . . the sea." The New York *Times* also believed Father Sherman was ill advised to have a cavalry escort as he retraced "one of the most harrowing memories of the war" for Southerners. The newspaper noted that Georgians in Washington were "much stirred up. . . . It has been a long time since so much bloody shirt waving has been done here." It cited a Georgia congressman's comments about the March to the Sea's "causeless vandalism" and absolute destruction. The cavalry escort, the *Times* said, was a "fool idea," and the whole thing a "tactless undertaking." The *Times* reported that Father Sherman attributed the failure of his proposed journey to "misinterpretation of his motives by the people of Georgia." The Jesuit was quoted as saying he had no idea of "affronting" the people of Georgia. It was a neat summation of the blunder, with one side seeing it as either a military study or a sort of historical review with soldiers along for mere classroom purposes, the other recalling outrages and terror, and seeing the soldiers as "bodyguards," an insult to Southern civility. The New York *Herald* wrote:

> So angered was Father Sherman at what he considered an insult by President Roosevelt that he took his baggage from the army wagon and had it moved into the home of his friend. . . . Father Sherman says he was an invited guest of the Federal Government. This invitation, he says, came unsought by him, was pressed upon him by one who is recognized as authorized to act for the Government in such matters,

namely, the president. It was not the first time a Sherman had crossed swords with a high government official.[27]

Confederate Veteran magazine illustrated the lingering resentment and even depth of misunderstanding and misinformation that followed the

March into the twentieth century. An article by William D. Pickett head-
lined "Why General Sherman's Name is Detested" ran in the wake of Father
Sherman's proposed march, accusing him of being "ignorant of the facts."
The article said the March "was truthfully characterized by the Nashville
American 'as such a record of burning, robbery, ravishing, and wanton destruction as finds no parallel in American history,' or it might be added, in
the history of modern warfare." Father Sherman, it noted, shared his father's
vanity in proposing such an indignity. Furthermore, the magazine criticized
the Northern press's surprise over the fuss, attributing it to being poorly informed:

> Surely they must have forgotten the records of the past; surely they must be ig-
> norant of the detestation that the name of W.T. Sherman conjures up to-day
> not only in Georgia and the Carolinas but throughout the South. . . . [The
> writer] has yet to find one among the women and noncombatants who has spo-
> ken a kind word of him. . . . His rough side, however, was almost invariably
> shown to women, and if irritated his manner bordered on the brutal.[28]

Pickett claimed the ill feelings demonstrated toward Father Sherman's
march were justified because his father had violated the rules of civilized warfare with his army of "one-hundred thousand men." Sherman's bummers
came in for special condemnation. The author said they "degenerated into a
band of robbers and plunderers whose acts of cruelty and outrage have made
infamous the name of 'Sherman.'" He even charged that "it is not believed
this famous march of Sherman to Savannah and thence to the seacoast in
North Carolina had a particle of effect on the termination of the war." He
tossed in a mention of Sherman's responsibility for burning Columbia, too.
The brew of resentment and disinformation was spiced with the resurrection
of the mythology of slaves having "kindly feelings" toward masters, and the
benign nature of slavery itself. Pickett was far from alone in his insistence on
the virtue of the Old South, and the vice of its conquerors.[29]

Pickett was writing at a time when the Lost Cause myth was undergoing
some adjustments. The myth had arisen shortly after the war with the publication of the journalist Edward Pollard's history of the Confederacy. The
myth evolved through the late nineteenth and early twentieth centuries,
however, and modern historians have pointed out its complexity through
these years. About the time of Father Sherman's march, according to David
W. Blight, the Lost Cause had two essential currents—reconciliation, on
Southern terms, and outright Southern partisanship. Both the United Confederate Veterans, which published *Confederate Veteran*, and the United
Daughters of the Confederacy, under the leadership of Mildred Rutherford,

co-opted the Lost Cause, and asserted authority in matters ranging from monuments and textbooks to white supremacy. An emerging group of "professional" historians countered some of the claims of the Lost Cause advocates, as did Mosby, the fabled "Gray Ghost" of the Confederacy. "That the Mildred Rutherfords prevailed in Southern memory over the John Mosbys demonstrates how and why the Lost Cause left such an enduring burden in national memory," according to Blight. While Father Sherman's march may have been conceived as a symbol of reconciliation, the turmoil among the mythmakers transformed the incident into a controversy. It was given a significance it probably didn't deserve, demonstrating that the nation remained uneasy about the Civil War even as it was looking outward after the Spanish-American War. Even thirteen years later Father Sherman's march was not forgotten. In 1919, an embittered former plantation owner in central Georgia told a passing journalist: "A year or so back Sherman's son said he was going to make a tour along the way his daddy had gone—to see what a wonderful thing his daddy had done. Lucky for him he changed his mind. We'd 'a' strung him to a pole, sure."[30]

Father Sherman's troubles continued after the aborted march. His erratic behavior became more pronounced, and his general health began to deteriorate. After a period of rest, and an apparent recovery, he had what was called a mental breakdown in 1911. The Atlanta *Constitution* reported that after threatening to shoot himself at the Jesuit Novitiate in Los Gatos, California, Father Sherman was now an "inmate" at the state hospital for the insane. Recalling the march in 1906, the newspaper, incredibly, told its readers that Father Sherman had "planned to lead an army of United States troops through the southern states, following the route his father took on his famous march to the sea." A contingent of fewer than a dozen soldiers on a ceremonial training junket had now become an "army" lead by a lunatic. Credulous Georgians, brandishing copies of the *Constitution*, had confirmation of what they may have long suspected, and perhaps needed to believe. If the son was insane, why not the father, too? The story could be twisted any way the interpreter desired. Either Father Sherman had tried to invade the South, or, filled with remorse for his father's crimes against the Confederacy, the son had joined a controversial religious order and gone insane.[31]

Father Sherman never really recovered. He resided for a time at sanatoria near Baltimore, Boston, and Buffalo, and then was in and out of Jesuit facilities and private accommodations for many years. He attempted to resign from the order, and believed he had, but his superiors would not release him in his mental condition. Paranoid and delusional, and sometimes violent, he nevertheless continued to travel in Europe and the United States, finally settling in

Santa Barbara, California, in the 1920s. At the end of his life he was cared for by the Jesuits and nuns at a sanatorium in Louisiana, where he died in 1933.[32]

"Up out of the Pit"

With the coming of the twentieth century, there was a feeling of increasing confidence in many cities of the South, especially Atlanta. Founded as a railroad junction in 1837, the future city was originally simply called Terminus. The name was changed to Atlanta to promote the city as a gateway from the Southern interior to the sea, which it literally became during Sherman's March. In 1895, Atlanta had staged the Cotton States and International Exposition, which was attended by more than three-quarters of a million people. Atlanta could also boast the South's first skyscraper. Newspapers were boosters for progress, and the new century gave them cause to proclaim the maturation of the New South and hail the coming of modernity, which would boost the community along with circulation and advertising revenue. For modern Atlanta, which saw itself in the image of the phoenix, Sherman could be summoned from the fires of history (and hell) to reprise his journey in awe and wonder at the achievements of the city and state he had wounded so grievously. In an editorial published on March 4, 1906, the Atlanta *Constitution* gushed:

> If it were possible for the disembodied spirit of William Tecumseh Sherman to trail again the path followed by his army of desolation, his second journey through the south would be one of surprises and encounters even more dramatic than those which marked his progress as a hostile invader. His broad wake, once blackened by fire and heaped with wreckage, is now obliterated by fruitful and smiling farms; where once the smoke of his cannon obscured the sun, there rises now the smoke of many factories; railroads criss-cross in the bewildering traffic of a new country, villages and towns have sprung up on the sites of his campfires and battle fields; everywhere the genius of development, of wealth, of aggression replaces the almost wholly agricultural civilization of that former era.
>
> The spirit of Sherman, on this imaginary invasion, would reach the climax of the metamorphosis on the arrival in Atlanta. His devastating host left a conglomeration of ruins and about 400 riddled dwellings and churches on the site of the city. Standing on the Whitehall street viaduct today, he would be unable to recognize the district his army swept with flame and grapeshot.
>
> Tall skyscrapers occupy the location of hospitals and whilom barracks; department stores of majestic mien tower high where once stood ancient warehouses, "general stores" or rambling commissariats; palatial hotels rise in place

of hostelries more famed for their hospitality than their appointments; an army of clerks has supplanted the corps in trim blue and ragged gray; a horde of shoppers and bustling captains of enterprise throng the spaces where once strode the patrols; mansions and dwelling houses have routed the forests and the red gashed gullies; the hum of industry sounds instead of the whine of the minie ball, and the smoke of a thousand factories ascends in welcome contrast to the deadly black pall over the smoldering ruins of an embryo city.[33]

This editorial made the burning of Atlanta sound like a desirable urban renewal project. The more desolation and destruction by Sherman, then the farther the South had come, and the greater its ultimate triumph. The destruction became the genesis of its rebirth. The bluster and bloviation, however, left things out, such as racial tensions, which erupted in a September race riot, and the retrograde bitterness left by the war. The editorial appeared only a few months before the uproar surrounding Father Tom Sherman's proposed march. It was one thing to conjure Sherman's ghost for civic purposes, quite another for his son actually to show up with an "army." While Father Sherman's proposed trek via horse and wagon reignited lingering resentments, however, the real invader had already arrived and made inroads, literally and figuratively, into the South, both the real and the remembered one. The automobile came to embody the democratization of modernity and industrialism. As geographic distance diminished, so did cultural distinctions. The North would come south again. For the Agrarian writer Lytle, no lover of Sherman, the paved highways were the problem, not the solution. In his essay in the Agrarian manifesto *I'll Take My Stand*, Lytle argued that road building benefited corporate interests at the expense of the small farmer, destroying the South's provincialism—"which prefers religion to science, handicrafts to technology, the inertia of the fields to the acceleration of industry, and leisure to nervous prostration." Sell the farmer an automobile, Lytle reasoned tendentiously, and you lure him away from the land and into the hands of charlatans who pick his pocket and destroy his homespun purity.[34]

In the first decade of the twentieth century, automobile travel was becoming a feature of American life. At first, automobiles were only for the rich and adventurous, but gradually mass production began to make vehicles affordable for working-class Americans, many of whom were enjoying prosperity and more leisure time. Motorists in the populous Northeast and Midwest cautiously ventured south to take advantage of the warmer climate and abundant natural beauty. Automobiles required roads, however, and the South lagged the rest of the nation in providing them. The inaccessibility of much of the South perpetuated its sense of romantic isolation, and there was resistance to road building.

The most popular route south initially was the National Highway running between New York and Atlanta by way of Philadelphia; Staunton, Virginia; Winston-Salem, North Carolina; and Spartanburg, South Carolina. The National Highway, which opened in 1908, was linked to other, less accessible highways. In 1908, R. H. "Pathfinder" Johnson, the advertising director of a Cleveland motorcar firm, made two journeys from North to South on the National Highway, and one along a more western route, as part of a promotional stunt to sell vehicles. Each journey included stretches of back road between Atlanta and Savannah. The next fall, some forty vehicles participated in a race from New York to Atlanta jointly sponsored by the Atlanta *Journal* and the New York *Herald*. When the vehicles rolled down Peachtree Street in Atlanta, the attendant publicity generated by newspaper boosterism demonstrated that the South had been breached by modernity just as surely as it had been breached by Sherman on his March to the Sea. Then, in 1911, Boston millionaire Charles Slidden led an expedition on the National Highway from New York to Atlanta, and then on to Jacksonville, Florida, accompanied by Georgia Governor Hoke Smith. The political endorsement encouraged further projects. In 1914 Miami real-estate baron Carl Fisher began promoting a new north-south highway that would speed midwesterners to his tropical paradise. One of his colleagues, William S. Gilbreath, went to Atlanta to sell the idea at the American Road Congress, and gained the support of another Georgia governor, John M. Slaton. Squabbling about the proposed route of the new highway immediately ensued, and the new "Dixie Highway" eventually became two main routes, both of them passing through Georgia. Work continued on the highway through the 1920s, eventually involving networks of roads in more than fifty counties in ten states.[35]

New South business interests were eager to promote commercial activity, tourism, and property development, not refight the Civil War, and that called for road building, not monuments. As early as 1903, residents in North Georgia had pushed for extending the road that ran through the Chickamauga military park, just south of Chattanooga, to Atlanta, "over territory as famous as that of Marengo or Waterloo." In 1911 five counties joined together to form a Battle Field Route Association, to promote the road and attract federal funds. At the heart of the matter was the supposition that the "Johnston-Sherman Highway" would be good for business. Said the Atlanta *Constitution*: "The advantages to be gained by increased automobile touring has [sic] become apparent to the people, and the prejudice that once was entertained against the luxurious machine is fast disappearing." Proposals were made to extend the road, and others, all the way to the coast, with the possibility of hundreds of thousands of tourists gawking at the scenery along the way. The old roads were wretched and precarious, but increasing numbers of automobiles were rumbling and clattering through territory once swept by Sherman's mighty army.[36]

All this road building brought the kind of excitement and anticipation that any new communications system creates. An Eatonton, Georgia, woman who had witnessed the March wrote a letter to the *Constitution* in which she celebrated the

> vision of a great highway made by war, consecrated by peace! A highway made by the very wheeltracks of Sherman's cannon, rolled and leveled by the grim engines of death and tramped to smoothness by 100,000 men, armed to kill and destroy, over which should travel a reunited nation. An army of brothers, marching to a common goal, construction not destruction.

The image was alluring if wildly inaccurate, Sherman and his inflated army as road builders crunching through Georgia in anticipation of a highway building program that would serve as a peace memorial half a century later.[37]

There would not be much history to see along the route, however, the detritus left by the army having all but disappeared with the passage of time. And yet the changes that were coming inevitably revived traditions that had been exacerbated in the wake of Sherman's March. The revival of the Ku Klux Klan at Stone Mountain near Atlanta in 1915 was just one of them. In the fall of 1919, Stephen Graham, a young British journalist who had fought in the First World War and traveled widely in Russia, set out from Atlanta to follow, mostly on foot, the route of Sherman's March. He had found Atlanta a prosperous city profiting from the cotton trade and filled with automobiles and skyscrapers. Leaving the city by way of the tawdry districts along a road of "bag-shops, gaudy cinema and vaudeville sheds, fruit-stalls, and booths of quack doctors and magic healers, venders of the devil's corn cure, [and] fortune-tellers," he passed into rural country, "on the lookout for the oldest folk along the way" who could tell him about the March. To the middle aged, he discovered, the Civil War was "somewhat of a joke, but the only thing the old folk will never laugh over is the great strife." Many had "pet stories" that seemed implausible, however. An old man told him how he and some boys had hidden behind a church and fired shotguns at Sherman as he rode by, narrowly missing him. The war was passing from memory into myth. The rural roads were in disrepair, yet he saw many cars as well as wagons, and was offered rides, although "people were a little dumfounded when I said I was following in Sherman's footsteps. . . . They said they knew nothing about it themselves, and then took me to the old folk who remembered. The old folk quavered forth, 'It's a long, long time ago now.'"[38]

What troubled Graham most about Georgia was the plight of the blacks, who were living in squalor, while whites of all classes incessantly condemned them for the conditions in which they lived. The North, many said, may have been right to end slavery, but had abandoned the blacks, as Sherman had on the March, to a condition of helplessness and peonage worse, Graham thought, than what he had seen in Russia. "Rural Georgia is not very much better off to-day than it was in slavery days," Graham wrote. Raw racism was evident everywhere, and blacks were being brutalized by mobs even in the districts through which he was walking. When he arrived at the sea he saw a stark contrast, passing first through the bawdy districts "luring colored youth to lowest pleasures, then to the grandeur and spaciousness of modern Savannah and the white man's civilization, up out of Georgia, up out of the pit, through the veil of the forest and of nature to the serene heights of world civilization."[39]

Graham had marched to the sea in Sherman's tracks, and he wrote a two-part account of his adventure for *Harper's Monthly* magazine. While sitting on a wayside stone along a disused rural road during his journey, he had the feeling "that Sherman's army has marched past me. It has gone over the hill and out of view. . . . It has gone on and on till it begins marching into the earth itself. For all that are left of Sherman's warriors are stepping inward into the quietness of earth to-day." Graham had followed Sherman at a time when modernity, symbolized by the automobile, was reawakening and reimagining the memory of the Old South in films like *The Birth of a Nation*. The roads along the coast had changed, too, as he observed "heavy touring-cars roll past on the way to Miami and Palm Beach." As the South became accessible to motorists passing through, the contrasts Graham had observed became more evident. Southerners might resist, striking out at blacks and outsiders in an attempt to delay feared changes, but they also increasingly profited from changes they often professed to deplore. Sherman's warriors might have marched into the earth, but Shermanism, the cannon blast of modernity decried by the Agrarians in the next decade, was marching on, and it was soon to be marching on paved highways. The Agrarians set themselves very purposefully against the current of the larger American culture. But their disdain for the road, whether asphalt or metaphor, also put them at odds with the inevitable. Americans build roads, whether into frontiers or to connect the disconnected. Lytle understood that roads invited—demanded—acceleration. And something would be left behind.[40]

White Columns and War Tours

The modernism that Sherman, industrialism, automobiles, and road building represented, newspaper boosterism extolled, and Lytle and the Agrarians decried was also seen as a victory for American initiative after the First World War. The Georgia-born journalist Edward Lowry had seen devastated cities in France and Belgium struggling to recover, and he concluded, in an article written for the *Saturday Evening Post*, that if Atlanta and the South could re- cover, so could the ruined cities along the Western Front, and without a handout from the Americans. "All this discussion of reconstruction problems is old stuff to me," he wrote after a visit to Atlanta. "I was raised on such talk. I have heard it ever since I can remember. I was born in Georgia eleven years after Lee's surrender. My people were in the path of Sherman's march to the sea." After the war, he claimed, people just got to work and rebuilt the South without much outside assistance, and prosperous Atlanta, "serene and un- troubled," and free of "reds," was in particular an example of what could be done. "A dear lady in Atlanta summed it all up for me," he wrote. "I asked her what she had left when Sherman had finished with Atlanta and gone on toward the sea. 'Nothing,' she replied 'but refinement and poverty.'" More- over, the South's devastation was greater than Europe's, more widespread ge- ographically, and more economically as well as culturally ruinous because of the racial situation. Sherman's March, then, was to be a parable for the twen- tieth-century wars of destruction. An army might do its worst in a place like Georgia or Flanders, or, later, in Germany, Japan, and Russia, but "total war" could never destroy the human spirit, American version. The task at hand was not to restore the ruined lands of Europe with American money, al- though some would be offered, but for Europe to follow Atlanta's example, get to work, and bust the buttons of civic pride in the best American way.[41]

Things may not have been as rosy at home as Lowry imagined, however. Further changes in central Georgia came with the collapse of the cotton crop during the 1920s, after the arrival of the boll weevil, followed by the Great Depression in the next decade. Entire communities disappeared as small farmers left for factory jobs in the North, and the dominant crop became corn. When geographer D. J. de Laubenfels followed the route of Sherman's March between Covington and Milledgeville in 1955, he found fewer rural residents but larger farms, with more pastures for cattle herds. The small ten- ant farms had practically vanished as land was consolidated into larger parcels, with the absence of labor encouraging further mechanization. Cov- ington, some thirty-five miles from Atlanta, was becoming a commuter sub- urb, as the automobile contributed to the sprawl of the city. Roads were still "axle-breakers" until the Second World War and the early postwar years, when road improvements became a greater priority. He also found antebel- lum homes, although dry rot was becoming more of a problem than Sher- man's firebugs had been.[42]

In 1922, Medora Field Perkerson, the assistant editor of the *Atlanta Journal Magazine*, helped Margaret Mitchell get a job as a cub reporter on the publication, which her husband, Angus, edited. Her long friendship with Mitchell continued until the author of *Gone with the Wind* was struck and killed by an automobile on Peachtree Street in 1949. Mitchell, who had done so much to create the popular image of the Old South, was herself a phenomenon of modernism, and the manner and place of her death were highly ironic. She had grown up on Peachtree Street and given the world enduring images of Georgia plantation mansions and of Sherman, who supposedly had swept them all away. The thoroughfare took on an almost mystical quality in the memory of the March. A few years after Mitchell's death, Perkerson set out to find the remaining antebellum mansions during a "happy pilgrimage" across Georgia. Although there were no plantations to be found on Peachtree Street, she wrote, "there are many roads branching off Peachtree that lead to other roads, and they, in turn, to others that lead eventually to . . . tall white columns [that] shine like a tourist's dream come true." She drove from Atlanta to Savannah along this ethereal web of Peachtree Street extensions, following the general route of the March, consulting old journals and military memoirs, and visiting homes where Sherman and his soldiers had tarried. Behind every standing antebellum home there seemed to be a fanciful story of why it was spared. The fact that she found so many old houses still standing refuted the myth that Sherman had burned most of them down. Why, then, she wondered, do Southerners remember the war? "I realized that the answer is simple," she wrote in her travelogue, *White Columns in Georgia*. "Invaded countries always remember."[43]

But what do they remember? A half century after Perkerson wrote *White Columns*, builders were outfitting new homes in the Atlanta suburbs, and throughout the South, with decorative white columns made not only of wood but of plastics, which are more durable and often less expensive. Builders had discovered that manufactured columns sell houses, creating the look of instant history. Homeowners could affordably live in Scarlett O'Hara's Tara in the suburbs, without the need for a plantation or field hands. The Old South was meeting the New South in the vicarious enjoyment of the past, without the necessity for actually knowing anything about it. This was an especially attractive option for newcomers to the South who might want to feel a bit Southern without getting too deeply into aspects of the culture that they might not understand or approve of. Those who preferred a sanitized history might look to the example of Riverside, Georgia, a "town" in the Atlanta area created in 1998 by a Miami urban planner and architect. Riverside was basically a gigantic apartment, office, and shopping complex in the New Urbanism style. The site's promoters invented a history for Riverside, complete with a fictional town father, faux historic buildings and nineteenth-century sepia photographs, a secret Civil War arsenal used by the Confederates during the Battle of Peachtree Creek, and even a rebuilding period during Reconstruction, the town presumably having been sacked by Sherman. The advertising campaign drew heavily on Ken Burns's documentary style, and on a fanciful narrative written by a fictional historian for the corporate owner. "We'd love for that history to be true. But we didn't have that history here, so we're creating our own," said the company's chairman. A real history professor from Emory University called the project "another example of the trivialization of the attempt to understand our past. When you make up history, you don't have to deal with the real thing." But in a sense, the "real thing" had already been manufactured by everyone from Sherman to Ken Burns.[44]

More recent travelers who wanted to follow the route of the March could rely on a number of guidebooks. Travelers more interested in terrain than military tactics could just pass through the countryside, scan a few historical markers, and enjoy the scenery along the state's "Blue and Gray Trail" with the blessing of Georgia tourism officials. Sue C. and William H. Bailey wrote *Cycling through Georgia: Tracing Sherman's March from Chickamauga to Savannah* as a guide for those who wanted to trace "probably the most familiar event in the state's history" while finding opportunities for "fun, adventure, and learning which transcend its Civil War theme." Union soldiers and bummers on the March may have found fun and adventure as well, even without bicycles. More history-minded travelers could consult Jim Miles's *To the Sea: A History and Tour Guide of the War in the West, Sherman's March across Georgia and through the Carolinas, 1864–1865.* Miles noted that while it is now easy to drive from Atlanta to Savannah, the tour requires leaving the interstates to travel through "small-town, pickup-truck country, where church and family are still the centers of life. A region of farmers and factories, it is a land where people nod or wave at those who pass them on the roadway; it is an America that is vanishing. Its passing should be mourned." The idyllic picture contrasts sharply with the squalor and murderous racism Graham had observed in 1919. Miles wisely warned travelers to stay off private property and not bother residents of private homes because there were "too many vandals and arsonists around to be tolerant toward uninvited visitors." Not much had changed since Sherman's March.[45]

Sherman's March and Vietnam

Other kinds of travel connected Sherman's March to more recent history. In the early 1980s, the United States had neither fully comprehended nor come to terms with the Vietnam War. Perhaps it never will; but at the time the memory of the war was still very raw, and boldly contested. A decade had passed since the Paris peace accords, American withdrawal, and the fall of Saigon. Journalists, politicians, scholars, and soldiers engaged in rancorous debate about the causes, conduct, and meaning of the war. The debate often was electric with words and concepts most Americans found problematic, even shocking—defeat, amnesty, atrocity, massacre, atonement, disloyalty, treason, genocide, political assassination. Into this debate came novelist and journalist James Reston, Jr., who had served in Army intelligence during the Vietnam War, after graduating from the University of North Carolina and working briefly as a reporter for the Chicago *Daily News*. By the 1980s he was widely published in leading magazines and had written several books.

Like many who had served, Reston was ambivalent, acknowledging that his "fascination for the war was at least as strong as my abhorrence of it." Although he did not serve in a combat role, he admitted he "would have been a willing participant. It would not have taken much to brutalize me." If it hadn't brutalized him, however, Reston believed the war had physically and morally maimed a generation of young Americans caught up in the conflict. "The war," he wrote, "made the whole nation howl, as surely as Sherman had done it to Georgia and South Carolina." Furthermore, the nation was unable to "bind up the nation's wounds" after Vietnam as Lincoln had intended after the Civil War.[46]

Amidst all the talk about American defeat in Vietnam, many Southerners were quick to point out the irony of the claim that defeat was somehow unprecedented in American history. Not only had the South been defeated in the Civil War, but, in the minds of many Southerners, the South had been morally vindicated by the alleged barbarism of Sherman's March. Reston claimed to see a parallel between Sherman's March and the "total war" mentality that inevitably had lead to terror tactics in Vietnam, although he knew the South's mythic Sherman—"a cardboard figure of our history," the barbarian who raped, plundered, and burned his way across the prostrated Confederacy—was largely an invention of the popular culture. Rather, he suggested, Sherman's legacy was "not so much his practice of 'total war' as his intellectual justification for it, his lack of remorse at it, his readiness to distort the record for psychological advantage. By denying any ethical gradations of warfare, he had moved the argument into the abyss." If war was "synonymous with hell, what point is there in standards of civilized behavior?" Reston asked. "Ethics in hell? The very notion is absurd. It is the philosophy of Sherman, and his selective outrage. . . . that leads conceptually straight to Dresden, Hiroshima, and Vietnam." In other words, Sherman unleashed the metaphor and made it bite. Start by burning a few plantations and swiping some chickens and silver spoons in Georgia, and then get philosophical about it, and pretty soon you're dropping atomic bombs and despoiling Vietnam with Agent Orange.[47]

Reston was not unique in connecting Sherman to Vietnam. The journalist Michael Herr, for example, in his famous book of war reportage, *Dispatches*, had also questioned the ways and means by which the American military sought to achieve its goals in Vietnam. "It was axiomatic that it was about ideological space, we were there to bring them choice, bringing it to them like Sherman bringing the Jubilee through Georgia, clean through it, wall to wall with pacified indigenous and scorched earth," he had written. Reston elaborated on Herr's "ideological space," beginning his journey at West Point to find out what Sherman had learned about ethical warfare as a cadet, as well as what military historians and ethicists had to say about the conduct of warfare after Vietnam. He then followed Sherman from Tunnel Hill, Georgia, to Savannah, and then north to Columbia, South Carolina, meeting historians, relic collectors, reenactors, teachers, students, guides, docents, shopkeepers, historical novelists, ministers, and Vietnam veterans; collecting anecdotes; breezily quoting from Sherman's *Memoirs* and other sources; and finally arriving at Bennett Place, where he thought Sherman had attempted to do what the Vietnam-era leaders had failed to accomplish: create a true peace based on magnanimity as a form of atonement.[48]

As a work of impressionistic journalism rather than history, Reston's *Sherman's March and Vietnam*, published in 1984, probably achieved its purpose, raising important, speculative questions during a troubling era about the conduct of war and the construction, and limitations, of historical memory. Not the least of these questions was how Southerners could censure Sherman for what he did in Georgia and South Carolina but condone what General William Westmoreland, a South Carolinian, did in Vietnam. But the historical debate about the origins and consequences of total war is well advanced, and too complex for drive-by narrative reporting. Reston discovered very little along the route of the March that he could not have found in a library. Even in Atlanta, he encountered more indifference to Sherman than interest. The city had long since moved on. "Amid the knarl of expressways, the glass towers, the overhead tramways, the three battlefields within the city limits are hard to find and hard to remember." The second part of the book, a polemical moral critique of the Vietnam War and its political legacy, while often eloquent, had little to do with the first part in which he followed Sherman's path. Reviewing the book in the New York *Times*, Civil War historian Stephen W. Sears thought that Reston had stretched his analogy too far, and that the precedent for excesses in Vietnam "is better found in past American responses to unconventional warfare, such as Indian hit-and-run raids, guerrilla bushwhacking or Japanese suicide tactics."[49]

The Deepest Wound

Writer Jerry Ellis viewed Sherman's March as the "the path of the South's deepest wound." By finding the scar left by the wound, he hoped to understand the modern South and come to terms with some unresolved issues, particularly racism. The result was *Marching through Georgia: My Walk with Sherman*. Previous hikes along the Cherokee Trail of Tears and the Pony Express Trail had provided source material for books, and in 1993 Ellis was looking for another walking adventure. The recent death of his father had prompted Ellis to reflect on family history. He conceived of the journey as a pilgrimage to honor his father's memory and to reassess his own Southern roots, complicated by the fact that his ancestors fought on both sides in the Civil War.[50]

Ellis took the literary and historical aspects of his journey rather lightly. He packed a copy of Major Henry Hitchcock's diary in his backpack and thought, "It'll be a hoot to compare and contrast what Hitchcock found in 1864 and what I find in 1993." He did not attempt to explain the grand military or political strategies in any detail. Instead, Ellis told the story primarily through his interaction with characters he met along the way. This strategy worked well enough when he encountered people who recounted plausible family legends bearing on the March itself, but too often Ellis became intrigued by eccentric and possibly demented drifters who spun tales that had nothing to do with the Civil War or much of anything else. He also had a tendency to generalize about the contemporary South based on conversations with young people who sometimes seemed to be putting him on. Ellis conflated his identity as a Southerner with what he saw as a broad-based cultural identity among those who lived in the region. We never know what South was included in his musings, which were deeply rooted in his own childhood experiences. He fell into stereotypes that would have been questionable even prior to 1960, when the South was more or less still a homogeneous region, merely concluding "the New South is a complex can of worms, crawling with a wide range of thoughts and feelings."[51]

As Ellis negotiated his three-hundred-mile walk across Georgia, his main problem was surviving the intense heat. Unlike Sherman, who began his journey in November, Ellis followed the route during the summer, thus compromising the historical narrative. He did find residual signs of the March, however. People told stories of their ancestors hiding possessions (and sometimes babies) from Sherman's soldiers. He discovered the foundations of burned buildings and bridges, visited rooms where Sherman supposedly slept, located battlefields, and handled the debris of a plundering army. The March seemed to have less to do with history than with the gathering and preservation of holy relics: "I see such fascination with Sherman everywhere I turn that it reminds me of how alleged pieces of Christ's cross and shawl were once sold like hotcakes to anyone desperate to get near immortality." The implication was that this was metaphorically a counterfeit faith built around bullet-and-button collections and folklore.[52]

In 1993, *Wall Street Journal* reporter Daniel Pearl was also in Georgia to write about Sherman's reputation in the South. He found that while Sherman remained "about as popular as Lucifer," his image might be starting to change. Pearl's interviews with Marszalek and Charles Edmund Vetter offered a more balanced view, and Marszalek noted that Sherman was still blamed for burnings that took place beyond the path of the March. Sherman's reputation as a terrorist seemed secure, however, as Pearl met Southerners who called Sherman a barbarian, a hooligan, and a war criminal. Pearl encountered real terrorists when he was kidnapped and murdered in Pakistan in 2002.[53]

Tony Horwitz, a former reporter for the *Wall Street Journal* and winner of the Pulitzer Prize for national reporting, wrote one of the most successful books about Southern memory, *Confederates in the Attic: Dispatches from the Unfinished Civil War*, published in 1998. Horwitz began his odyssey through the South after he returned from a decade abroad as a foreign correspondent in the Balkans, Iraq, and Northern Ireland. Meanwhile, millions of Americans had developed an interest in the Civil War after seeing popular films such as *Glory* and *Gettysburg*, or watching Ken Burns's documentary, *The Civil War*. The latter devoted about fifteen minutes to the March, dwelling heavily in narration and pictures on the destruction of property. It left the impression of absolute desolation in the general's wake, a perspective highly congruent with conventional wisdom about the March. Horwitz found such public interest out of character for an America otherwise afflicted with historical amnesia. He also saw "a hardening ideological edge to Confederate remembrance." In Atlanta, he discovered "the anti-South: a crass, brash city built in the image of the Chamber of Commerce and overrun by carpetbaggers, corporate climbers and conventioneers," all lacking historical consciousness. But in nearby Jonesboro, site of the mythical Tara, Horwitz found a hoop-skirt, *Gone with the Wind* tourism industry, and located what may have been the derelict remains of the actual modest farmhouse where Mitchell's great-grandparents once lived, the original site of the structure surrounded by housing developments. Heading east from Atlanta he followed Sherman's tracks, reflecting on the exaggerated, discredited claims of damage surrounding the March, yet meeting passionate apologists for the Confederacy who expressed even more bitterness toward the general than Graham had found in 1919. Attending a meeting of the Sons of Confederate Veterans in Conyers, he heard a speaker who "performed a peculiar call-and-response. Mixing recent news stories about Bosnia with accounts of Sherman's March, she asked the audience to guess each time if the perpetrators were Serbs or Yankees." The speaker, according to Horwitz, concluded that "there isn't much difference between what Sarajevo and Georgia suffered."[54]

The kind of stories Horwitz heard were collected and analyzed by Elissa R. Henken, who taught folklore and Celtic studies at the University of Georgia. In 2003, she published the results of her fourteen-year study of Civil War stories and legends in the state. Predictably, Sherman the evil destroyer was a factor in many of them. But given the mythology that Sherman destroyed everything in his path, she was surprised to find more stories about places he spared than those he did not. One explanation was that if Sherman was considered so destructive, a town or home that was spared had some explaining to do, or the good fortune might be attributed to collaboration with the enemy. In most cases, these stories involved women, such as tales that he spared a home because he once knew a woman who lived there, or because a kindly woman cooked him a chicken dinner. These stories followed certain narrative patterns. Sherman might in some way be awed by a town's beauty, or the town's friendly inhabitants. Or he was scolded, challenged, shamed, bluffed, or civilized by women, or simply so stunned by their beauty and spunk that he could not bear to see them or their homes harmed. "What strikes me most forcefully is this image of Sherman as the ravaging monster, going through Georgia but pausing, being tamed by some civilizing aspect of the South," Henken said in an interview. The stories also fit the folklore of monsters being tamed or fooled by the small and helpless.[55]

The explanation that a town or home was spared because of its hospitality also plays into another Southern myth. Because the South sees itself as cultured, virtuous, courteous, and hospitable even to Northern barbarians, it is redeemed in the stories by its civility. When Sherman destroys, he is a villain. When he doesn't destroy he is a villain who is humbled by the South's virtues, confirming his own unworthiness, or briefly recovering his stunted sense of decency like a schoolboy chastened by a teacher. The legends often came with a great deal of pride, as if the site were spared because of some special grace, virtue, or strength attached to it. Another curious aspect of these stories is that Sherman seems to be everywhere during the March. It is always Sherman personally who spares the house and the town or offers the magnanimous gesture. This adds importance to the legend as it is repeated. Far better for the great Sherman himself to have burned, or spared, a home than for a lowly corporal to have done the deed. Henken also found that many of these stories were similar to those she found in Celtic myths, as if the memory of the March had been shaped by the myths of an older culture.[56]

In 2007 the History Channel featured a 50-minute segment on Sherman's March in its *Save Our History* series. Host and producer Steve Thomas, who, ironically, had been seen most frequently on television on *This Old House*, a program about home restoration, began "Sherman's Total War Tactics" by standing on top of an office building's parking deck on Vinings Mountain, near the spot where the general first saw the city during the war. From there the travelogue followed the route of Sherman's "state of the art" fighting force to "discover how he brought total war to America." Interviews with historians were interspersed with period photographs and footage of reenactors, who built pontoon bridges and twisted railroad ties. The episode soon became a kind of treasure hunt, as historical sleuths looked for the exact site of the Ebenezer Creek crossing, bridges, and graves. At the end of the road trip, Thomas concluded that "Sherman's total war tactics pioneered a major shift in American military strategy. His legacy and the legacy of Sherman's March remains strong to this day." The legacy remains. Just what that legacy eventually might turn out to be remains a mystery.[57]

Notes

1. William Tecumseh Sherman to Ellen Sherman, June 26, 1864, in M. A. DeWolfe, editor, *Home Letters of General Sherman* (New York: Charles Scribner's Sons, 1909), 298.

2. John Townsend Trowbridge, *The South: A Tour of Its Battlefields and Ruined Cities, a Journey through the Desolated States, and Talks With the People, 1867*, edited by J. H. Segars (Macon, GA: Mercer University Press, 2006; orig. pub. 1867), 323–24.

3. Chicago *Tribune*, Apr. 26, 1865.

4. *Army and Navy Journal* 34 (June 19, 1897): 783, cited in Stanley P. Hirshson, *The White Tecumseh: A Biography of William T. Sherman* (New York: Wiley, 1997), 122; Whitelaw Reid, *After the War: A Tour of the Southern States, 1865–1866*, edited by C. Vann Woodward (New York: Harper and Row, 1965; orig. pub. 1866), 355–56, 360.

5. John Richard Dennett, *The South as It Is: 1865–1866*, edited by Henry M. Christman (New York: Viking, 1965), 267–68.

6. Trowbridge, *The South*, 459, 464.

7. Ibid., 479–80.

8. Ibid., 453, 480.

9. John Henry Kennaway, *On Sherman's Track, or The South after the War* (London: Seeley, Jackson, and Halliday, 1867), v–vii, 7, 11.

10. Ibid., 13, 109, 162–63.

11. Milton Lomask, "Sgt. Bates March, Carrying the Stars and Stripes Unfurled, from Vicksburg to Washington, and from Gretna Green to London," *American Heritage* 16:6 (October 1965), 12–16; Mark Twain, "More Westonism," Virginia City (NV) *Territorial Enterprise*, Feb. 27, 1868.

12. "The March of Sergeant Bates," New York *Times*, Mar. 5, 1868; Gilbert H. Bates, *Triumphal March of Sergeant Bates from Vicksburg to Washington* (Washington, DC: Intelligencer Printing House, 1868), 15.

13. New York *Times*, Mar. 12, 1868; Mar. 19, 1868; Apr. 15, 1868; Bates, *Triumphal March of Sergeant Bates from Vicksburg to Washington*, 283.

14. W. E. B. Du Bois, *The Souls of Black Folk*, edited by Brent Hayes Edwards (Oxford: Oxford University Press, 2007; orig. pub. 1903), 15, 18–19, 54–57, 77–78.

15. General Sherman to Major Henry Turner, Mar. 9, 1879, Eleanor Sherman Fitch Papers, cited in Joseph T. Durkin, *General Sherman's Son: The Life of Thomas Ewing Sherman, S.J.* (New York: Farrar, Straus and Cudahy, 1959), 193.

16. Edmund Wilson, *Patriotic Gore: Studies in the Literature of the American Civil War* (New York: Oxford University Press, 1962), 209–18; Paul Ashdown and Edward Caudill, *The Mosby Myth: A Confederate Hero in Life and Legend* (Wilmington, DE: Scholarly Resources, 2002), 12–13.

17. John F. Marszalek, *Sherman: A Soldier's Passion for Order* (New York: Free Press, 1993), 410–11; Durkin, *General Sherman's Son*, 52–56; Wilson, *Patriotic Gore*, 210.

18. Marszalek, *Sherman*, 413–14.

19. W. T. Sherman to Minnie Sherman, Aug. 26, 1880, cited in Durkin, *General Sherman's Son*, 68; see Charles Royster, *The Destructive War: William Tecumseh Sherman, Stonewall Jackson, and the Americans* (New York: Knopf, 1991), 366–404, on Sherman's philosophy; Thomas Sherman to W. Tecumseh Sherman, Feb. 24, 1890, cited in Durkin, 110.

20. Wilson, *Patriotic Gore*, 212; Durkin, *General Sherman's Son*, 123, 127.

21. *Proceedings of the Society of the Army of the Tennessee*, St. Louis, Nov. 17, 1892, cited in Durkin, *General Sherman's Son*, 138; W. T. Sherman to T. T. Gantt, May 6, 1878, W. T. Sherman Papers, Library of Congress, cited in Royster, *Destructive War*, 400.

22. *Chicago Herald*, Feb. 6, 1894, cited in Durkin, *General Sherman's Son*, 148.

23. *The Catholic Forester*, March 1949; Milwaukee *Journal*, Jan. 22, 1904, cited in Durkin, *General Sherman's Son*, 181–82.

24. Durkin, *General Sherman's Son*, 190–93.

25. *Atlanta Constitution*, May 1, 1906.

26. *Atlanta Constitution*, May 1, 1906; May 2, 1906; May 3, 1906; May 4, 1906; May 6, 1906; May 9, 1906; New York *Herald*, May 2, 1906.

27. Chicago *Daily Tribune*, May 4, 1906; New York *Times*, May 2, 1906; May 4, 1906; May 7, 1906; New York *Herald*, May 2, 1906.

28. William D. Pickett, "Why General Sherman's Name is Detested," *Confederate Veteran* 14 (1906): 295.

29. Ibid.

30. David W. Blight, *Race and Reunion: The Civil War in American Memory* (Cambridge, MA: Harvard University Press, 2001), 258, 272–81, 295–99; Stephen Graham, "Marching through Georgia, Following Sherman's Footsteps To-day," Part I, *Harper's Monthly* 140 (April 1920), 619.

31. Atlanta *Constitution*, Sept. 22, 1911.

32. Durkin, *General Sherman's Son*, 193–240.

33. Russell Duncan, "Atlanta 1895 Cotton States and International Exposition," in John E. Findling and Kimberly D. Pelle, editors, *Historical Dictionary of World's Fairs and Expositions, 1851–1988* (Westport, CT: Greenwood Press, 1990), 139–41; "Men Who Made Atlanta," Atlanta *Constitution*, Mar. 4, 1906.

34. Howard Lawrence Preston, *Dirt Roads to Dixie: Accessibility and Modernization in the South, 1885–1935* (Knoxville: University of Tennessee Press, 1991), 168–69; Andrew Lytle, "The Hind Tit," in John Crowe Ransom et al., *I'll Take My Stand* (New York: Harper, 1962; orig. pub. 1930), 234.

35. Preston, *Dirt Roads to Dixie*, 48–49, 52–60, 98–103.

36. "A Historic Military Road," Atlanta *Constitution*, July 12, 1903; "Five Counties Blaze Trail to Sherman-Johnson Boulevard," Atlanta *Constitution*, June 23, 1911; "History, Sentiment and Scenic Beauty Combined in Johnston-Sherman Highway," Atlanta *Constitution*, July 2, 1911.

37. "Highway Following Sherman's March to the Sea Eloquently Advocated by Mrs. B. W. Hunt," Atlanta *Constitution*, Dec. 20, 1914.

38. Graham, "Marching through Georgia, Following Sherman's Footsteps To-day," Part I, 612–16; "Marching through Georgia, Following Sherman's Footsteps To-day," Part II *Harper's Monthly* 140 (May 1920), 822.

39. Graham, "Marching through Georgia, Following Sherman's Footsteps To-day," Part II, 817, 819–823.

40. Graham, "Marching through Georgia, Following Sherman's Footsteps To-day," Part I, 616; Part II, 822.

41. Edward Lowry, "Reconstruction, or Atlanta, For Instance," *Saturday Evening Post* 192:51 (June 19, 1920), 18–19, 113, 116, 120, 122.

42. D. J. de Laubenfels, "Where Sherman Passed By," *Geographical Review* 47:3 (1957), 381–95.

43. Anne Edwards, *Road to Tara: The Life of Margaret Mitchell* (New York: Dell, 1983), 91–92; Medora Field Perkerson, *White Columns in Georgia* (New York: Bonanza Books, 1952), 3, 83, 343.

44. Ellen Barry, "Pillars of Southern Charm," Charlotte *Observer*, May 14, 2005, www.charlotte.com/mld/observer (accessed May 19, 2005); Craig Schneider, "A Charming Fictional Story: Plan Invents Past in Present; Planners of Riverside in

North Atlanta Decided the Development Needed a Past—So They Created It," Atlanta *Constitution*, Mar. 23, 1998; Ann Carrns, "How a Brand-New Development Came by Its Rich History," *Wall Street Journal*, Oct. 18, 1998.

45. Sue C. Bailey and William H. Bailey, *Cycling through Georgia: Tracing Sherman's March from Chickamauga to Savannah* (Atlanta: Susan Hunter, 1989), ix–x; Jim Miles, *To the Sea: A History and Tour Guide of the War in the West, Sherman's March across Georgia and through the Carolinas, 1864–1865* (Nashville, TN: Cumberland House, 2002), 9–10.

46. James Reston, Jr., *Sherman's March and Vietnam* (New York: Macmillan, 1984), 172, 198–99.

47. Ibid., 6, 51,92.

48. Michael Herr, *Dispatches* (New York: Knopf, 1977), 43.

49. Reston, *Sherman's March and Vietnam*, 43; Stephen W. Sears, "From Atlanta to the South China Sea," New York *Times*, Feb. 17, 1985; see, for example, Lance Janda, "Shutting the Gates of Mercy: The American Origins of Total War, 1860–1880," *Journal of Military History* 59:1 (January 1995), 7–26.

50. Jerry Ellis, *Marching through Georgia: My Walk With Sherman* (New York: Delacorte Press, 1995), 8.

51. Ibid., 31, 117–18, 236–37.

52. Ibid., 239.

53. Daniel Pearl, "Pariah in the South, William T. Sherman Is Getting a Makeover," *Wall Street Journal*, June 9, 1993.

54. Tony Horwitz, *Confederates in the Attic: Dispatches from the Unfinished Civil War* (New York: Vintage, 1999), 283, 294, 301–14.

55. Elissa R. Henken, "Taming the Enemy: Georgian Narratives about the Civil War," *Journal of Folklore Research* 40:3 (2003), 289–307; Steven N. Koppes, "Folklore—Where Fact Meets Fiction," *University of Georgia Research Magazine*, Spring 2000, www.ovpr.uga.edu/researchnews/spring2000/fact.html.

56. Henken, "Taming the Enemy: Georgian Narratives about the Civil War," 289–307.

57. "Save Our History: Sherman's Total War Tactics," The History Channel, A&E Television Networks, 2007.

Epilogue
The March and Its Myths

The featured speaker for the evening had briefly addressed a sizable crowd that damp summer evening in Columbus, Ohio. A master of ceremonies noted that an earlier crowd had raised a few shouts at about this point, and the audience took the opportunity to call for remarks from "Uncle Billy." Others applauded the idea, even stood on chairs in a show of enthusiasm for remarks from the general. The crowd was a conglomeration, reflected in the various attire—top hats and coats, hoop skirts, and military uniforms. There were some shabby-looking individuals in garb that looked better suited to barrooms and brothels than dinner with dignitaries. Even a few professors lurked about, taking extra dessert. "Uncle Billy" arose and strode purposefully to the stage, as the cheers arose anew. As the noise subsided, he warned that he hadn't prepared remarks. But in the course of his speech, the general delivered oft-quoted, memorable words: "War is all hell." Then the "veterans" in the audience erupted again, with even more enthusiasm and appreciation. It was the high point for the 2005 Sherman festival, commemorating the 125th anniversary of the famous speech in the same city.

Go south a few states, and people can point out "Sherman's sentinels," the brick or stone chimneys that remained after the March and the torch. Sherman biographer John F. Marszalek has pointed out in a few cases that Sherman and his troops were not within a hundred miles of a given "sentinel." He changed no minds and only succeeded in aggravating a few diehards. The chimneys' designations are one example of how the March became synonymous with Sherman's name, and how interpretations sometimes were based on memories of things that never happened—such as the absolute destruction, or wanton pillage and rape.[1]

Sherman aggrandized the myth and the teller. Even if one's property was not in the path, it should have been. That would mean it was important enough, distinct enough, to draw the attention of the barbarians, drawn like moths out of the darkness to its light.

The myths of Sherman and the March were shaped in a divided nation by people dedicated to the sanctity of their histories. A multitude of national identities began emerging after the war, defined along innumerable and mutable lines that included region, race, religion, ancestry, and livelihood. Such cultural dynamics inevitably challenged conventions of a singular past and demanded new versions of history. Reconstruction exacted a measure of revenge while regional differences grew into economic chasms between industrial North and agrarian South. The imperative of remembering and reconstructing stumbled along in a national fog of meaning about nation, fundamental values, and citizenship, and the meaning of progress at a time when science, evolution, and imperialism were in the ascendancy.

While the grinding war meant death and deprivation for many, it was an awakening to a new reality for others, even in terms of their faith. Private John Brobst was an infantryman during the March. His letters home do not show him to be an especially religious man, but he was familiar with Bible stories. He apparently believed in a just God, but reveals himself to be a free-spirited thinker about applying scriptural lessons:

> Sherman is our guide, like Moses of old was guide for the children of Israel, but he did not smote the waters of the Cattahoocha river as Moses did the red sea, but we had to wade, swim or roll through it. . . . In place of smoting the rock for water, he smotes the seller [sic] doors, and the wine, brandy, gin, and whiskey flows in the place of water. Sherman is rather ahead of Moses if he gets us through the wilderness all rite [sic], I think.[2]

The entry illustrates the diametric opposition of cultural myths, because the wilderness to which he refers, the South, saw itself as the citadel of civilization and culture, and saw Sherman as chief barbarian. In other circumstances, Northern oraters even spoke of Sherman as having gone through the South "like the plow of God."[3] But even into the next century, Southerners such as the Agrarians insisted it was they who inhabited Eden, threatened not by God's plow but Attila's sword. Where Grant had fought on the borders and appendages of the South, Sherman cut through its heart. If that were not bad enough, Sherman shamed the South not by vanquishing it in slaughter, an accusation leveled against Grant, but by winning with a minimum of bloodshed.

So the South could not even celebrate a "heroic" demise, and instead simply crumbled before Sherman. Thief, perhaps, but not executioner.

The March demonstrated, empirically, the brute superiority of industrialism and modernism. Or did it show the destruction of culture, via a godless goal-driven system without regard for the traditions that enrich and give meaning to human existence? The North tended to see a tragic necessity, a virtuous military action in which Sherman was a progressive innovator, whose recognition of war's reality facilitated the inevitable conclusion in an efficient fashion, and minimized losses in doing so. But for the South, that same event was an assault on a civilization. In the Lost Cause mythology, it was akin to the ancient barbarians' conquest of Rome, in which military superiority did not mean cultural superiority.

A Multitude of Marches

The myths of the March endure despite the fact that the South of the twenty-first century is not the rural, agrarian South of the late nineteenth and early twentieth centuries. North and South drew on the same mythic traditions to create different Marches, different Shermans. The general was complex, and his life and actions were conducive to a complex myth, one adaptable to numerous American myths—such as Horatio Alger, the frontier, science-technology as progress, individualism, and the Garden. He was an upscale version of the Alger myth because he had no advantage of privilege, and in some respects his early life was difficult. There was something of an everyman in the adult Sherman, in his rumpled appearance, his plain speech, and his soldiers calling him "Uncle Billy." His individualism came to be celebrated, particularly in the North, where his quirks of character, such as wandering about camp in his long johns at night, became charming eccentricities. Southern myth did not make such adaptations, which would not have served its memory. Instead, it retained the madman the Northern press discovered early in the war. He never became eccentric, and the nature of the March and its success was evidence that a very calculating madman had been in the culture's midst. Thus, the South could retain some dignity in defeat by attributing the loss, in part, to its own superiority. And the North was able to celebrate a unique event and individual. In American myth, there seems never to have been a strong challenge to the idea that the earthly Garden was in America, but only to where it might be, and how it might be manifest—whether in a wilderness, utopian communities, or idyllic farms and small towns. Wherever one found it, there was a place for Sherman, who could be the uncivilized invader or the cultivator pruning diseased branches.

The same traits made him both a tactical genius and a barbarian. His conduct of war was humane because he attacked property rather than people, a tactic others deemed terrorism. His industrial efficiency in "hard war" was heroic in the North, villainous in the South.

A Good Story, Then and Now

Journalists have marked the March's myths as clearly as Sherman's army did the Georgia countryside. Though the general would have blanched at the idea, he was entwined or embroiled with the press almost all of his adult life, from his California banking days (when he threatened to throw an editor out a window) to his public feuds over statements in the Memoirs. The March itself was notable for the lack of press coverage. But the silence elevated the daring, the mystery, the story. The press abhors a vacuum. The result in the Southern press was a Sherman more terrible in tale than in reality. In the North, the March became a modern epic, replete with all the elements of a great story: a just cause, obstacles and ingenuity, colorful characters, and eventual triumph.

The earliest hint of the "dual Sherman" arose in the Northern Civil War press. His transformation from insanity to mere eccentricity was a result of the March. In addition, eccentricity can be rather charming, and a great ingredient for a story. In the North, eccentricity became central to the myth, and in modern myth such behavior is a stereotypical trait of genius. The March and its success were seen as prima facie evidence for the validity of this version of Sherman. In the Southern version, the madman endured. But Sherman was transformed in the Southern myth, too, into a rational madman, ultimately even more menacing than a deranged general, who could be easily marginalized in any recounting. It is difficult to dismiss reasoned passion for a just cause and the calculated passion to achieve it.

In 1864, the Union was desperate for good news and a hero. The hero myth came to life in the March and Sherman, and the myth dilemma was created. The dilemma resides in the fact that the part of Southern culture which had glorified war was left to bemoan the very acts that comprise war. Violence is a critical part of the frontier myth, according to Richard Slotkin, author of Gunfighter Nation. Using Slotkin's logic, the fact that Sherman—the mythic "gunfighter"—might kill a lot of people only enhances the myth. It is what he is supposed to do. Cognitive contortions were needed if one were to aggrandize war and then condemn one of a generation's foremost practitioners of it.[4]

Sherman used his celebrity to gain access to the press, which in turn found him to be a good story in both fact and fiction. The March alone does not explain Sherman's national acclaim or notoriety, although it was the genesis of it. The importance of facility with the press is demonstrated not just in the legend of Sherman, but also in the legends of Mosby and Forrest—as is the importance of longevity. Mosby and Forrest operated in more limited theaters of the war, and both won national attention. Mosby and Sherman were skilled writers and orators, and they lived long after the war, giving them more time for more public exposure than was available to Forrest, who died in 1877. Forrest, unlike Sherman and Mosby, was poorly educated, a man of action rather than letters. But the Sherman myth is more nuanced and complex than either Forrest's or Mosby's. Sherman's long life and skill as orator and writer meant he had some control over the story of the March, an advantage that Forrest clearly lacked in such notorious episodes of his career as the Fort Pillow massacre or the leadership of the Ku Klux Klan. Both taint his myth. For example and in contrast, Sherman contributed to a convincing case that he was not responsible for the burning of Columbia. Mosby's legend is inordinately large if it is considered with respect to his impact on the war. But he told his own story well and often, living until 1916. Like Sherman, he had a substantial hand in creating his myth.

The myth of the March and Sherman is a democratic one, understood across cultures, even when people hold opposing views. It is a useful and accessible myth because it taps into conventional mythic templates, such as the frontier or the Garden. Like the soldier's Old Testament hero, this mythic marcher is known by all, whether or not they accept him as prophet. Southern agrarianism and gallantry found its antithesis in Sherman and the March. Northern industrialism and pragmatism saw an exemplar of modernism's virtues.

The March's myth had its beginnings in the popular press and its pursuit of a good story. The March was great drama, its leading man born to the role, whether or not one liked the story line. As it moved from news pages to literature, to film and theater, the culture absorbed it, to the point of universal recognition in American society. Even when people are at odds over the meaning of the March, they comprehend the rival reading. Invoking Sherman is a statement of values, akin to waving a Confederate flag or burning one. The March, like the flag, has become shorthand for a complex set of values, perspectives, and traditions.

War Is Still Hell

"Hero or terrorist? Leader or butcher?" the History Channel asked in the opening to its April 2007 program on Sherman and the March. In the first fifteen minutes of the show, the audience learned that this "father of total war," who remained "controversial to this day," would "ravage the South." Before the first commercial break, viewers also heard that Sherman's proposed march from Atlanta would put 60,000 men "at risk." Lincoln was nervous. Grant had doubts. Sherman was sure. The opening artfully sketched an innovative military genius, and set up a story of fall and redemption (from alleged insanity back to command), depicting a martial spirit dedicated to nation and a just cause. His appeal—the show's appeal—was confirmed with its first two commercials: Samuel Adams beer and Maxiderm, a "male enhancement" drug. American legend. American revolutionary. American male. Legends and myths, like beer and prescriptions, are packaged for consumption. The show went on to provide an overview and assessment of Sherman's March and the Carolinas campaign, stressing their accomplishments. It also noted the less-than-admirable facts of Sherman and the March, especially treatment of newly freed slaves at Ebenezer Creek, and the killing of a Confederate prisoner of war in retaliation for the Confederate execution of Union cavalrymen. For the South, historian Steven E. Woodworth tells us, Sherman had become the "new Attila the Hun." Such status would make Sherman an extremely important figure in inventing a memory of magnolias and knights—because he was neither. He was the villain in the memory, a corrosive agent in mythology's armor.[5]

The national memory industry remains fully engaged with the Civil War. And the dynamic cultural landscape means reinventing the war for each generation. There is no conciliation in sight for the myth of the March. If nothing else, the war is more than the culture has made of it—a national Iliad that succumbed to modernism, a media epic replete with special effects, a tragedy, a romance, a morality tale, and more.

One bitterly cold winter morning in 2007, two aging journalists could be seen stumbling through the dark woods near Sherman's camp at Shiloh. Other journeys had taken them from Lancaster, Ohio, to San Francisco; to Tunnel Hill, Georgia; to Savannah; and to Bennett Place. But Shiloh seemed the best place to have a final séance with William Tecumseh Sherman. The journalists followed in the footsteps of thousands who had looked for—what?—in Sherman's tracks in that awful place. The ground was covered with dead leaves. No melancholy ghosts appeared in the damp morning haze. But men had died there. That seemed reason enough to stand on hallowed ground and ponder myths and memories, the tellers of tales, and the deep shadows of the past.

Notes

1. John F. Marszalek, personal interview, Jan. 19, 2007, Starkville, MS.

2. A. Reed Taylor, "The War History of Two Soldiers: A Two-Sided View of the Civil War," *Alabama Review* 23:2 (April 1970), 103.

3. Lloyd Lewis, *Sherman: Fighting Prophet* (New York: Harcourt, Brace, 1932), 619.

4. Richard Slotkin, *Gunfighter Nation: The Myth of the Frontier in Twentieth-Century America* (New York: HarperCollins, 1992), 10–16.

5. Steven E. Woodworth, "West versus East," *America's Civil War* 20:5 (November 2007), 28–37.

The melancholy winter woods at Shiloh surround the site of Sherman's headquarters. A pyramid of cannonballs stacked on a plinth suggests the intrusion of industrial power in the peaceful landscape. Edward Caudill

Bibliography

Periodicals

Atlanta Constitution, 1864, 1868, 1874, 1875, 1879, 1880, 1884, 1885, 1888, 1889, 1891, 1903, 1906, 1911, 1914, 1941.
Century, 1888, 1893.
Charleston *News & Courier*, 1879.
Chattanooga *Daily News*, 1879.
Chicago *Daily Tribune*, 1906.
Chicago *Herald*, 1891.
Chicago *Tribune*, 1865, 1879.
Cincinnati *Daily Gazette*, 1865.
Columbus (OH) *Dispatch*, 1993.
Frank Leslie's Illustrated Newspaper, 1865.
Literary Digest, 1891.
Louisville *Times*, 1891.
New York *Herald*, 1864, 1906.
New York *Times*, 1865, 1868, 1880, 1891, 1906, 1939.
North American Review, 1887, 1888, 1890.
Washington *Chronicle*, 1864.
Washington *Post*, 1889.

Books and Monographs

Aaron, Daniel, *The Unwritten War: American Writers and the Civil War*, Madison: University of Wisconsin Press, 1987; orig. pub. 1973.

Adams, Richard, *Traveller*, New York: Knopf, 1988.

Alexander, Bevin, *How Great Generals Win*, New York: Norton, 1993.

Allen, Patrick, editor, *Margaret Mitchell: Reporter*, Athens, GA: Hill Street Press, 2000.

Ashdown, Paul, *A Cold Mountain Companion*, Gettysburg, PA: Thomas Publications, 2004.

Ashdown, Paul, and Edward Caudill, *The Mosby Myth: A Confederate Hero in Life and Legend*, Wilmington, DE: Scholarly Resources, 2002.

———, *The Myth of Nathan Bedford Forrest*, Lanham, MD: Rowman & Littlefield, 2005.

Babe, Thomas, *Rebel Women*, New York: Dramatists Play Service, 1977.

Bailey, Anne J., *War and Ruin: William T. Sherman and the Savannah Campaign*, Wilmington, DE: Scholarly Resources, 2003.

Bailey, Sue C., and William H. Bailey, *Cycling through Georgia: Tracing Sherman's March from Chickamauga to Savannah*, Atlanta, GA: Susan Hunter, 1989.

Bartley, Numan V., editor, *The Evolution of Southern Culture*, Athens: University of Georgia Press, 1988.

Bass, Cynthia, *Sherman's March*, New York: Villard, 1994.

Bates, Gilbert H., *Triumphal March of Sergeant Bates from Vicksburg to Washington*, Washington, DC: Intelligencer Printing House, 1868.

Bierce, Ambrose, *Tales of Soldiers and Civilians*, New York: United States Book Co., 1891.

Bird, Edward G., *Sherman's "March to the Sea," or Fighting His Way through Georgia*, Old Cap Collier Library no. 398, New York: Old Cap Collier Library, Mar. 2, 1891.

Blight, David W., *Race and Reunion: The Civil War in American Memory*, Cambridge, MA: Harvard University Press, 2001.

Boles, John B., *The South through Time: A History of an American Region*, Englewood Cliffs, NJ: Prentice Hall, 1995.

Bowman, Kent A., *Voice of Combat: A Century of Liberty and War Songs, 1765–1865*, Westport, CT: Greenwood Press, 1987.

Boynton, Henry Van Ness, *Sherman's Historical Raid: The Memoirs in Light of the Record*, Cincinnati, OH: Wilstach, Baldwin, 1875.

Brick, John, *Jubilee*, New York: Doubleday, 1956.

Byers, S. H. M., *Twenty Years in Europe; A Consul-General's Memoirs of Noted People, with Letters from General W. T. Sherman*, Chicago: Rand, McNally, 1900.

Campbell, Jacqueline Glass, *When Sherman Marched North from the Sea: Resistance on the Confederate Home Front*, Chapel Hill: University of North Carolina Press, 2003.

Cashman, Sean Dennis, *America in the Gilded Age: From the Death of Lincoln to the Rise of Theodore Roosevelt*, 3rd edition, New York: New York University Press, 1993.

Cassidy, John M., *Civil War Cinema*, Missoula, MT: Pictorial Histories, 1986.

Castel, Albert, *Decision in the West: The Atlanta Campaign of 1864*, Lawrence: University Press of Kansas, 1992.

Chadwick, Bruce, *The Reel Civil War: Mythmaking in American Film*, New York: Knopf, 2001.

Churchill, Winston, *The Crisis*, New York: Macmillan, 1901.

Coburn, Mark, *Terrible Innocence: General Sherman at War*, New York: Hippocrene Books, 1993.

Commager, Henry Steele, editor, *The Blue and the Gray*, Vol. 1, Indianapolis, IN: Bobbs-Merrill, 1950.

Coyningham, David P., *Sherman's March through the South, with Sketches and Incidents of the Campaign*, New York: Sheldon, 1865.

Cullen, Jim, *The Civil War in Popular Culture: A Reusable Past*, Washington, DC: Smithsonian Institution Press, 1995.

Davidson, Donald, *The Tennessee*, Vol. 2: *The New River, Civil War to TVA*, New York, Rinehart, 1948.

Davis, Burke, *Sherman's March*, New York: Vintage Books, 1988.

Davis, Jefferson, *The Rise and Fall of the Confederate Government*, New York: Appleton, 1881.

Davis, Stephen, *Atlanta Will Fall: Sherman, Joe Johnston, and the Yankee Heavy Battalions*, Wilmington, DE: Scholarly Resources, 2001.

Dennett, John Richard, *The South as It Is: 1865–1866*, edited by Henry M. Christman, New York: Viking, 1965.

DeWolfe, M. A., *Home Letters of General Sherman*, New York: Charles Scribner's Sons, 1909.

Doctorow, E. L., *The March*, New York: Random House, 2005.

Du Bois, W. E. B., *The Souls of Black Folk*, edited by Brent Hayes Edwards, Oxford: Oxford University Press, 2007; orig. pub. 1903.

Dunn, Byron A, *Battling for Atlanta*, Chicago: McClurg, 1900.

———, *From Atlanta to the Sea*, Chicago, IL: McClurg, 1901.

Durkin, Joseph T., *General Sherman's Son: The Life of Thomas Ewing Sherman, S.J.*, New York: Farrar, Straus and Cudahy, 1959.

Dyer, Thomas G., *Secret Yankees: The Union Circle in Confederate Atlanta*, Baltimore, MD: Johns Hopkins University Press, 1999.

Edwards, Anne, *Road to Tara: The Life of Margaret Mitchell*, New York: Dell, 1983.

Ellis, Jerry, *Marching through Georgia: My Walk with Sherman*, New York: Delacorte Press, 1995.

Erhart, Margaret, *Crossing Bully Creek*, Minneapolis, MN: Milkweed Editions, 2005.

Eyles, Allen, *John Wayne and the Movies*, South Brunswick, NJ: A. S. Barnes, 1976.

Fahs, Alice and Joan Waugh, editors, *The Memory of the Civil War in American Culture*, Chapel Hill: University of North Carolina Press, 2004.

Fellman, Michael, *Citizen Sherman: A Life of William Tecumseh Sherman*, New York: Random House, 1995.

Flood, Charles Bracelin, *Grant and Sherman: The Friendship That Won the Civil War*, New York: Farrar, Straus and Giroux, 2005.

Forbes, Ida B., *Gen'l Wm. T. Sherman, His Life and Battles, or From Boy-Hood, to His "March to the Sea," Mostly in One Syllable Words*, New York: McLoughlin, 1886.

Garner, Stanton, *The Civil War World of Herman Melville*, Lawrence: University Press of Kansas, 1993.

Gaston, Paul M., *The New South Creed: A Study in Southern Mythmaking*, New York: Knopf, 1970.

Glatthaar, Joseph T., *The March to the Sea and Beyond: Sherman's Troops in the Savannah and Carolinas Campaigns*, Baton Rouge: Louisiana State University Press, 1985.

Goss, Warren Lee, *Tom Clifton, or Western Boys in Grant and Sherman's Army, '61–'65*, New York: Crowell, 1892.

Grantham, Dewey W., *The South in Modern America*, New York: HarperCollins, 1994.

Graves, Charles P., *William Tecumseh Sherman: Champion of the Union*, Champaign, IL: Garrard, 1968.

Grimsley, Mark, *The Hard Hand of War: Union Military Policy toward Southern Civilians, 1861–1865*, New York: Cambridge University Press, 1995.

Gurganus, Allan, *Oldest Living Confederate Widow Tells All*, New York: Knopf, 1989.

Gylanders, S. C., *The Better Angels of Our Nature*, New York: Random House, 2006.

Haeger, Diane, *My Dearest Cecelia: A Novel of the Southern Belle Who Stole General Sherman's Heart*, New York: St. Martin's, 2003.

Hanson, Victor Davis, *The Soul of Battle: From Ancient Times to the Present Day, How Three Great Liberators Vanquished Tyranny*, New York: Anchor Books, 2001.

Harris, Brayton, *Blue and Gray in Black and White*, Washington, DC: Brassey's 1999.

Harrison, Harry, *Stars and Stripes Forever*, New York: Del Rey, 1999.

——, *Stars and Stripes in Peril*, New York: Del Rey, 2000.

——, *Stars and Stripes Triumphant*, New York: Del Rey, 2003.

Harwell, Richard, *"Gone with the Wind" as Book and Film*, Columbia: University of South Carolina Press, 1983.

——, editor, *Margaret Mitchell's "Gone with the Wind" Letters, 1936–1949*, New York: Macmillan, 1976.

Hawk, Richard L., *Moonstalker: The Adventures of Gen. Sherman's Drummer Boy*, Lancaster, OH: Beechwood Books, 1993.

Heaps, Willard, and Porter Heaps, *The Singing Sixties: The Spirit of Civil War Days down from the Music of the Times*, Norman: University of Oklahoma Press, 1960.

Herr, Michael, *Dispatches*, New York: Knopf, 1977.

Hirshson, Stanley P., *The White Tecumseh: A Biography of William T. Sherman*, New York: Wiley, 1997.

Hobson, Fred, *Tell about the South: The Southern Rage to Explain*, Baton Rouge: Louisiana State University Press, 1983.

Horwitz, Tony, *Confederates in the Attic: Dispatches from the Unfinished Civil War*, New York: Vintage, 1999.

Jakes, John, *Savannah, or A Gift for Mr. Lincoln*, New York: Dutton, 2004.

John, Arthur, *The Best Years of the Century: Richard Watson Gilder, Scribner's Monthly, and the "Century" Magazine, 1870–1909*, Urbana: University of Illinois Press, 1981.

Johnston, Mary, *Cease Firing*, Boston: Houghton Mifflin, 1912.

Jones, Katharine M., *When Sherman Came: Southern Women and the "Great March,"* Indianapolis, IN: Bobbs-Merrill, 1964.

Kammen, Michael, *Mystic Chords of Memory: The Transformation of Tradition in American Culture*, New York: Vintage Books, 1993.

Kantor, MacKinlay, *If the South Had Won the Civil War*, New York: Bantam, 1961.

Kennaway, John Henry, *On Sherman's Track, or The South after the War*, London: Seeley, Jackson and Halliday, 1867.

Kennedy, Sara Beaumont, *Cicely: A Tale of the Georgia March*, Garden City, NY: Doubleday, Page, 1911.

Kennett, Lee B., *Marching through Georgia: The Story of Soldiers and Civilians during Sherman's Campaign*, New York: Harper Perennial, 2001.

———, *Sherman: A Soldier's Life*, New York: HarperCollins, 2001.

Kilpatrick, Judson, and J. Owen Moore, *Allatoona: An Historical and Military Drama in Five Acts*, New York: Samuel French, 1875.

King, Richard H., *A Southern Renaissance: The Cultural Awakening of the American South, 1930–1955*, New York: Oxford University Press, 1980.

Kinnard, Ray, *The Blue and the Gray on the Silver Screen*, Secaucus, NJ: Birch Lane, 1996.

Lewis, Lloyd, *Sherman: Fighting Prophet*, New York: Harcourt, Brace, 1932.

Liddell Hart, B. H., *Sherman: Soldier, Realist, American*, New York: Dodd, Mead, 1929.

———, *Sherman: Soldier, Realist, American*, New York: Praeger, second printing, 1958.

Lockridge, Ross, Jr., *Raintree County*, Boston: Houghton Mifflin, 1948.

Longstreet, Helen Dortch, *In the Path of Lee's "Old War Horse,"* Atlanta: A. B. Caldwell, 1917.

Lucas, Marion B., *Sherman and the Burning of Columbia*, College Station: Texas A&M University Press, 1976.

Luvaas, Jay, *The Military Legacy of the Civil War: The European Inheritance*, Chicago: University of Chicago Press, 1959.

Marszalek, John F., *Sherman: A Soldier's Passion for Order*, New York: Free Press, 1993.

———, *Sherman's Other War: The General and the Civil War Press*, Kent, OH: Kent State University Press, 1981.

Martin, Samuel J., *Kill-Cavalry: Sherman's Merchant of Terror: The Life of Union General Hugh Judson Kilpatrick*, Madison, NJ: Fairleigh Dickinson University Press, 1996.

Martinez, J. Michael, *Life and Death in Civil War Prisons: The Parallel Torments of Corporal John Wesley Minnich, C.S.A. and Sergeant Warren Lee Goss, U.S.A.*, Nashville, TN: Rutledge Hill, 2004.

McMurry, Richard M., *Atlanta 1864: Last Chance for the Confederacy*, Lincoln: University of Nebraska Press, 2000.

Melville, Herman, *The Battle-Pieces of Herman Melville*, edited by Hennig Cohen, New York: Yoseloff, 1963.

Merrill, James M., *William Tecumseh Sherman*, New York: Rand McNally, 1971.

Miers, Earl Schenck, *The General Who Marched to Hell: William Tecumseh Sherman and His March to Fame and Infamy*, New York: Knopf, 1951.

Miles, Jim, *To the Sea: A History and Tour Guide of the War in the West, Sherman's March across Georgia and through the Carolinas, 1864–1865*, Nashville, TN: Cumberland House, 2002.

Mills, Lane, editor, *War is Hell: William T. Sherman's Personal Narrative of His March through Georgia*, Savannah, GA: Beehive Press, 1974.

Mitchell, Margaret, *Gone with the Wind*, New York: Macmillan, 1936.

Murphy, Paul V., *The Rebuke of History: The Southern Agrarians and American Conservative Thought*, Chapel Hill: University of North Carolina Press, 2001.

Nevin, David, *Sherman's March*, Alexandria, VA: Time-Life Books, 1986.

Nichols, George W., *The Sanctuary*, New York: Harper, 1866.

——, *The Story of the Great March*, New York: Harper, 1865.

Nixon, Raymond B., *Henry W. Grady: Spokesman of the New South*, New York: Knopf, 1943.

O'Connor, Richard, *Company Q*, Garden City, NY: Doubleday, 1957.

Owens, David M., *The Devil's Topographer: Ambrose Bierce and the American War Story*, Knoxville: University of Tennessee Press, 2006.

Palmer, Leonard, *The Sherman Letter*, Aurora, CO: Write Way, 1994.

Peck, William Henry, *The M'Donalds, or The Ashes of Southern Homes*, New York: Metropolitan Record Office, 1867.

Perkerson, Medora Field, *White Columns in Georgia*, New York: Bonanza Books, 1952.

Preston, Howard Lawrence, *Dirt Roads to Dixie: Accessibility and Modernization in the South, 1885–1935*, Knoxville: University of Tennessee Press, 1991.

Ransom, John Crowe, Donald Davidson, Frank Lawrence Owsley, John Gould Fletcher, Lyle H. Lanier, Allen Tate, Herman Clarence Nixon, et al., *I'll Take My Stand: The South and the Agrarian Tradition, by Twelve Southerners*, New York: Harper, 1930.

Ratner, Lorman A., and Dwight L. Teeter, Jr., *Fanatics and Fire-Eaters: Newspapers and the Coming of the Civil War*, Urbana: University of Illinois Press, 2003.

Rawl, Miriam Freeman, *From the Ashes of Ruin*, Columbia, SC: Summerhouse, 1999.

Reasoner, James, *Savannah*, Nashville, TN: Cumberland House, 2003.

Reid, Whitelaw, *After the War: A Tour of the Southern States, 1865–1866*, edited by C. Vann Woodward, New York: Harper & Row, 1965; orig. pub. 1866.

Reston, James, Jr., *Sherman, the Peacemaker: A Play in Two Acts*, typescript, North Carolina Collection, University of North Carolina Library, Chapel Hill, revised September 1980.

——, *Sherman's March and Vietnam*, New York: Macmillan, 1984.

Roberts, Randy, and James S. Olson, *John Wayne, American*, New York: Free Press, 1995.

Royster, Charles, *The Destructive War: William Tecumseh Sherman, Stonewall Jackson, and the Americans*, New York: Knopf, 1991.

Saum, Lewis O., *The Popular Mood of America, 1860–1900*, Lincoln: University of Nebraska Press, 1990.

Senour, F. (Faunt LeRoy), *Major General William T. Sherman and His Campaigns*, Chicago: Henry M. Sherwood, 1865.

Shenk, Joshua Wolf, *Lincoln's Melancholy: How Depression Challenged a President and Fueled His Greatness*, Boston: Houghton Mifflin, 2005.

Sherman, William Tecumseh, *Memoirs of General W. T. Sherman*, edited with an introduction by Michael Fellman, New York: Penguin Books, 2000.

———, *Memoirs of W. T. Sherman*, New York: Library of America, 1984; orig. pub. 1875.

Slaughter, Frank G., *Lorena*, Garden City, NY: Doubleday, 1959.

Slotkin, Richard, *Gunfighter Nation: The Myth of the Frontier in Twentieth-Century America*, New York: HarperCollins, 1992.

Spears, Jack, *The Civil War on the Screen, and Other Essays*, South Brunswick, NJ: A. S. Barnes, 1977.

Stone, Geoffrey, *Melville*, New York: Sheed and Ward, 1949.

Stout, Harry S., *Upon the Altar of the Nation: A Moral History of the Civil War*, New York: Viking, 2006.

Street, James, *Captain Little Ax*, Philadelphia: Lippincott, 1956.

Sword, Wiley, *Southern Invincibility: A History of the Confederate Heart*, New York: St. Martin's Griffin, 1999.

Titus, Warren I., *Winston Churchill*, New York: Twayne, 1963.

Trowbridge, John Townsend, *The South: A Tour of its Battlefields and Ruined Cities, A Journey through the Desolated States, and Talks with the People, 1867*, edited by J. H. Segars, Macon, GA: Mercer University Press, 2006; orig. pub. 1867.

Turtledove, Harry, *Marching through Peachtree*, Riverdale, NY: Baen, 2001.

Tyndall, George Brown, *America: A Narrative History*, New York: Norton, 1984.

Upson, Theodore, *With Sherman to the Sea: The Civil War Letters, Diaries, and Reminiscences of Theodore F. Upson*, Baton Rouge: Louisiana State University Press, 1943.

Vetter, Charles Edmund, *Sherman: Merchant of Terror, Advocate of Peace*, Gretna, LA: Pelican Publishing, 1992.

Walters, John Bennett, *Merchant of Terror: General Sherman and Total War*, New York: Bobbs-Merrill, 1973.

Watterson, Henry, *"Marse Henry": An Autobiography*, 2 vols., New York: Doran, 1919.

Webb, James, *How the Scots-Irish Shaped America*, New York: Broadway Books, 2004.

White, Karen, *In the Shadow of the Moon*, New York: Dorchester, 2000.

Whitney, Louisa M., *Goldie's Inheritance: A Story of the Siege of Atlanta*, Burlington, VT: Free Press, 1903.

Williams, Philip Lee, *A Distant Flame*, New York: St. Martin's, 2004.

Wills, Brian Steel, *Gone with the Glory: The Civil War in Cinema*, Lanham, MD: Rowman & Littlefield, 2007.

Wills, Charles Wright, *Army Life of an Illinois Soldier, Including a Day by Day Record of Sherman's March to the Sea*, Washington, DC: Globe Printing, 1906.

Wilson, Edmund, *Patriotic Gore: Studies in the Literature of the American Civil War*, New York: Oxford University Press, 1962.

Winik, Jay, *April 1865: The Month That Saved America*, New York: HarperCollins, 2001.

Woodfin, Henry Grady, editor, *The New South Writings and Speeches of Henry Grady*, Savannah, GA: Beehive Press, 1971.

Woodworth, Steven E., *Nothing but Victory: The Army of the Tennessee, 1861–1865*, New York: Knopf, 2005.

Yarbro, Chelsea Quinn, *In the Face of Death: An Historical Horror Novel*, Dallas, TX: BenBella Books, 2001.

Young, Stark, *So Red the Rose*, with an introduction by Donald Davidson, New York: Charles Scribner's Sons, 1953; orig. pub. 1934.

Articles and Chapters

Aaron, Daniel, "On Ross Lockridge, Jr.'s *Raintree County*," in David Madden and Peggy Bach, editors, *Classics of Civil War Fiction*, Jackson: University Press of Mississippi, 1991.

Allred, Randal W., "Marching Through Georgia," in M. Paul Holsinger, editor, *War and American Popular Culture*, Westport, CT: Greenwood Press, 1999.

Ambrose, Stephen, "William T. Sherman: A Personality Profile," *American History Illustrated* 1 (1967), 5–12, 54–57.

Barry, Ellen, "Pillars of Southern Charm," Charlotte *Observer*, May 14, 2005, www.charlotte.com/mld/observer (accessed May 19, 2005).

Beale, Lewis, "History Through Art's Prism," Los Angeles *Times*, Sept. 18, 2005.

Berg, Gordon, "'Phantoms of a Blood-Stained Period,'" *Civil War Times* 44:4 (October 2005), 42–48.

Bonner, James D., "Sherman at Milledgeville, in 1864," *Journal of Southern History* 22 (1956), 273–91.

Bower, Stephen E., "The Theology of the Battlefield: William Tecumseh Sherman and the U.S. Civil War," *Journal of Military History* 64:4 (October 2000), 1005–34.

Bynum, Hartwell T., "Sherman's Expulsion of the Roswell Women in 1864," *Georgia Historical Quarterly* 54 (1970), 169–82.

Carrns, Ann, "How a Brand-New Development Came by Its Rich History," *Wall Street Journal*, Oct. 18, 1998.

Castel, Albert, "Prevaricating through Georgia: Sherman's Memoirs as a Source on the Atlanta Campaign," *Civil War History* 40:1 (March 1994), 48–71.

Castel, Albert, and Steven E. Woodworth, "How Good a General Was Sherman?" *North and South* 7:2 (March 2004), 62–73.

Chesney, Charles, "Sherman's Campaigns in Georgia," *Journal of the R.U.S.I.* 9 (1866), 205–6.

Coulter, E. Merton, "Sherman and the South," *North Carolina Historical Review* 8:1 (January 1931), 41–54.

DeLaubenfels, D. J., "Where Sherman Passed By," *Geographical Review* 47:3 (1957), 381–95.

Doctorow, E. L., "The Unfeeling President," East Hampton (NY) *Star*, Sept. 9, 2004.

"Doctorow Booed after Anti-Bush Speech," *USA Today*, May 26, 2004.

"Doctorow Is In," *U.S. News & World Report*, Oct. 10, 2005.

Duncan, Russell, "Atlanta 1895 Cotton States and International Exposition," in John E. Findling and Kimberly D. Pelle, editors, *Historical Dictionary of World's Fairs and Expositions, 1851–1988*, Westport, CT: Greenwood Press, 1990.

Freeman, John, "Marching through Georgia," Louisville (KY) *Courier-Journal*, Sept. 18, 2005.

Ghaemi, Nassir, "Sherman's Demons," *Atlanta*, November 2006, 76–82.

Gilder, Richard Watson, "Sherman," in Lois Hill, editor, *Poems and Songs of the Civil War*, New York: Gramercy Books, 1990.

Graham, Stephen, "Marching through Georgia, Following Sherman's Footsteps To-day," Part I, *Harper's Monthly* 140 (April 1920), 612–20.

——, "Marching through Georgia, Following Sherman's Footsteps To-day," Part II, *Harper's Monthly* 140 (May 1920), 813–23.

Guelzo, Allen, "Bierce's Civil War: One Man's Morbid Vision," *Civil War Times* 44:4 (October 2005), 35–40, 60.

Gurganus, Allan, "Sherman's Ghost," *New York Times Magazine*, Sept. 23, 2001, 101.

Henken, Elissa R., "Taming the Enemy: Georgian Narratives About the Civil War," *Journal of Folklore Research* 40:3 (2003), 289–307.

Huff, Lawrence, "'A Bitter Draught We Have Had to Quaff': Sherman's March through the Eyes of Joseph Addison Turner," *Georgia Historical Quarterly* 72 (1988), 306–26.

Janda, Lance, "Shutting the Gates of Mercy: The American Origins of Total War, 1860–1880," *Journal of Military History* 59:1 (January 1995), 7–26.

Kapoor, Mini, "Is There a Good War?" *Sunday Indian Express* (Mumbai, India), Nov. 20, 2005.

Kirn, Walter, "Making War Hell," *New York Times Book Review*, Sept. 25, 2005.

Koppes, Steven N., "Folklore—Where Fact Meets Fiction," *University of Georgia Research Magazine*, Spring 2000, www.ovpr.uga.edu/researchnews/spring2000/fact.html.

Lomask, Milton, "Sgt. Bates March, Carrying the Stars and Stripes Unfurled from Vicksburg to Washington, and from Gretna Green to London," *American Heritage* 16:6 (October 1965), 12–16.

Lowry, Edward, "Reconstruction, or Atlanta, for Instance," *Saturday Evening Post* 192:51 (June 19, 1920), 18–19, 113, 116, 120, 122.

Lucas, Marion B., "William Tecumseh Sherman v. the Historians," *Proteus: A Journal of Ideas* 7:2 (Fall 2000), 15–21.

MacArthur, John R., "Sherman's Vast Ambivalence," Providence (RI) *Journal*, Feb. 8, 2006.

Marszalek, John F., "Celebrity in Dixie: Sherman Tours the South, 1879," *Georgia Historical Quarterly* 66:3 (Fall 1982), 368–83.

———, "Sherman Called It the Way He Saw It," *Civil War History* 40:1 (March 1994), 73–78.

Maslin, Janet, "Using History as a Guide, but Skipping the Details," New York *Times*, Sept. 27, 2005.

Matchett, Stephen, "Power of the Patriot," *Australian* (Sydney), Sept. 30, 2006.

Melville, Herman, "The March to the Sea," *Harper's New Monthly* 32 (February 1866), 366–67.

Menand, Louis, "Dispossession," *New Yorker*, Oct. 2, 2006, 92.

Neeley, Mark E., Jr., "Was the Civil War a Total War?" *Civil War History* 50:4 (December 2004), 434–58.

Passaro, Vince, "Another Country," *Nation* 36.281:14 (Oct. 31, 2005), 32–36.

Patten, Irene M., "The Civil War as Romance: Of Noble Warriors and Maidens Chaste," *American Heritage* 22:3 (April 1971), 48–53.

Pearl, Daniel, "Pariah in the South, William T. Sherman is Getting a Makeover," *Wall Street Journal*, June 9, 1993.

Pickett, William D., "Why General Sherman's Name is Detested," *Confederate Veteran* 14 (1906), 295–98.

Randall, James G., "The Newspaper Problem and Its Bearing upon Military Secrecy during the Civil War," *American Historical Review* 23 (January 1918), 303–23.

Sachs, Lloyd, "E. L. Doctorow Brilliantly Retells Sherman's March," Chicago *Sun-Times*, Sept. 18, 2005.

Schneider, Craig, "A Charming Fictional Story: Plan Invents Past in Present; Planners of Riverside in North Atlanta Decided the Development Needed a Past—So They Created It," Atlanta *Constitution*, Mar. 23, 1998.

Sears, Stephen W., "From Atlanta to the South China Sea," New York *Times*, Feb. 17, 1985.

Shelton, William Henry, "Uncle Obadiah's Uncle Billy," *Century*, June 1893, 307–12.

Sherman, William T., "The Grand Strategy of the War of the Rebellion," *Century* 13 (February 1888), 582–98.

———, "Grant, Thomas, Lee," *North American Review* 144 (May 1887), 437–50.

———, "Old Shady, with a Moral," *North American Review* 147 (October 1888), 361–68.

———, "Our Army and Militia," *North American Review* 151 (August 1890), 129–45.

Silver, Nina, "The Northern Myth of the Rebel Girl," in Christie Ann Farnham, editor, *Women of the American South: A Multiracial Reader*, New York: New York University Press, 1997.

Smythe, Ted Curtis, and Paulette Kilmer, "The Press in Industrial America, 1865–1883," in William David Sloan, editor, *The Media in America: A History*, 5th edition, Northport, AL: Vision Press, 2002.

Street, James, "All Out with Sherman," *Collier's*, Dec. 19, 1942, 72–77.

Taylor, A. Reed, "The War History of Two Soldiers: A Two-Sided View of the Civil War," *Alabama Review* 23:2 (April 1970), 83–109.

Tribble, Edwin, "'Marching through Georgia,'" *Georgia Review* 21:4 (1967), 423–29.

Twain, Mark, "More Westonism," Virginia City (NV) *Territorial Enterprise*, Feb. 27, 1868.

Updike, John, "A Cloud of Dust," *The New Yorker*, Sept. 12, 2005, 98.

Van Dyke, Henry, "The Statue of Sherman by St. Gaudens," in *Music and Other Poems*, New York: Charles Scribner's Sons, 1904.

Van Tuyll, Debra Reddin, "Journalists First, Rebels Second: An Examination of Editorial Reaction to the President's Proposed Conscription of Newspapermen," in David B. Sachsman, S. Kittrell Rushing, and Debra Reddin van Tuyll, editors, *The Civil War and the Press*, New Brunswick, NJ: Transaction, 2000.

Vidal, Gore, "Honor," in A. S. Burack, editor, *Television Plays for Writers*, Boston: The Writer, 1957.

———, "On the March to the Sea," in *Three Plays*, London: Heinemann, 1962.

Walters, John Bennett, "General William T. Sherman and Total War," *Journal of Southern History* 14:4 (November 1948), 447–80.

Weeks, Jerome, "Gen. Sherman Marches to the Sea in Doctorow's New Novel," Lincoln (NE) *Journal Star*, Oct. 20, 2005.

Welsh, Willard, "Civil War Theater: The War in Drama," *Civil War History* 2 (1955), 251–80.

Wolseley, Garnet, "General Sherman," *United Service Magazine*, N.S. 3 (May–July, 1891), 99–103.

Woodworth, Steven E., "November 1864: The March to the Sea," in *1864: Grinding, Relentless War* (Leesburg, VA: Primedia Enthusiast Group, 2004), 70–78.

———, "West versus East," *America's Civil War* 20:5 (November 2007), 28–37.

Woodworth, Steven E., Reid Mitchell, Gordon C. Rhea, John Y. Simon, Steven H. Newton, and Keith Poulter, "Who Were the Top Ten Generals? A Panel of Historians Discusses the Strengths and Weaknesses of Leading Civil War Commanders," *North and South* 6:4 (May 2003), 14–22.

Zuck, Barbara, "Ensemble Shows Its Versatility in Southern Theatre Debut," Columbus (OH) *Dispatch*, May 8, 2006.

Audio Recording

Swenson, Warren Michel, *Battle Pieces*, CD, Albany Records.

Index

About the Authors

Edward Caudill (Ph.D., University of North Carolina at Chapel Hill) and **Paul Ashdown** (Ph.D., Bowling Green State University) are professors of journalism and electronic media at the University of Tennessee. They are coauthors of *The Myth of Nathan Bedford Forrest* (2005) and *The Mosby Myth: A Confederate Hero in Life and Legend* (2002). Caudill is author of *Darwinian Myths: The Legends and Misuses of a Theory* (1997) and coauthor of *The Scopes Trial: A Photographic History* (2000). Ashdown is editor of *James Agee: Selected Journalism* (1985, 2004) and author of *A Cold Mountain Companion* (2004).